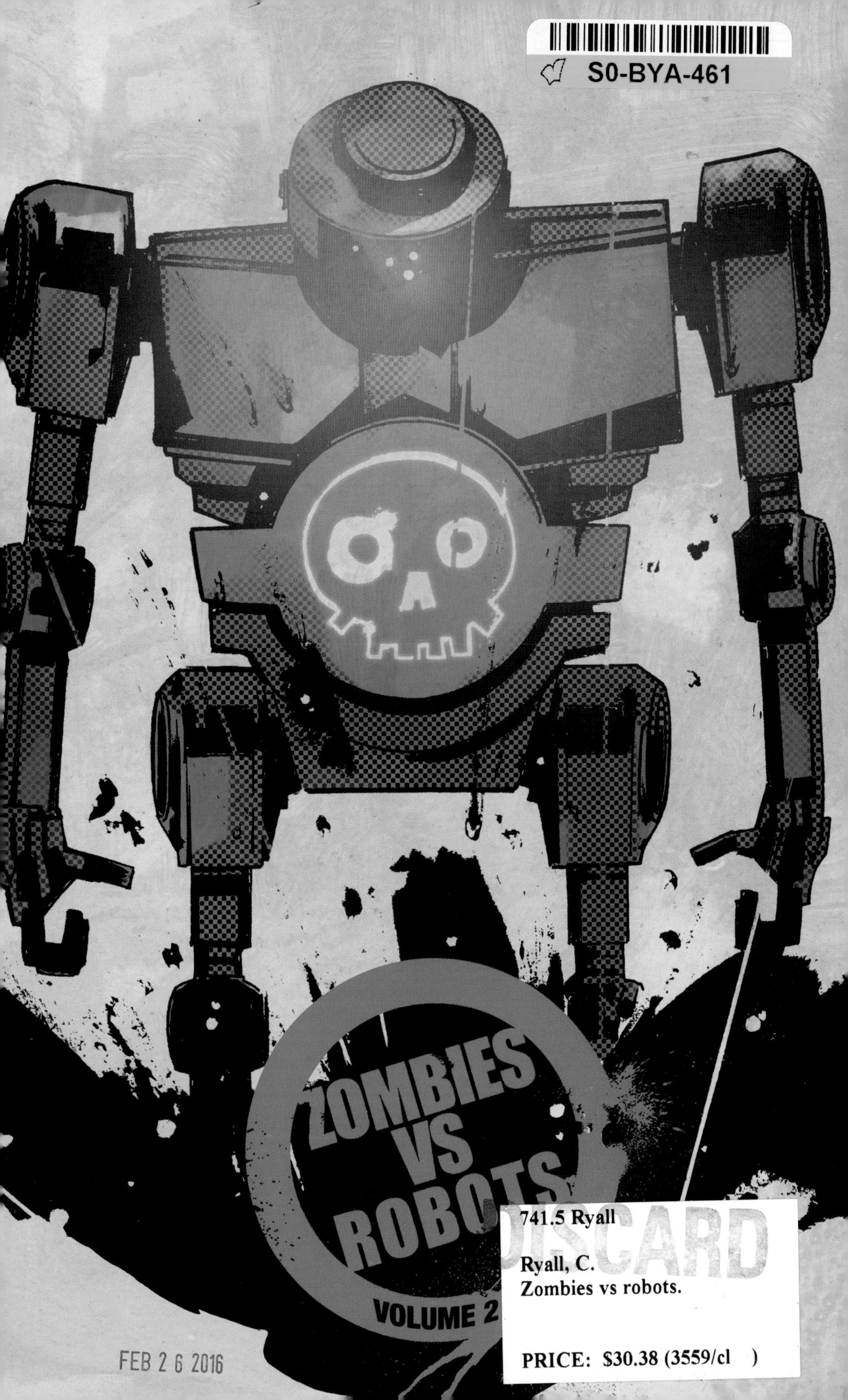
ZOMBIES
VS
ROBOTS
VOLUME 2

ISBN: 978-1-63140-524-2

19 18 17 16   1 2 3 4

Ted Adams, CEO & Publisher
Greg Goldstein, President & COO
Robbie Robbins, EVP/Sr. Graphic Artist
Chris Ryall, Chief Creative Officer/Editor-in-Chief
Matthew Ruzicka, CPA, Chief Financial Officer
Dirk Wood, VP of Marketing
Lorelei Bunjes, VP of Digital Services
Jeff Webber, VP of Licensing, Digital and Subsidiary Rights
Jerry Bennington, VP of New Product Development

www.IDWPUBLISHING.com
IDW founded by Ted Adams, Alex Garner, Kris Oprisko, and Robbie Robbins

Facebook: **facebook.com/idwpublishing**
Twitter: **@idwpublishing**
YouTube: **youtube.com/idwpublishing**
Tumblr: **tumblr.idwpublishing.com**
Instagram: **instagram.com/idwpublishing**

Written by Chris Ryall

The Man on the Moon
Artist: Paul Davidson
Additional Artists: James McDonald,
Valentin Ramon, and James Kochalka
Colorist: Jay Fotos

War! 'Bots!
Artist: Antonio Fuso
Colorist: Stefano Simeone

Tales of ZvR
Storyteller/Artist: Ashley Wood
Dialogue/Lettering: Chris Ryall

One Day
Writer: Lucy Ryall
Art/Colors/Letters: Nico Peña

Zombies vs Robots created by Chris Ryall & Ashley Wood

Series Editor: Chris Ryall
Editorial Assist: Michael Benedetto
Letterer: Shawn Lee

Cover Artist: Ashley Wood
Collection Editors: Justin Eisinger & Alonzo Simon
Collection Designer: Clyde Grapa

For Lucy Ryall, the next generation of ZvR - Chris

THE MAN ON THE MOON

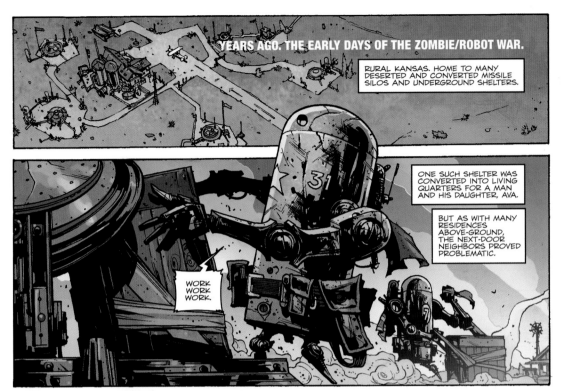

YEARS AGO. THE EARLY DAYS OF THE ZOMBIE/ROBOT WAR.

RURAL KANSAS. HOME TO MANY DESERTED AND CONVERTED MISSILE SILOS AND UNDERGROUND SHELTERS.

ONE SUCH SHELTER WAS CONVERTED INTO LIVING QUARTERS FOR A MAN AND HIS DAUGHTER, AVA.

BUT AS WITH MANY RESIDENCES ABOVE-GROUND, THE NEXT-DOOR NEIGHBORS PROVED PROBLEMATIC.

WORK WORK WORK.

I TELLYA, I DON'T WANT NONE'A YOR WARBOTS AROUND ME OR MY FAMILY, T'AIN'T SAFE!

YOU SAY THAT NOW, BUT WHEN THE GATHERING STORM FINALLY HITS KANSAS, YOU'LL BE GLAD THEY'RE HERE.

THOSE CREATURES ARE OVERSEAS AN' SHIT, NOT HERE, MISTER!

AND THEM ROBOTS IS MURDEROUS, I TELL YOU!

IF THE SHIT REACHES US, YOU BETTER HOPE THAT'S TRUE.

AHH, SCREW THIS. LET'S GET BELOW AND SEAL OFF OUR BUNKER. THAT'LL KEEP OUT ANYTHIN', EVEN THOSE SCUMMY 'BOTS.

DADDY? THE SKY'S CLEAR, WHY'D YOU TELL THAT MAN THERE'S A STORM?

TRUST ME, MY LITTLE AVA, THE STORM MIGHT NOT BE THERE YET...

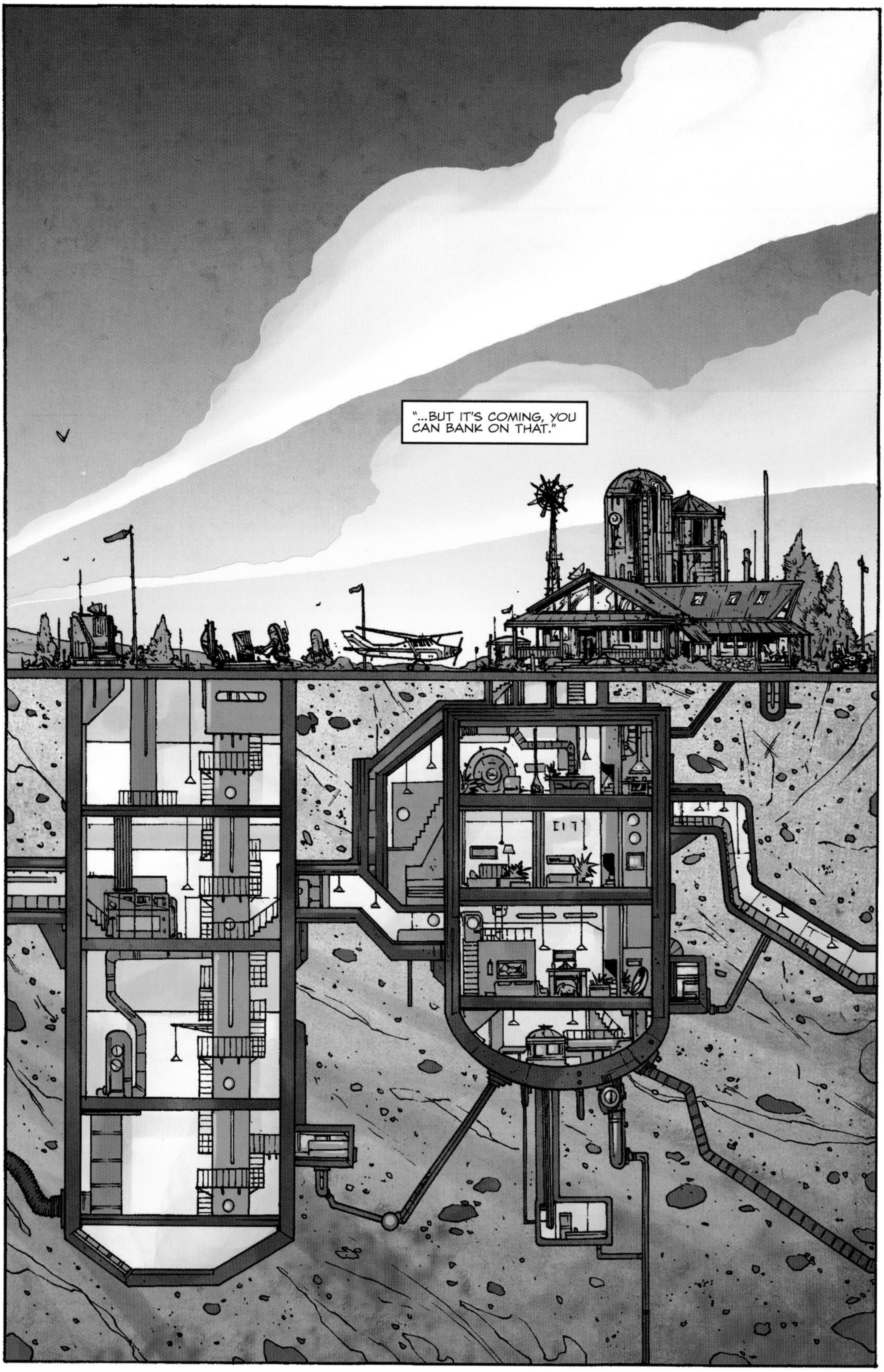
"...BUT IT'S COMING, YOU CAN BANK ON THAT."

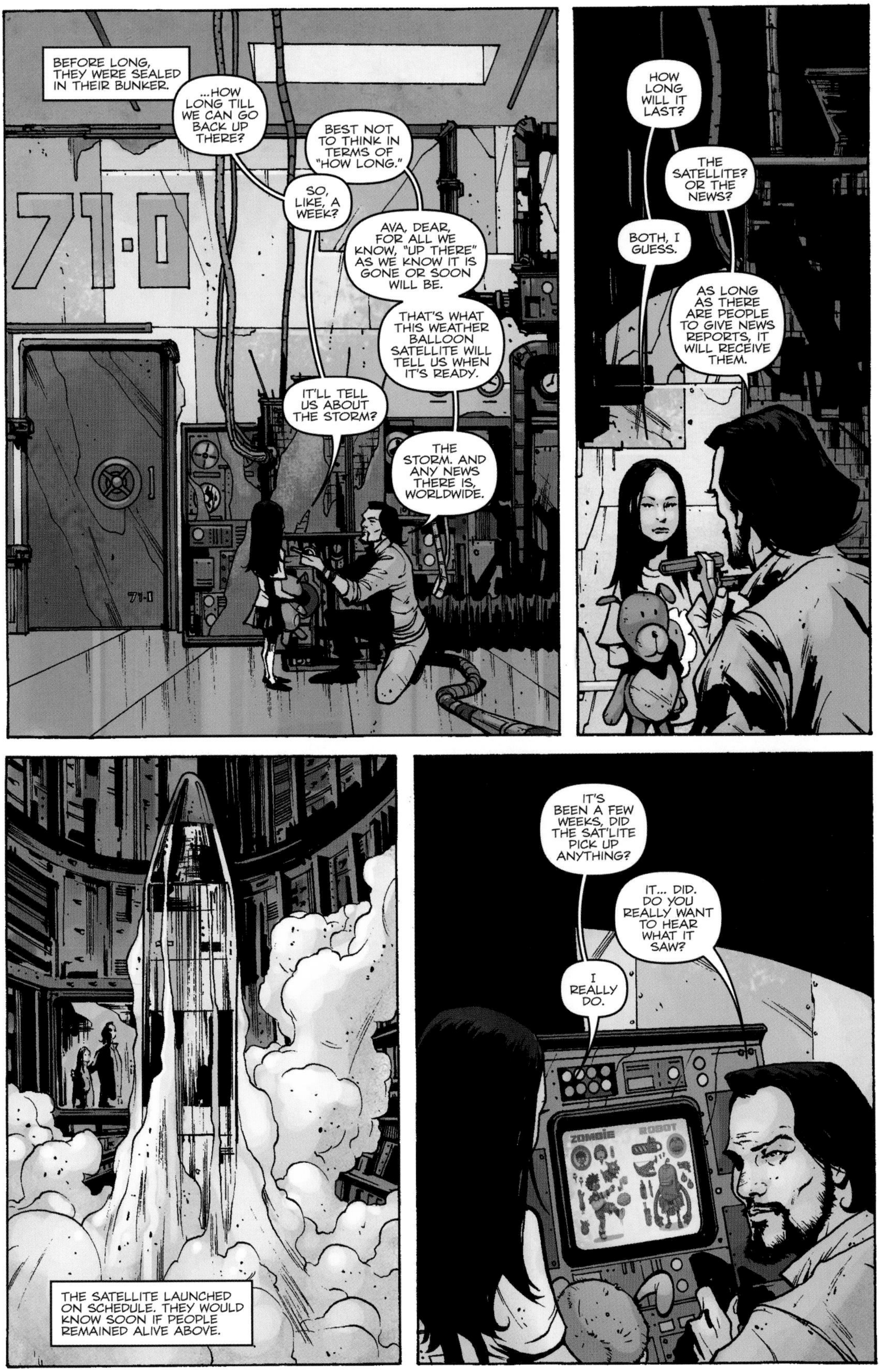

BEFORE LONG, THEY WERE SEALED IN THEIR BUNKER.
...HOW LONG TILL WE CAN GO BACK UP THERE?
BEST NOT TO THINK IN TERMS OF "HOW LONG."
SO, LIKE, A WEEK?
AVA, DEAR, FOR ALL WE KNOW, "UP THERE" AS WE KNOW IT IS GONE OR SOON WILL BE.
THAT'S WHAT THIS WEATHER BALLOON SATELLITE WILL TELL US WHEN IT'S READY.
IT'LL TELL US ABOUT THE STORM?
THE STORM. AND ANY NEWS THERE IS, WORLDWIDE.
71-0
71-1
HOW LONG WILL IT LAST?
THE SATELLITE? OR THE NEWS?
BOTH, I GUESS.
AS LONG AS THERE ARE PEOPLE TO GIVE NEWS REPORTS, IT WILL RECEIVE THEM.
THE SATELLITE LAUNCHED ON SCHEDULE. THEY WOULD KNOW SOON IF PEOPLE REMAINED ALIVE ABOVE.
IT'S BEEN A FEW WEEKS, DID THE SAT'LITE PICK UP ANYTHING?
IT... DID. DO YOU REALLY WANT TO HEAR WHAT IT SAW?
I REALLY DO.
ZOMBIE
ROBOT

ZOMBIE

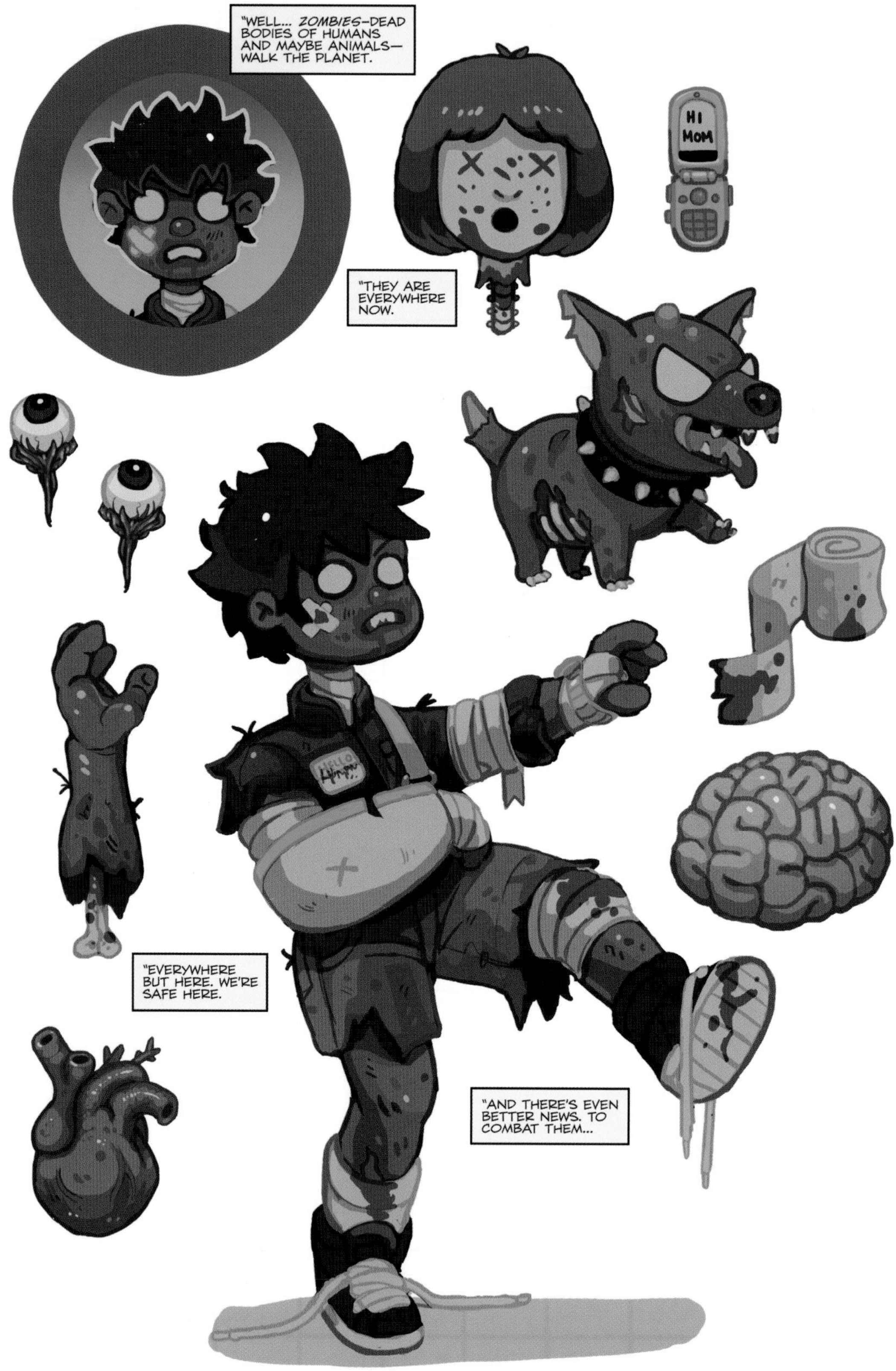
"WELL... *ZOMBIES*—DEAD BODIES OF HUMANS AND MAYBE ANIMALS—WALK THE PLANET.
HI MOM
"THEY ARE EVERYWHERE NOW.
"EVERYWHERE BUT HERE. WE'RE SAFE HERE.
"AND THERE'S EVEN BETTER NEWS. TO COMBAT THEM...

ROBOT

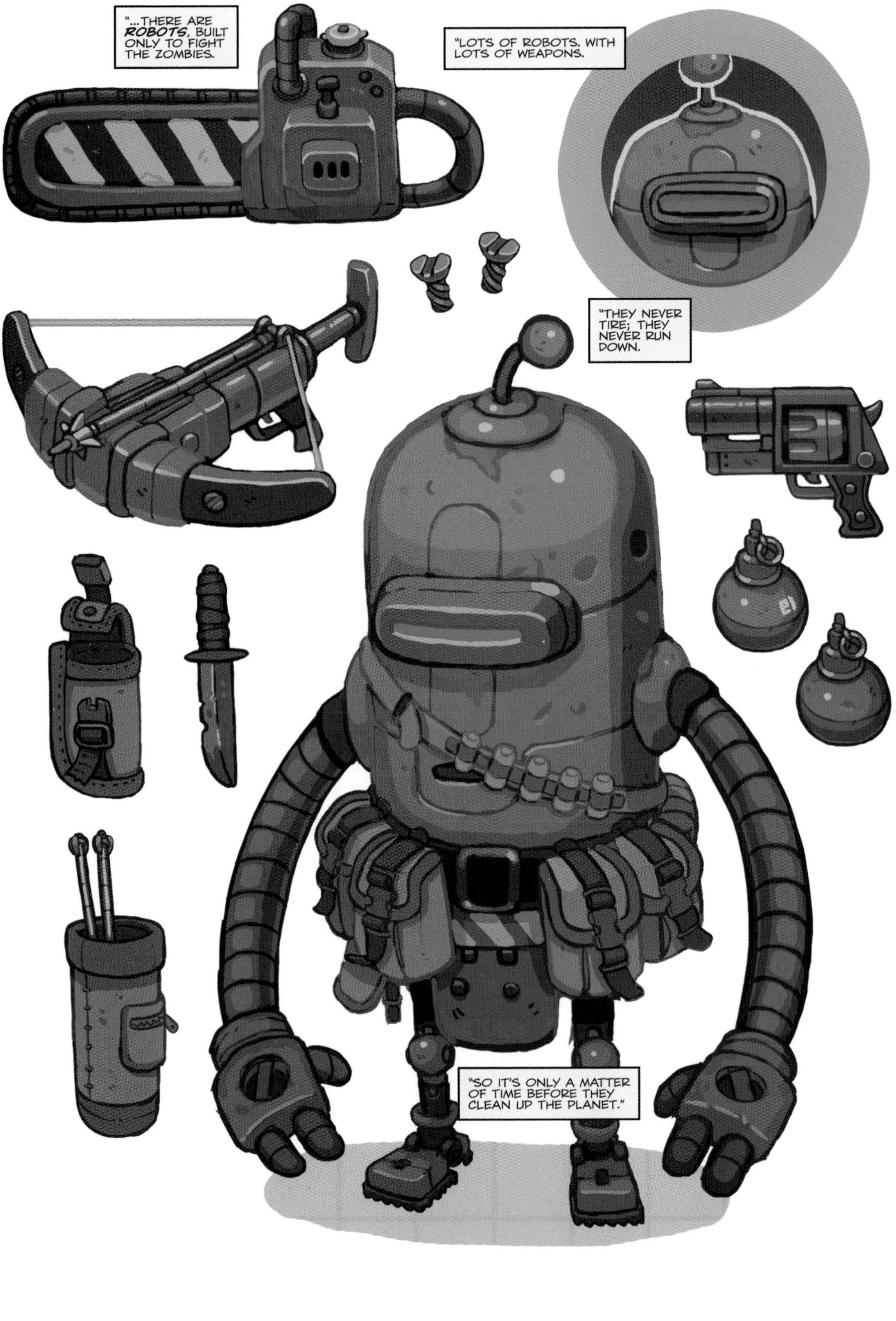
"...THERE ARE *ROBOTS*, BUILT ONLY TO FIGHT THE ZOMBIES.
"LOTS OF ROBOTS. WITH LOTS OF WEAPONS.
"THEY NEVER TIRE; THEY NEVER RUN DOWN.
"SO IT'S ONLY A MATTER OF TIME BEFORE THEY CLEAN UP THE PLANET."

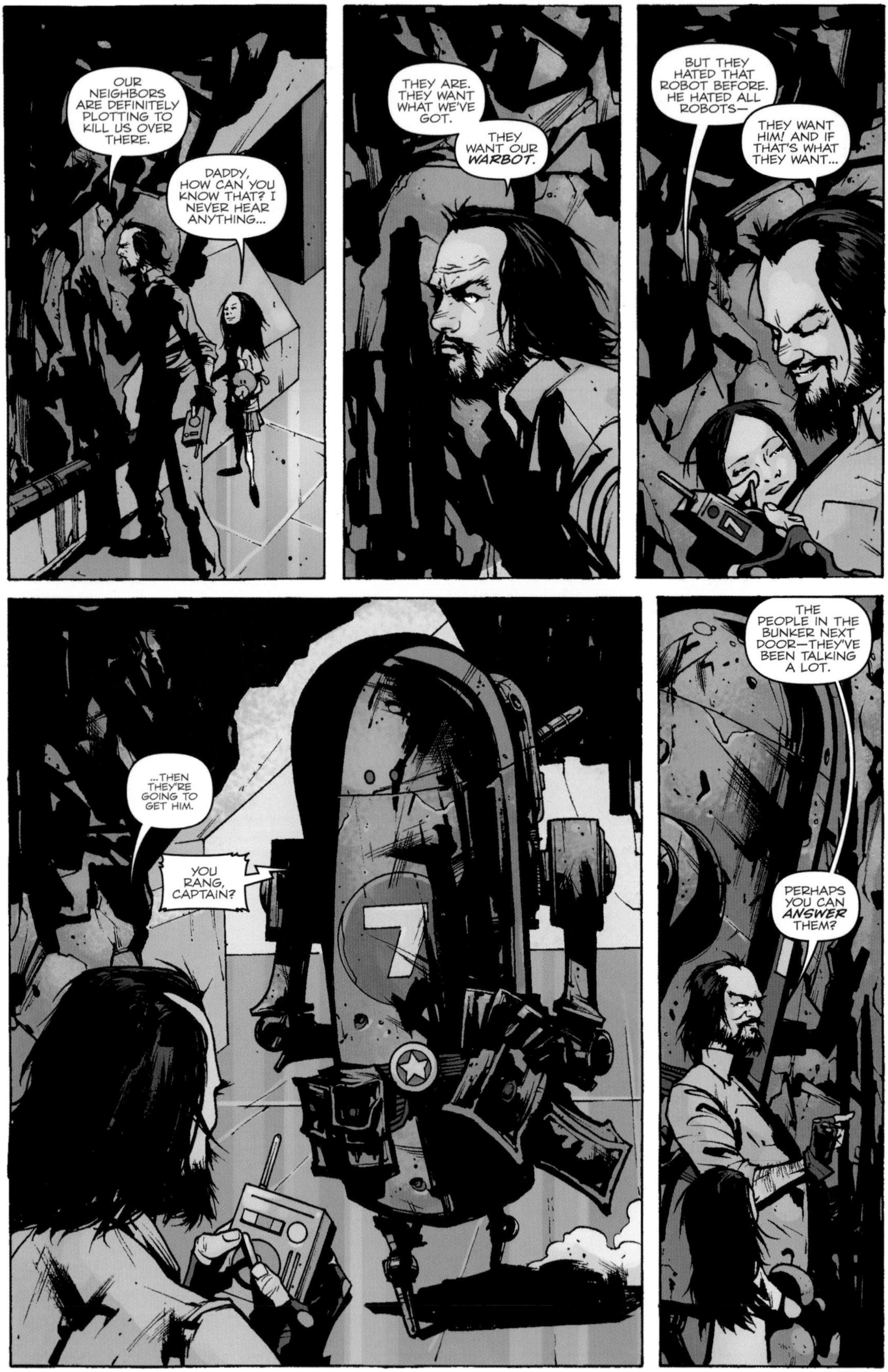
OUR NEIGHBORS ARE DEFINITELY PLOTTING TO KILL US OVER THERE.
DADDY, HOW CAN YOU KNOW THAT? I NEVER HEAR ANYTHING...
THEY ARE. THEY WANT WHAT WE'VE GOT.
THEY WANT OUR WARBOT.
BUT THEY HATED THAT ROBOT BEFORE. HE HATED ALL ROBOTS—
THEY WANT HIM! AND IF THAT'S WHAT THEY WANT...
...THEN THEY'RE GOING TO GET HIM.
YOU RANG, CAPTAIN?
THE PEOPLE IN THE BUNKER NEXT DOOR—THEY'VE BEEN TALKING A LOT.
PERHAPS YOU CAN ANSWER THEM?

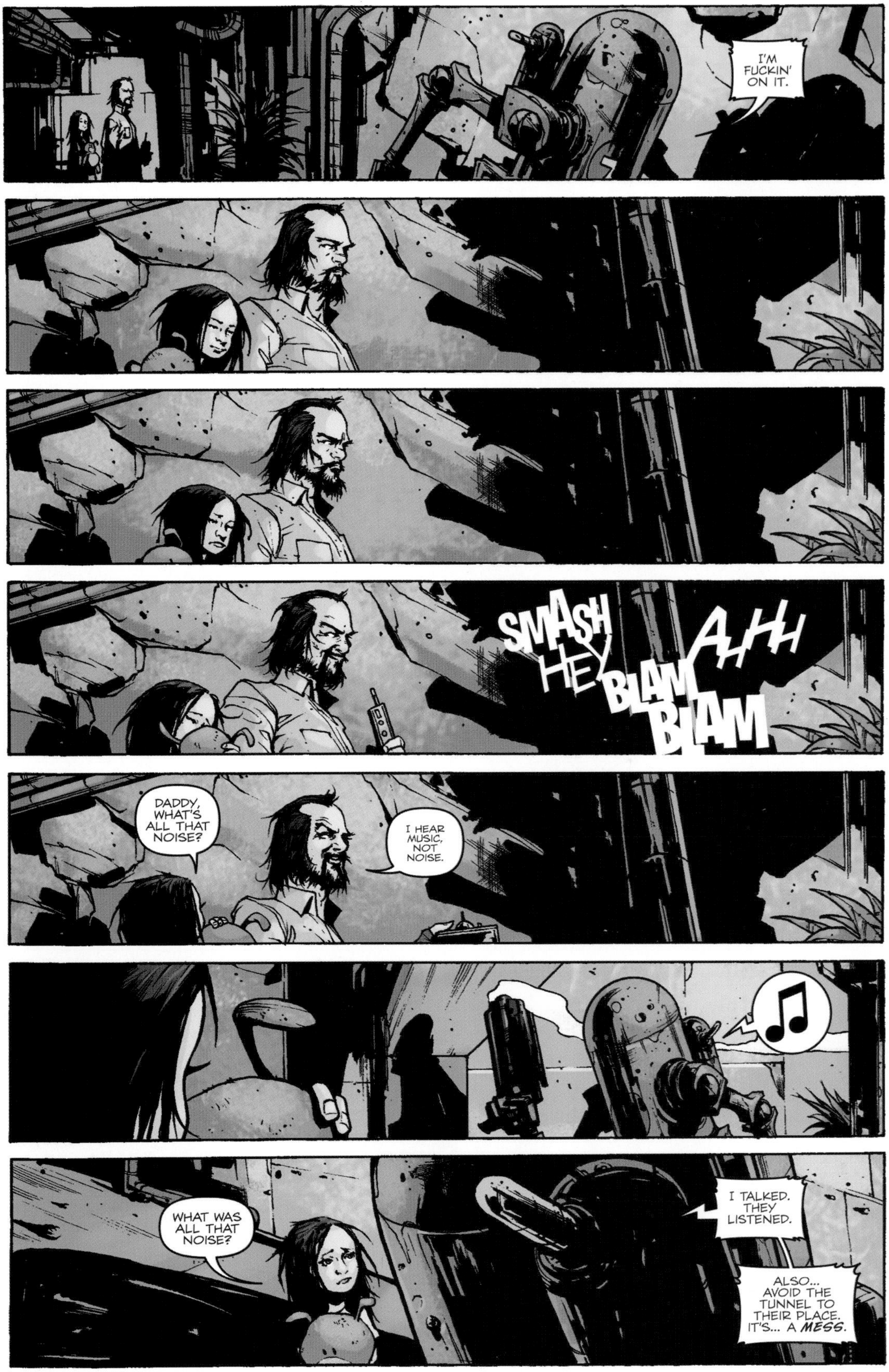
I'M FUCKIN' ON IT.
SMASH
HEY
AHH
BLAM
BLAM
DADDY, WHAT'S ALL THAT NOISE?
I HEAR MUSIC, NOT NOISE.
WHAT WAS ALL THAT NOISE?
I TALKED. THEY LISTENED.
ALSO... AVOID THE TUNNEL TO THEIR PLACE. IT'S... A *MESS*.

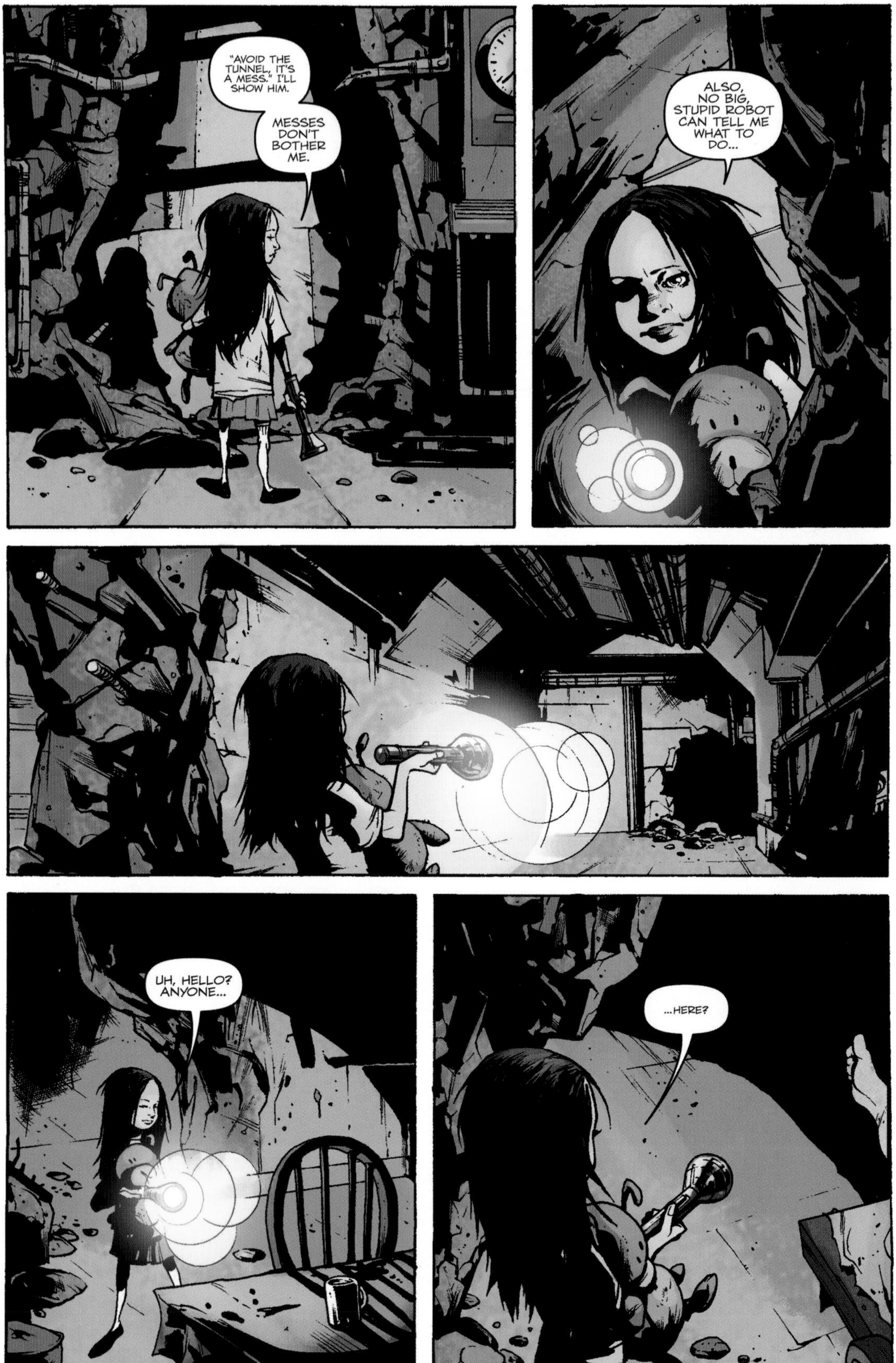
"AVOID THE TUNNEL, IT'S A MESS." I'LL SHOW HIM.
MESSES DON'T BOTHER ME.
ALSO, NO BIG, STUPID ROBOT CAN TELL ME WHAT TO DO...
UH, HELLO? ANYONE...
...HERE?

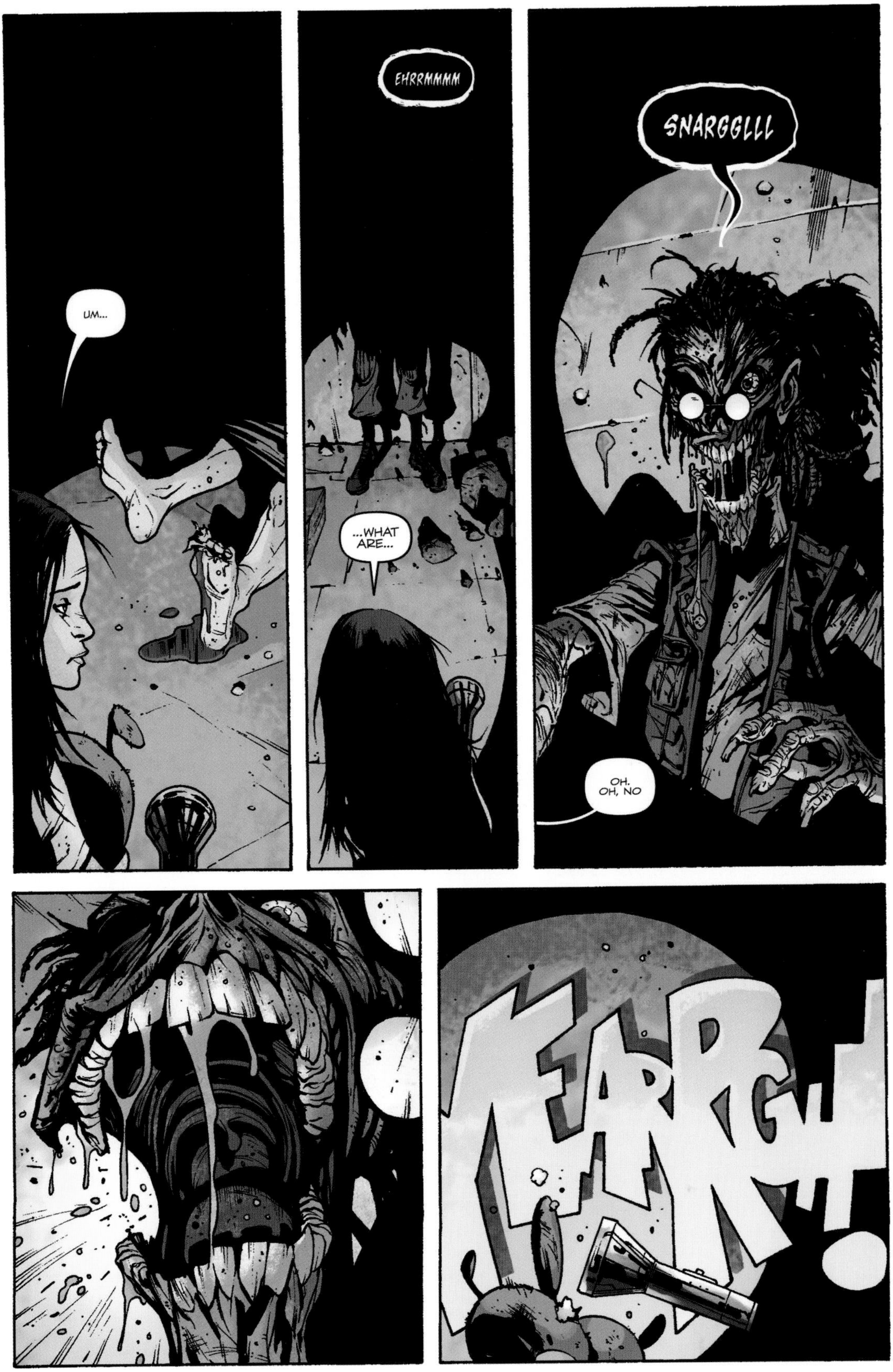
UM...
EHRRMMMM
...WHAT ARE...
SNARGGLLL
OH. OH, NO
NEARRGH!

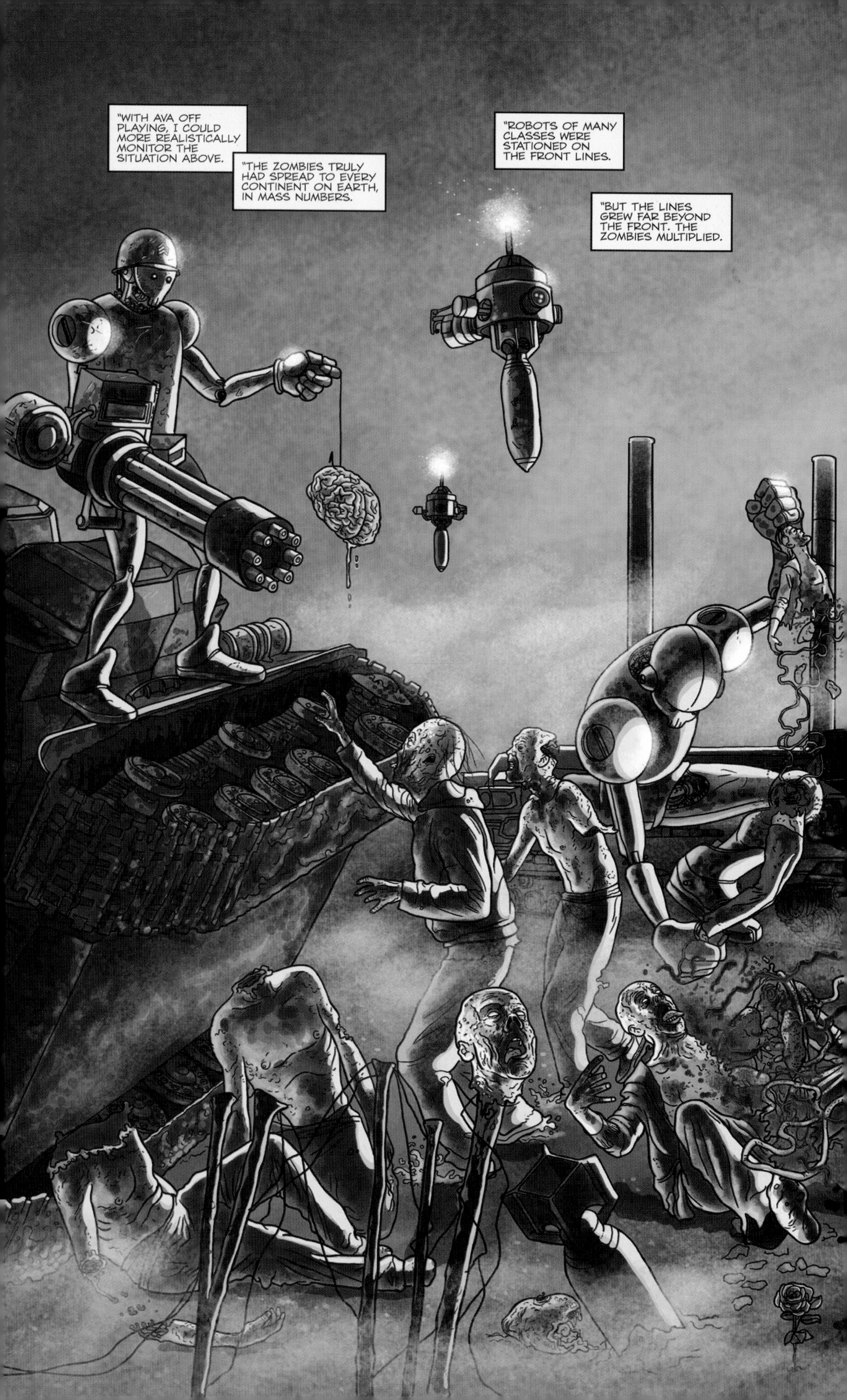
"WITH AVA OFF PLAYING, I COULD MORE REALISTICALLY MONITOR THE SITUATION ABOVE.
"THE ZOMBIES TRULY HAD SPREAD TO EVERY CONTINENT ON EARTH, IN MASS NUMBERS.
"ROBOTS OF MANY CLASSES WERE STATIONED ON THE FRONT LINES.
"BUT THE LINES GREW FAR BEYOND THE FRONT. THE ZOMBIES MULTIPLIED.

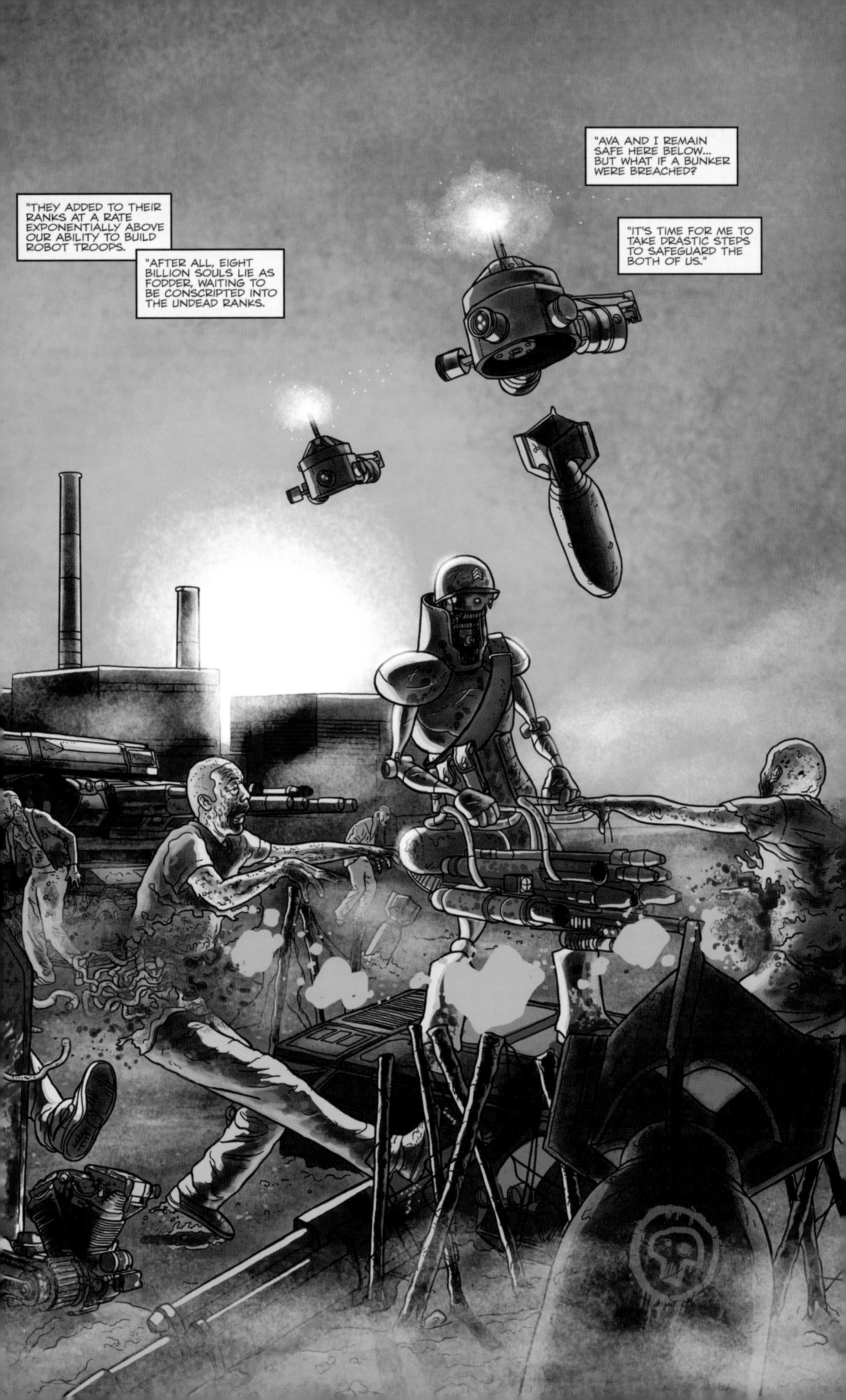
"THEY ADDED TO THEIR RANKS AT A RATE EXPONENTIALLY ABOVE OUR ABILITY TO BUILD ROBOT TROOPS.
"AFTER ALL, EIGHT BILLION SOULS LIE AS FODDER, WAITING TO BE CONSCRIPTED INTO THE UNDEAD RANKS.
"AVA AND I REMAIN SAFE HERE BELOW... BUT WHAT IF A BUNKER WERE BREACHED?
"IT'S TIME FOR ME TO TAKE DRASTIC STEPS TO SAFEGUARD THE BOTH OF US."

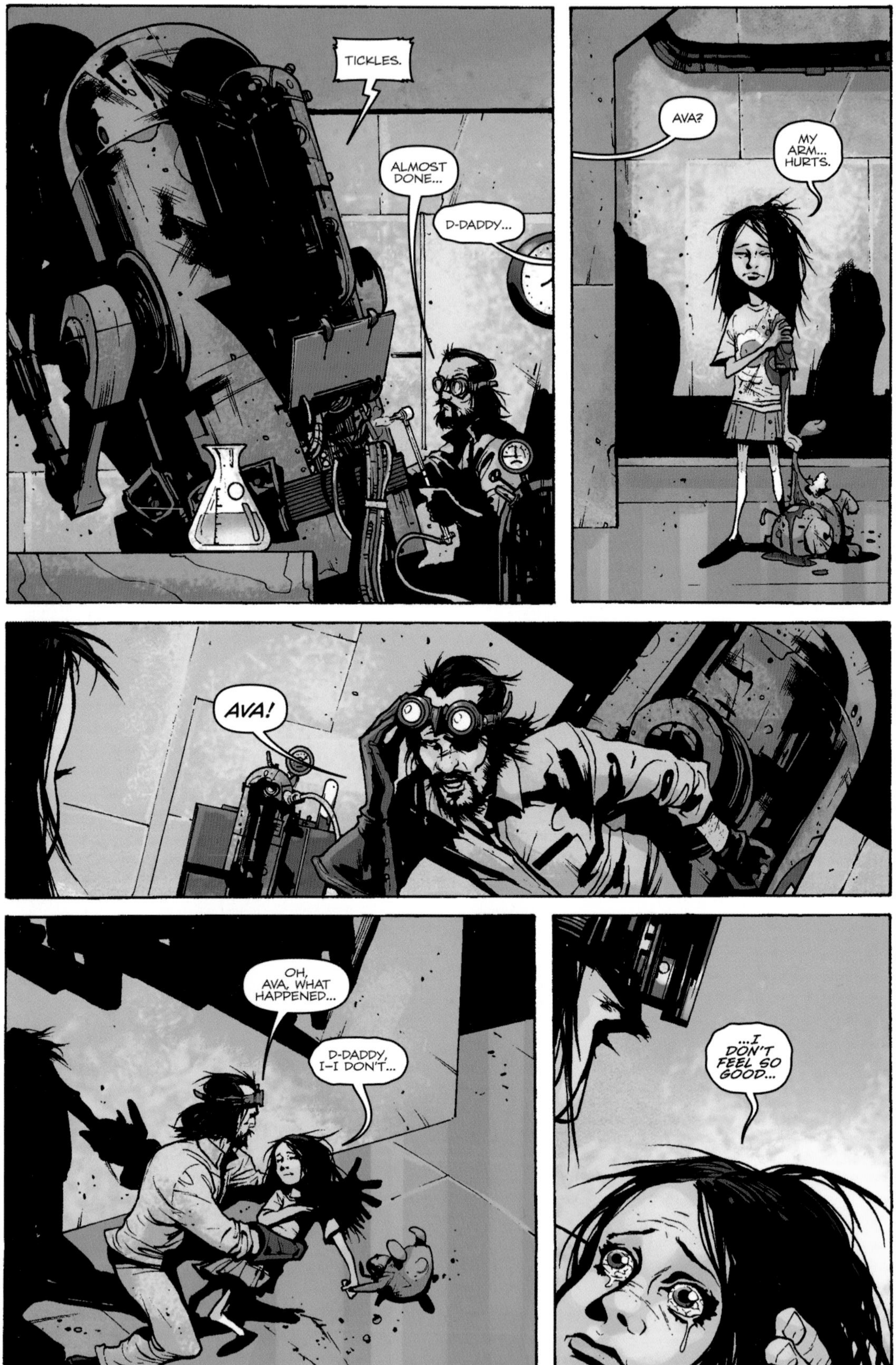
TICKLES.
ALMOST DONE...
D-DADDY...
AVA?
MY ARM... HURTS.
AVA!
OH, AVA, WHAT HAPPENED...
D-DADDY, I-I DON'T...
...I DON'T FEEL SO GOOD...

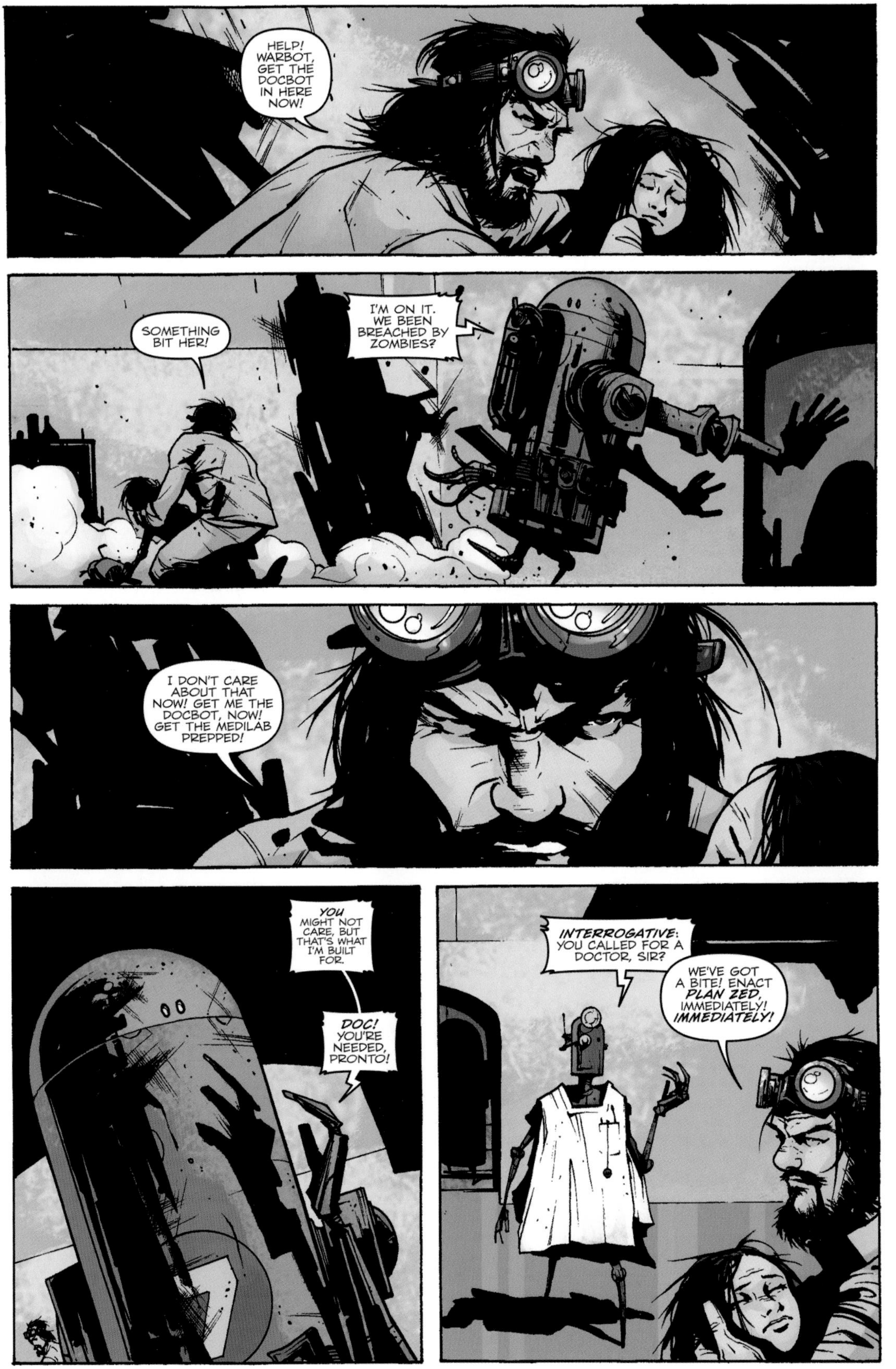
HELP! WARBOT, GET THE DOCBOT IN HERE NOW!
SOMETHING BIT HER!
I'M ON IT. WE BEEN BREACHED BY ZOMBIES?
I DON'T CARE ABOUT THAT NOW! GET ME THE DOCBOT, NOW! GET THE MEDILAB PREPPED!
YOU MIGHT NOT CARE, BUT THAT'S WHAT I'M BUILT FOR.
DOC! YOU'RE NEEDED, PRONTO!
INTERROGATIVE: YOU CALLED FOR A DOCTOR, SIR?
WE'VE GOT A BITE! ENACT PLAN ZED, IMMEDIATELY! IMMEDIATELY!

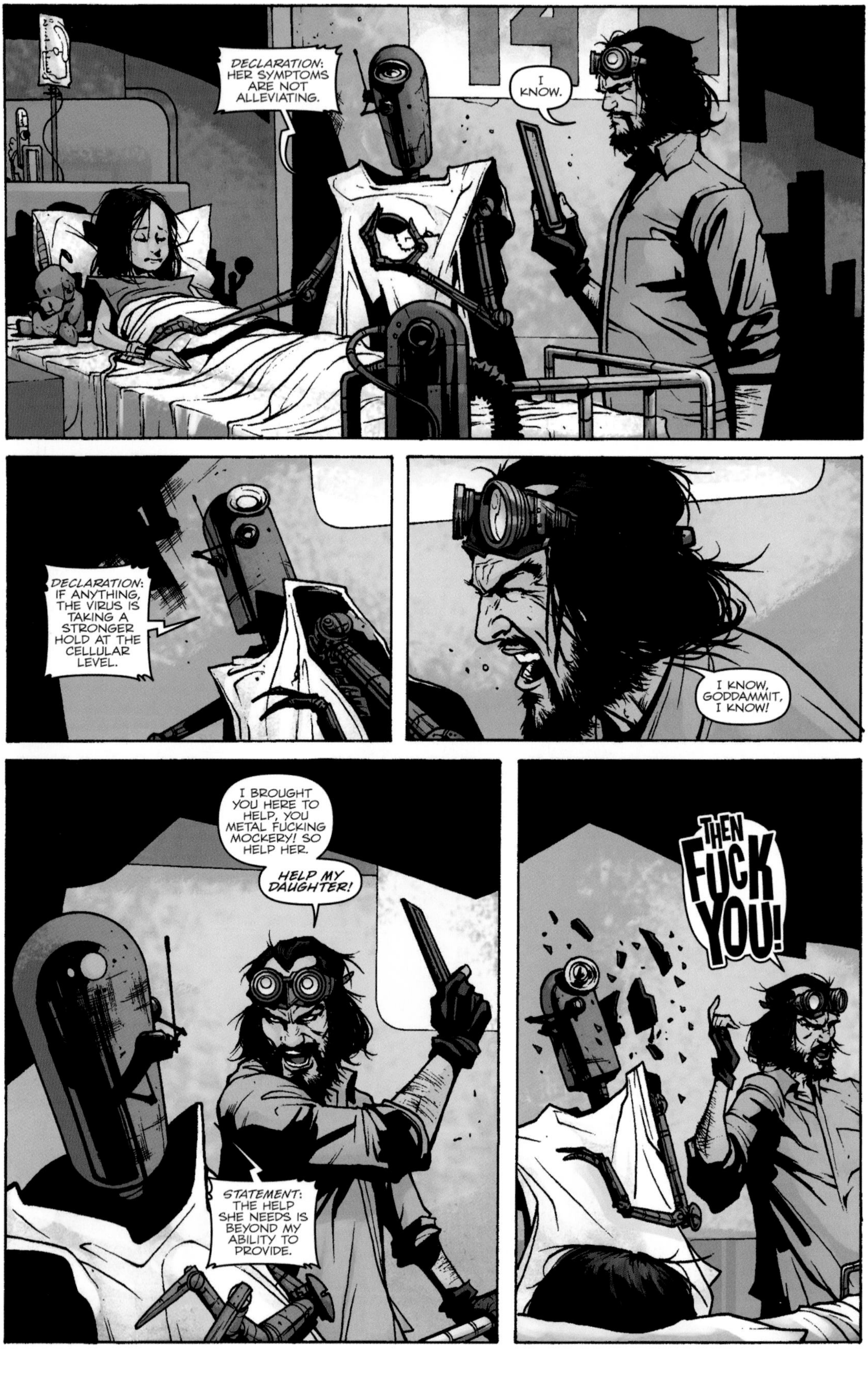
DECLARATION: HER SYMPTOMS ARE NOT ALLEVIATING.
I KNOW.
DECLARATION: IF ANYTHING, THE VIRUS IS TAKING A STRONGER HOLD AT THE CELLULAR LEVEL.
I KNOW, GODDAMMIT, I KNOW!
I BROUGHT YOU HERE TO HELP, YOU METAL FUCKING MOCKERY! SO HELP HER.
HELP MY DAUGHTER!
STATEMENT: THE HELP SHE NEEDS IS BEYOND MY ABILITY TO PROVIDE.
THEN FUCK YOU!

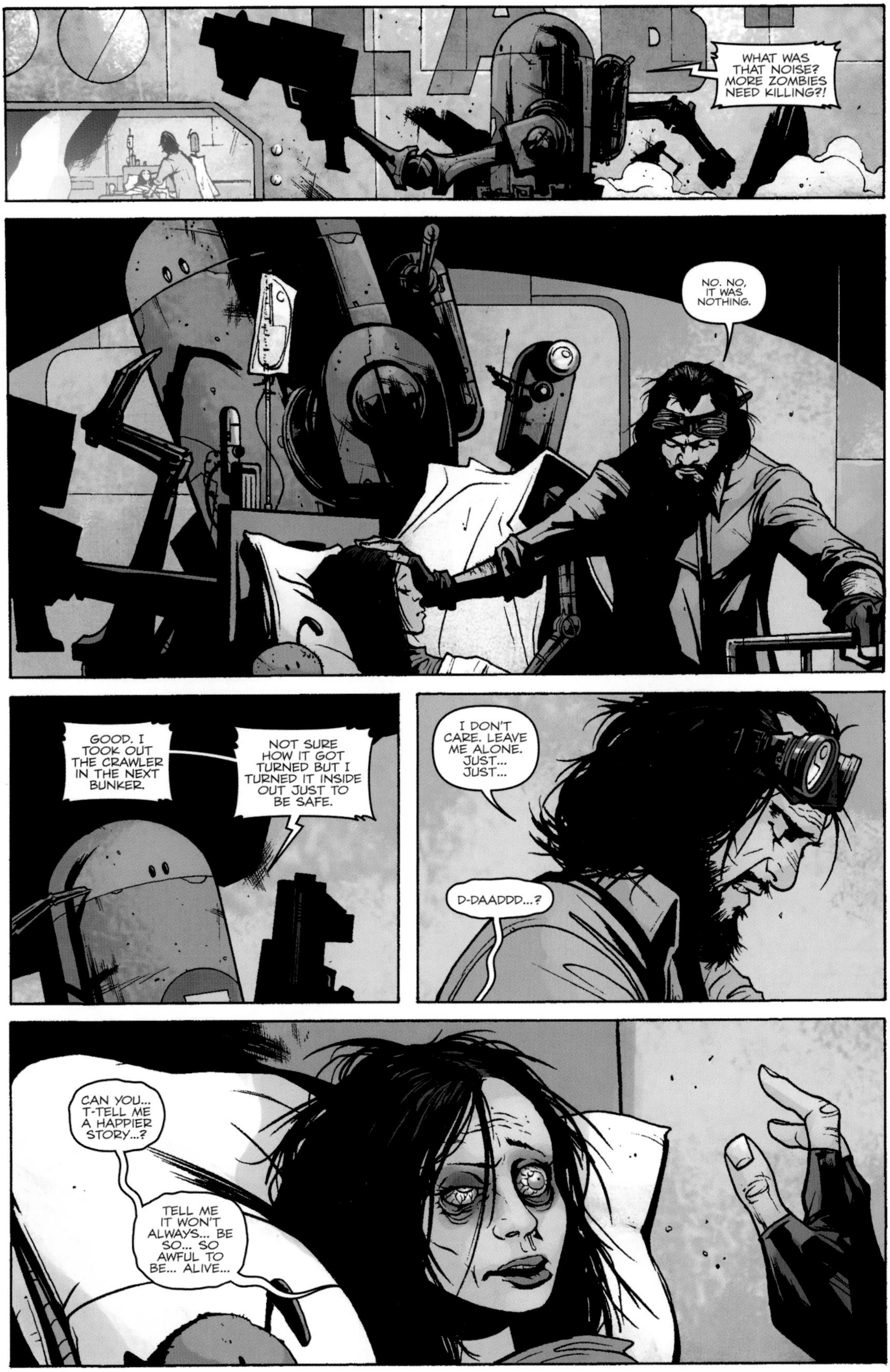
WHAT WAS THAT NOISE? MORE ZOMBIES NEED KILLING?!
NO. NO, IT WAS NOTHING.
GOOD. I TOOK OUT THE CRAWLER IN THE NEXT BUNKER.
NOT SURE HOW IT GOT TURNED BUT I TURNED IT INSIDE OUT JUST TO BE SAFE.
I DON'T CARE. LEAVE ME ALONE. JUST... JUST...
D-DAADDD...?
CAN YOU... T-TELL ME A HAPPIER STORY...?
TELL ME IT WON'T ALWAYS... BE SO... SO AWFUL TO BE... ALIVE...

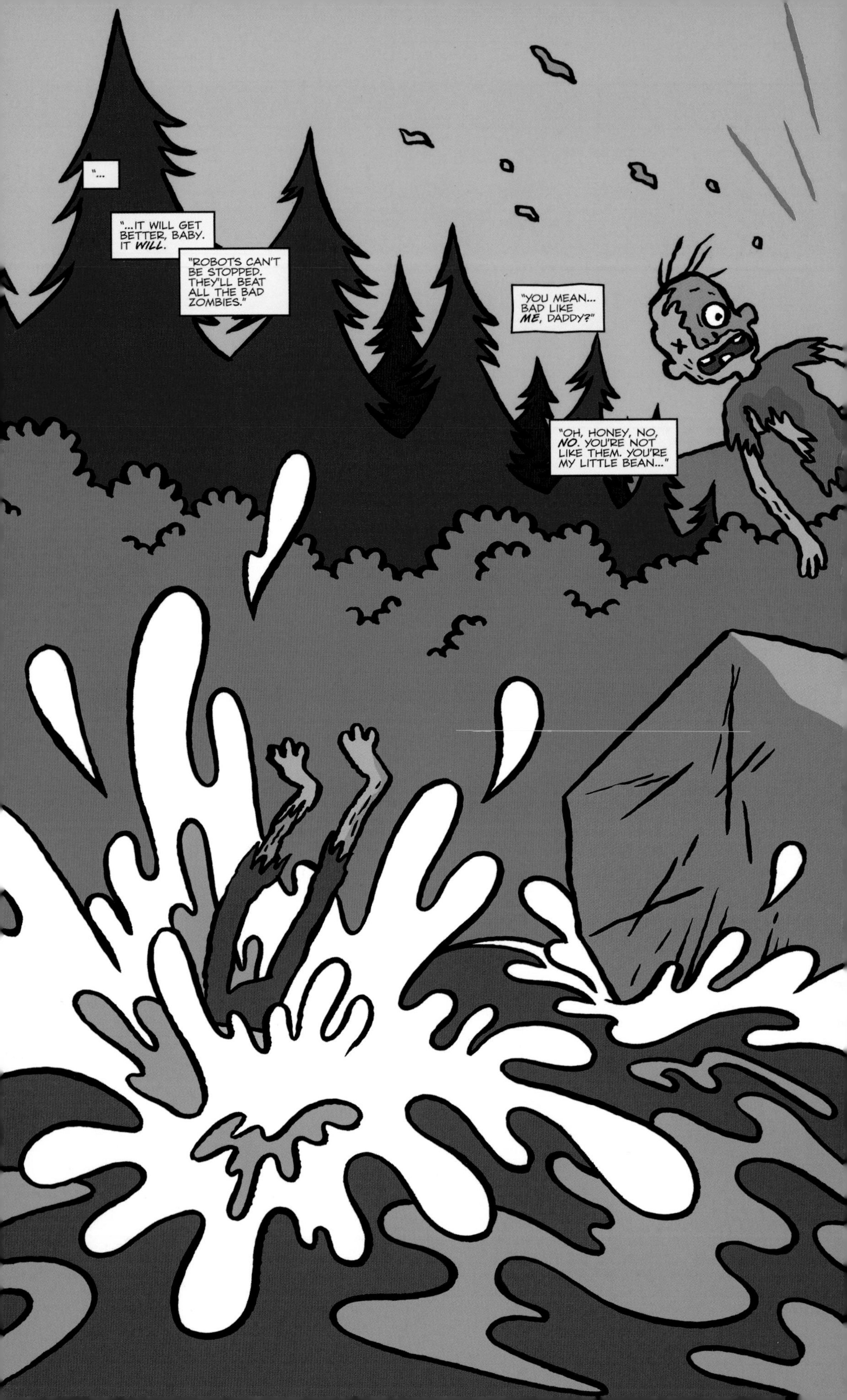
"...
"...IT WILL GET BETTER, BABY. IT *WILL*.
"ROBOTS CAN'T BE STOPPED. THEY'LL BEAT ALL THE BAD ZOMBIES."
"YOU MEAN... BAD LIKE *ME*, DADDY?"
"OH, HONEY, NO, *NO*. YOU'RE NOT LIKE THEM. YOU'RE MY LITTLE BEAN..."

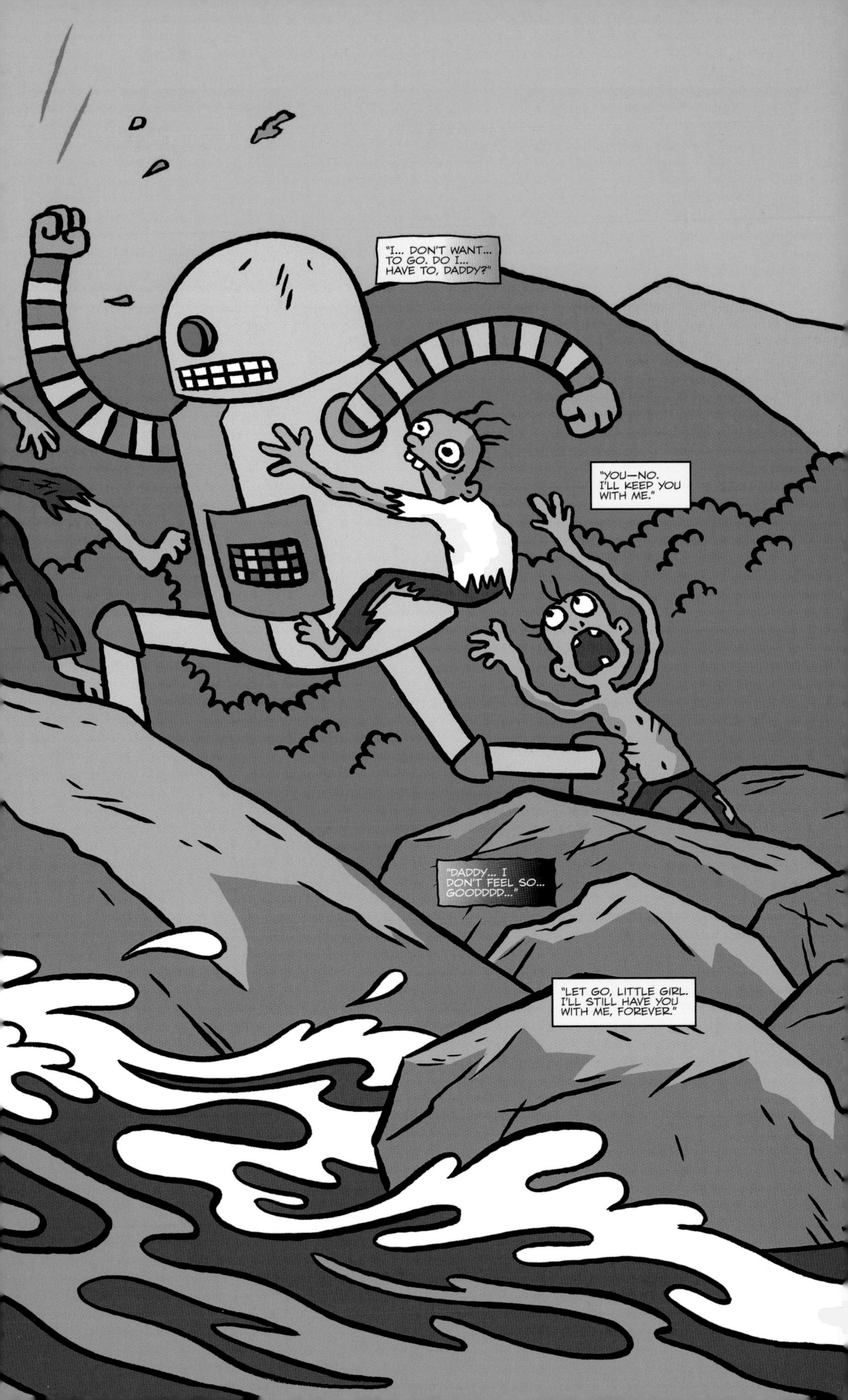
"I... DON'T WANT... TO GO. DO I... HAVE TO, DADDY?"
"YOU—NO. I'LL KEEP YOU WITH ME."
"DADDY... I DON'T FEEL SO... GOODDDD..."
"LET GO, LITTLE GIRL. I'LL STILL HAVE YOU WITH ME, FOREVER."

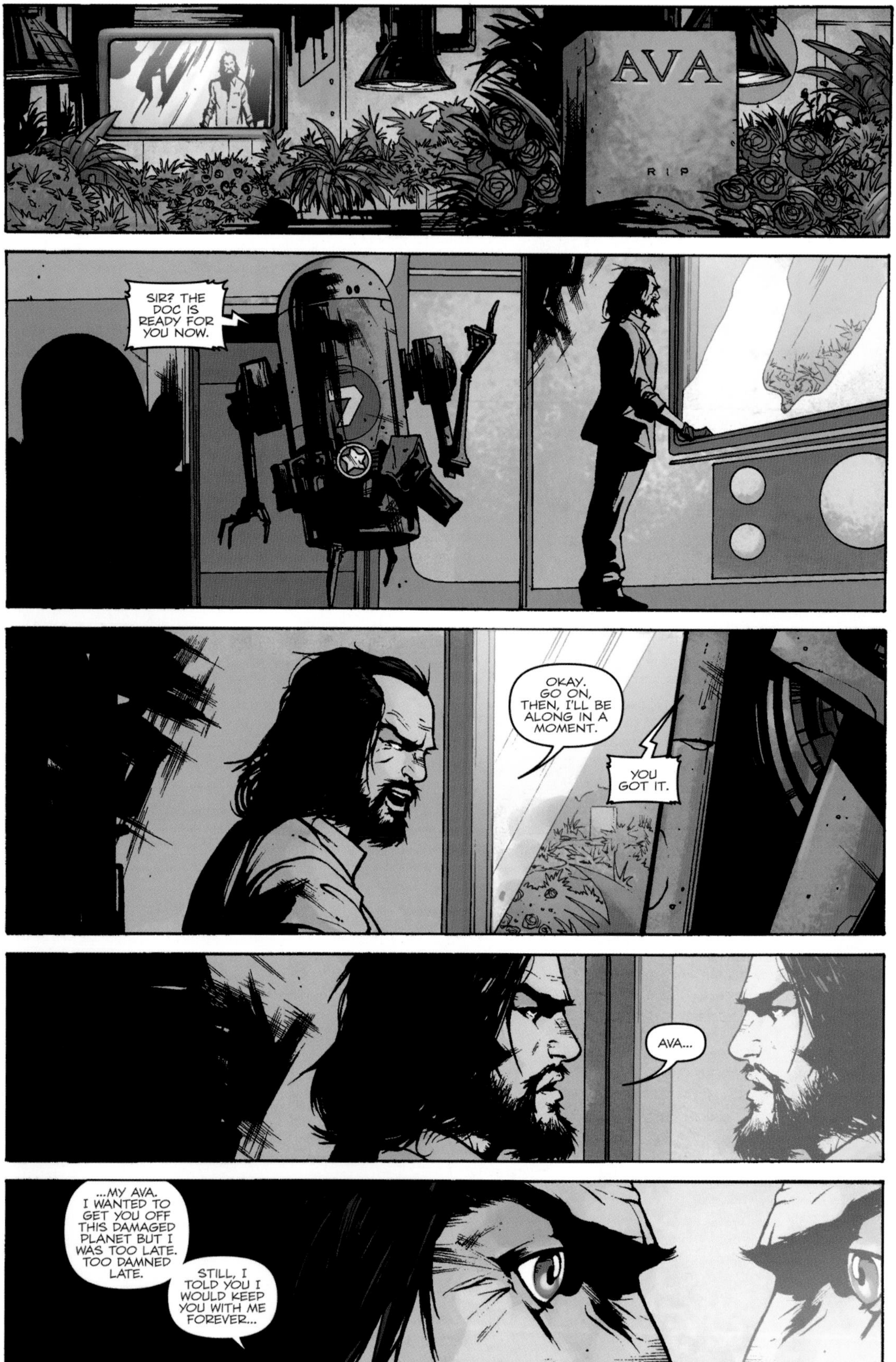
AVA
RIP
SIR? THE DOC IS READY FOR YOU NOW.
OKAY. GO ON, THEN, I'LL BE ALONG IN A MOMENT.
YOU GOT IT.
AVA...
...MY AVA. I WANTED TO GET YOU OFF THIS DAMAGED PLANET BUT I WAS TOO LATE. TOO DAMNED LATE.
STILL, I TOLD YOU I WOULD KEEP YOU WITH ME FOREVER...

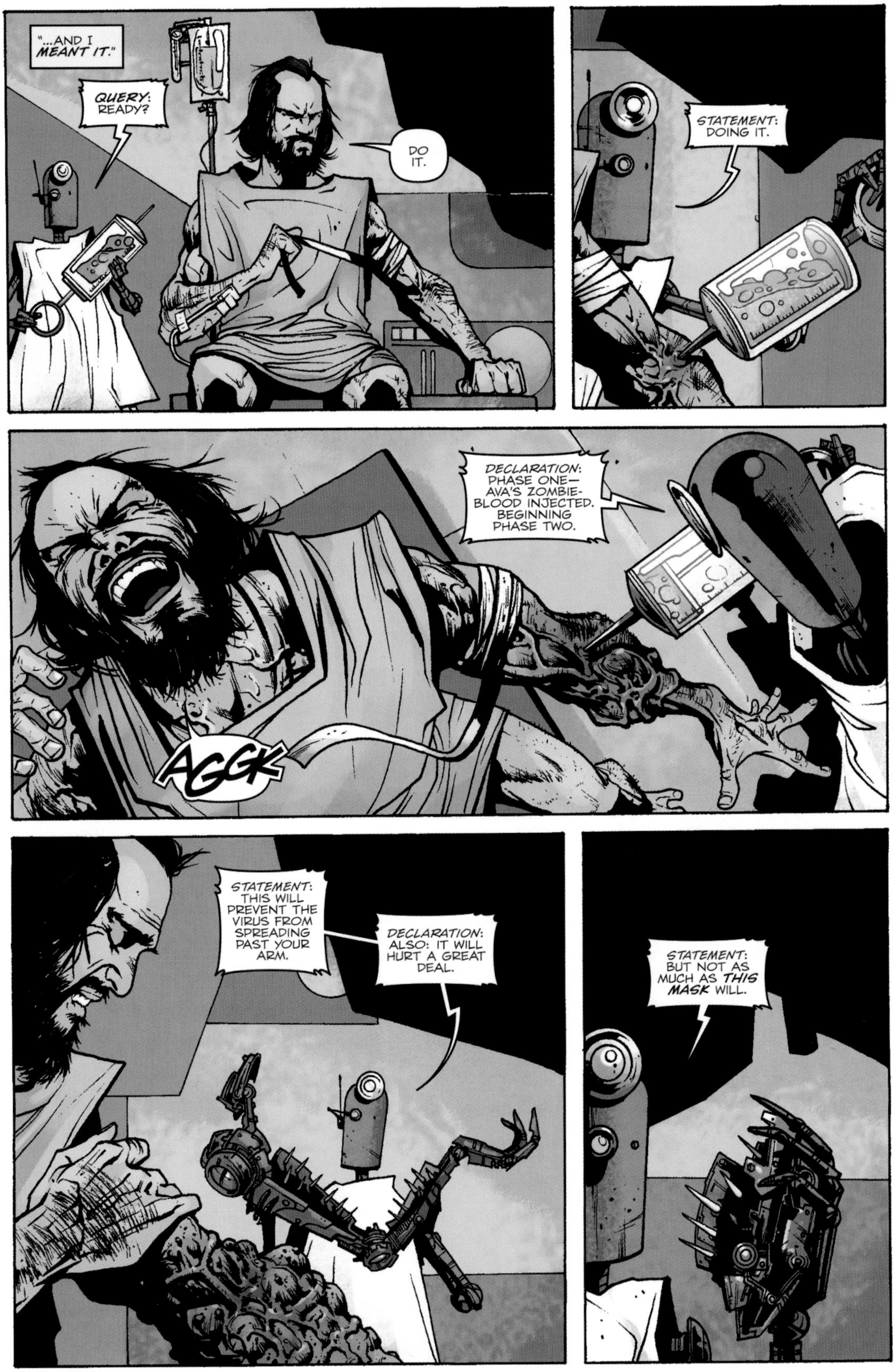

"...AND I *MEANT IT.*"
QUERY: READY?
DO IT.
STATEMENT: DOING IT.
DECLARATION: PHASE ONE— AVA'S ZOMBIE-BLOOD INJECTED. BEGINNING PHASE TWO.
AGGK
STATEMENT: THIS WILL PREVENT THE VIRUS FROM SPREADING PAST YOUR ARM.
DECLARATION: ALSO: IT WILL HURT A GREAT DEAL.
STATEMENT: BUT NOT AS MUCH AS *THIS MASK* WILL.

SOON...
PRESENTATION: HERE IS THE HARD DRIVE CONTAINING BUILDER'S PLANS FOR THE WARBOTS, A WORKABLE VIRUS MODEL, AND ASSORTED DRONE-BOTS.
THE ROCKET IS READY FOR LIFT-OFF NOW.
EXCELLENT.
YOU HEAD ON INTO THE ROCKET.
I'LL NEED YOU TO START THE REPLICATION PROCESS IMMEDIATELY AFTER ESTABLISHING THE BASE.
REMEMBER, BUILD THE 'BOTS AND PUT THEM IN SLEEP MODE UNTIL I NEED THEM.
YOU GOT IT, BOSS.
MY AVA, THIS PLANET HAS FAILED YOU. AND WILL PAY FOR IT DEARLY BEFORE LONG.
BUT FIRST, TO ESCAPE THIS EARTHLY PLANE AND PREPARE OUR REVENGE.
"TO THE MOON, AVA!"

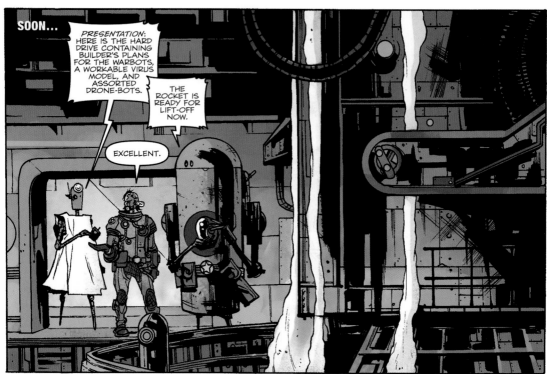

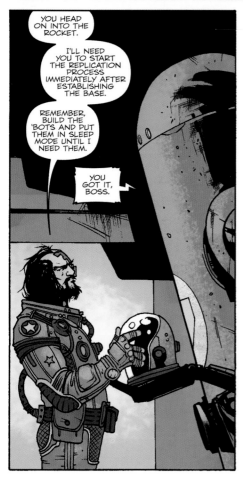

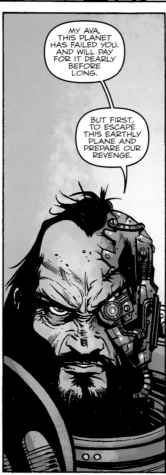

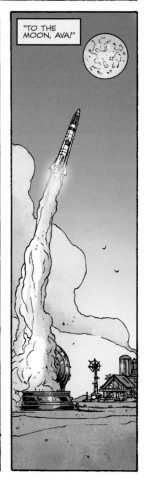

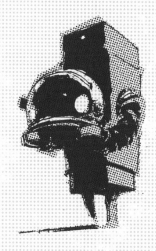

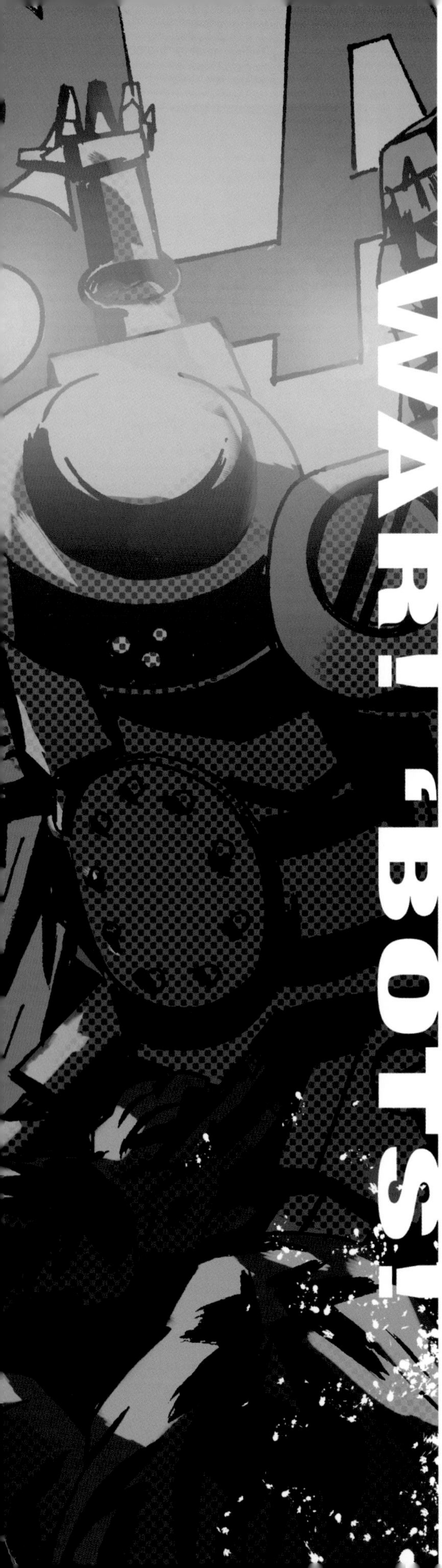
WAR of BOTS!

THE KIRTLAND MUNITIONS COMPLEX. THEN

...SOON ENOUGH, I SHALL LEARN WHAT LIES ON THE OTHER SIDE OF MY GATEWAY.

PHILLIPPE SATTERFIELD: Inventor of this inter-dimensional gateway

OUR GATEWAY. AND I STILL SAY I SHOULD GO.

FRITZ WINTERBOTTOM: Part of Satterfield's team; Iron person armor-maker

SORRY, CANNOT HEAR YOU WITH MY HELMET ON.

NOW STAND AND WATCH AS HISTORY IS MADE.

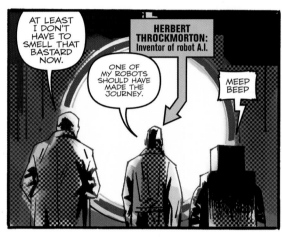

AT LEAST I DON'T HAVE TO SMELL THAT BASTARD NOW.

ONE OF MY ROBOTS SHOULD HAVE MADE THE JOURNEY.

HERBERT THROCKMORTON: Inventor of robot A.I.

MEEP BEEP

SOON ENOUGH.

C'MON BACK THROUGH, YOU ARROGANT—

—STUMP...?!

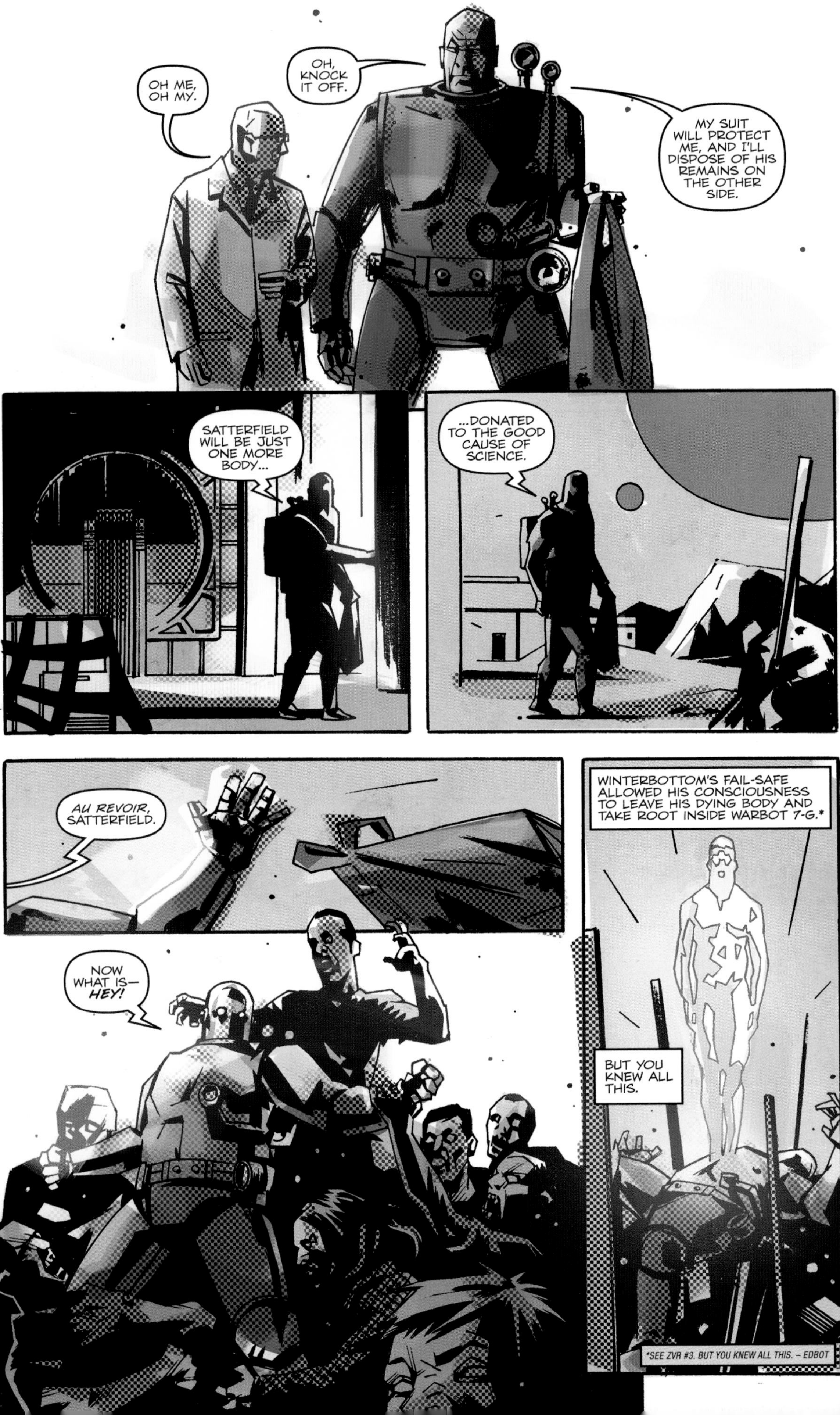

OH ME, OH MY.
OH, KNOCK IT OFF.
MY SUIT WILL PROTECT ME, AND I'LL DISPOSE OF HIS REMAINS ON THE OTHER SIDE.
SATTERFIELD WILL BE JUST ONE MORE BODY...
...DONATED TO THE GOOD CAUSE OF SCIENCE.
AU REVOIR, SATTERFIELD.
NOW WHAT IS— HEY!
WINTERBOTTOM'S FAIL-SAFE ALLOWED HIS CONSCIOUSNESS TO LEAVE HIS DYING BODY AND TAKE ROOT INSIDE WARBOT 7-G.*
BUT YOU KNEW ALL THIS.
*SEE ZVR #3. BUT YOU KNEW ALL THIS. – EDBOT

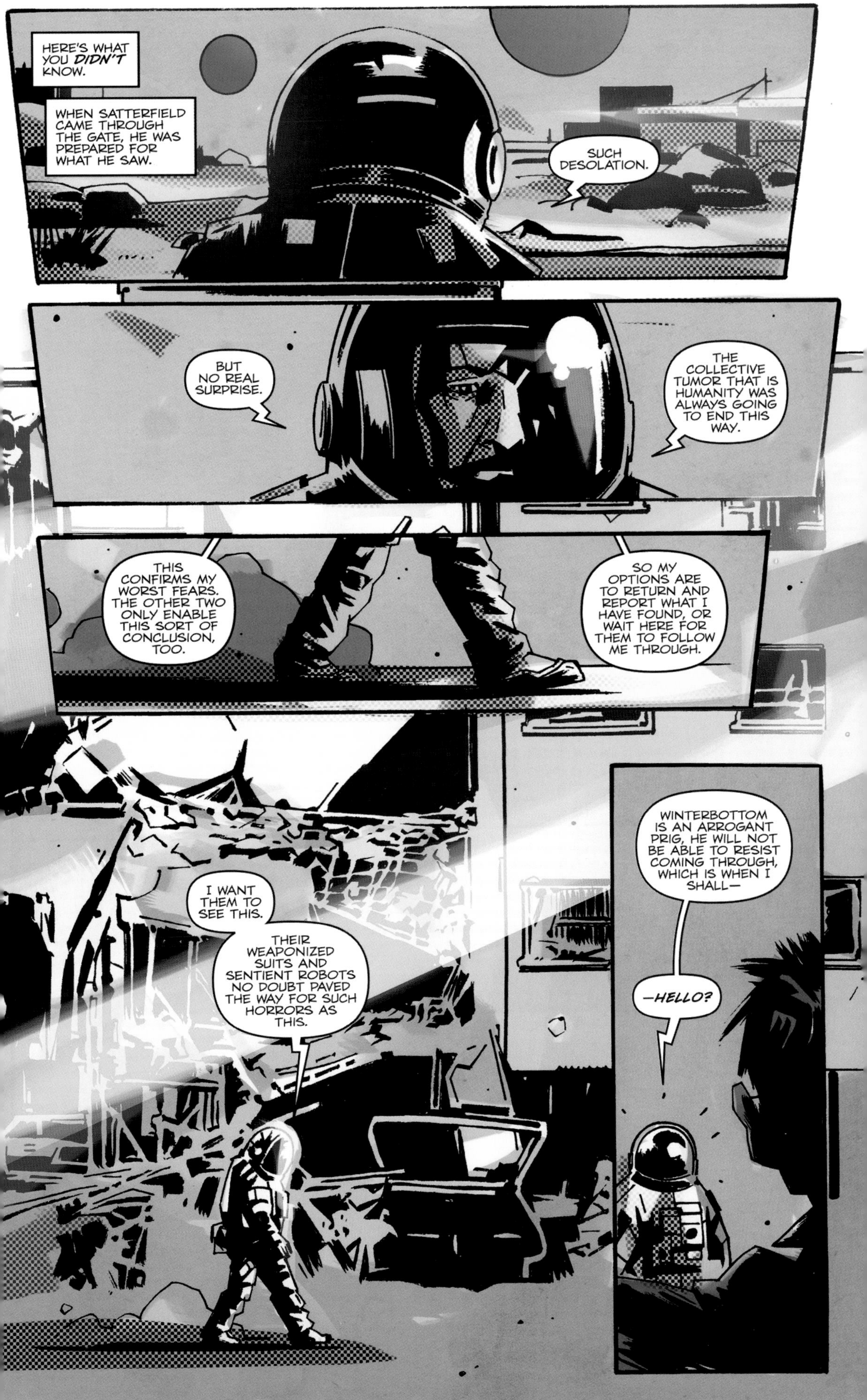
HERE'S WHAT YOU *DIDN'T* KNOW.
WHEN SATTERFIELD CAME THROUGH THE GATE, HE WAS PREPARED FOR WHAT HE SAW.
SUCH DESOLATION.
BUT NO REAL SURPRISE.
THE COLLECTIVE TUMOR THAT IS HUMANITY WAS ALWAYS GOING TO END THIS WAY.
THIS CONFIRMS MY WORST FEARS. THE OTHER TWO ONLY ENABLE THIS SORT OF CONCLUSION, TOO.
SO MY OPTIONS ARE TO RETURN AND REPORT WHAT I HAVE FOUND, OR WAIT HERE FOR THEM TO FOLLOW ME THROUGH.
I WANT THEM TO SEE THIS.
THEIR WEAPONIZED SUITS AND SENTIENT ROBOTS NO DOUBT PAVED THE WAY FOR SUCH HORRORS AS THIS.
WINTERBOTTOM IS AN ARROGANT PRIG, HE WILL NOT BE ABLE TO RESIST COMING THROUGH, WHICH IS WHEN I SHALL—
—*HELLO?*

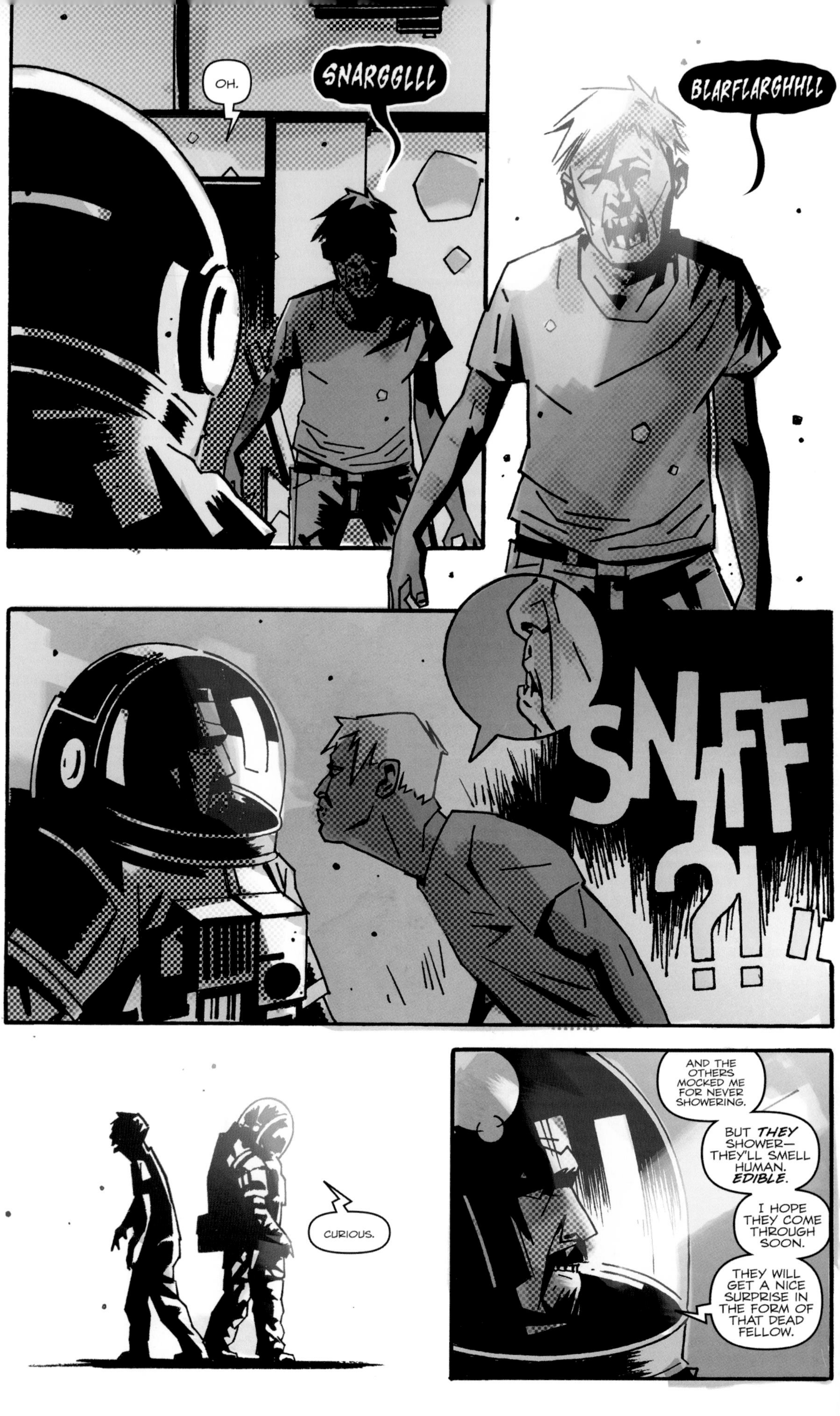
OH.
SNARGGLLL
BLARFLARGHHLL
SNIFF
?!!
CURIOUS.
AND THE OTHERS MOCKED ME FOR NEVER SHOWERING.
BUT *THEY* SHOWER— THEY'LL SMELL HUMAN. ***EDIBLE***.
I HOPE THEY COME THROUGH SOON.
THEY WILL GET A NICE SURPRISE IN THE FORM OF THAT DEAD FELLOW.

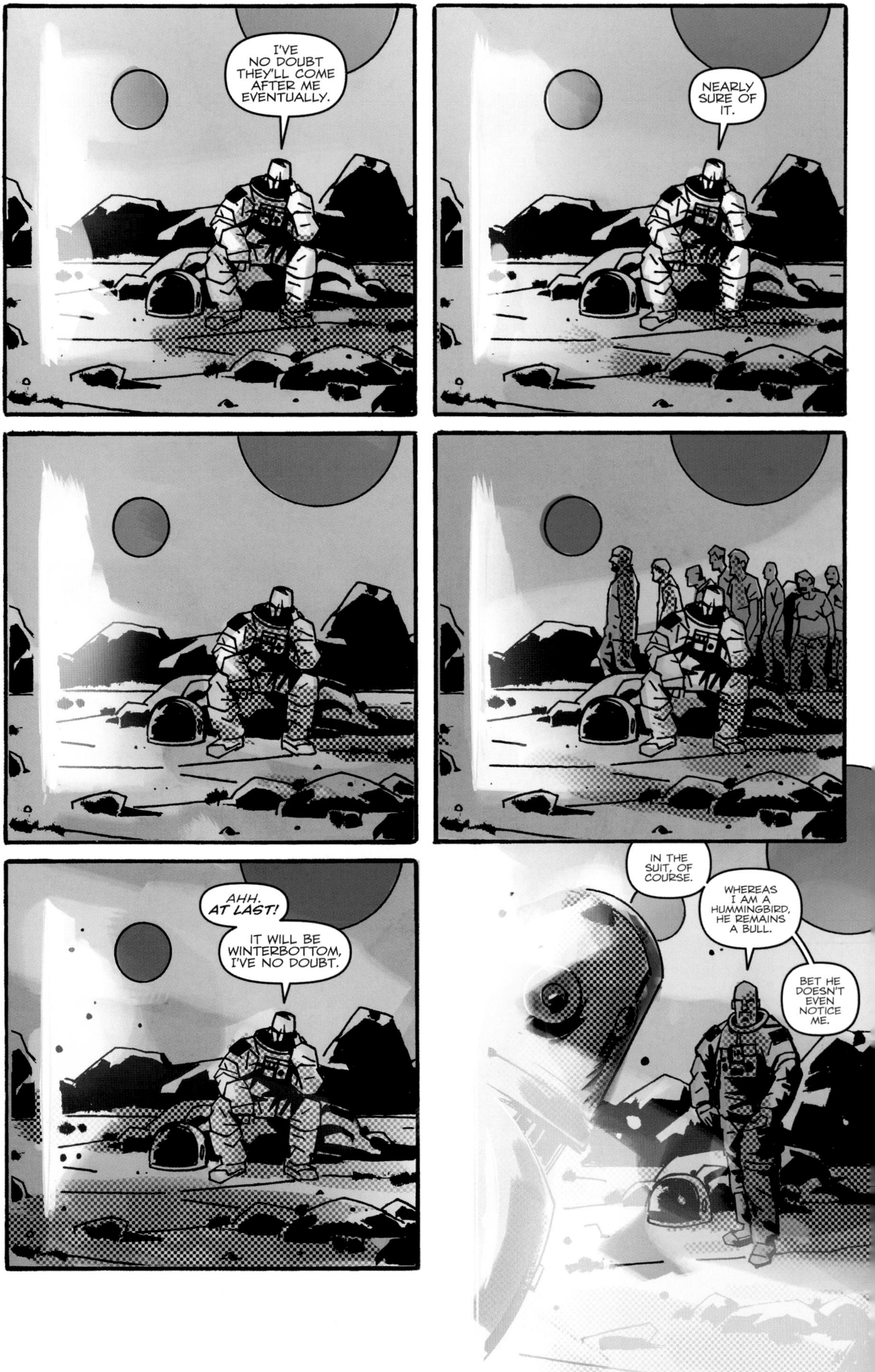
I'VE NO DOUBT THEY'LL COME AFTER ME EVENTUALLY.
NEARLY SURE OF IT.
AHH. AT LAST!
IT WILL BE WINTERBOTTOM, I'VE NO DOUBT.
IN THE SUIT, OF COURSE.
WHEREAS I AM A HUMMINGBIRD, HE REMAINS A BULL.
BET HE DOESN'T EVEN NOTICE ME.

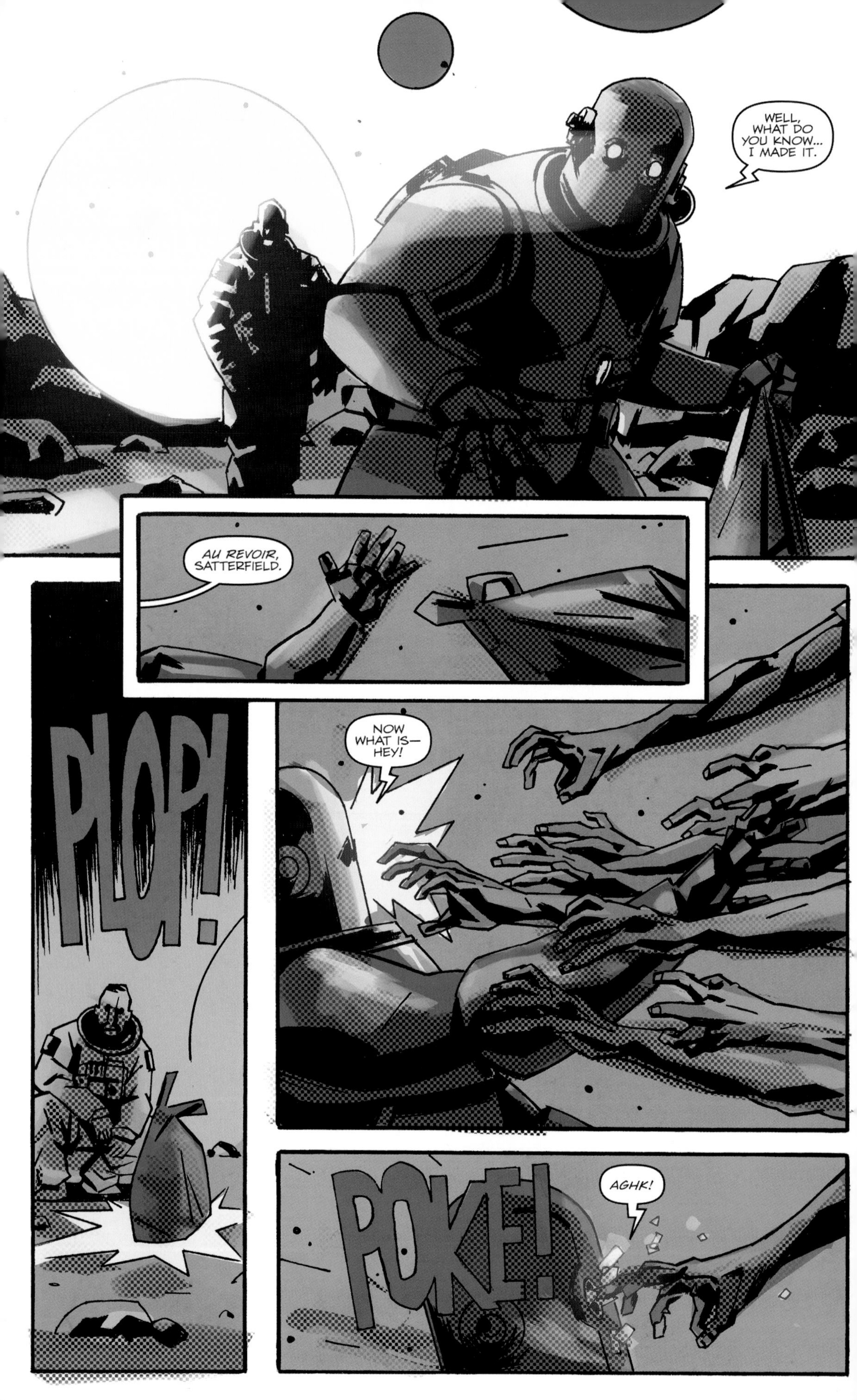
WELL, WHAT DO YOU KNOW... I MADE IT.
AU REVOIR, SATTERFIELD.
PLOP!
NOW WHAT IS— HEY!
POKE!
AGHK!

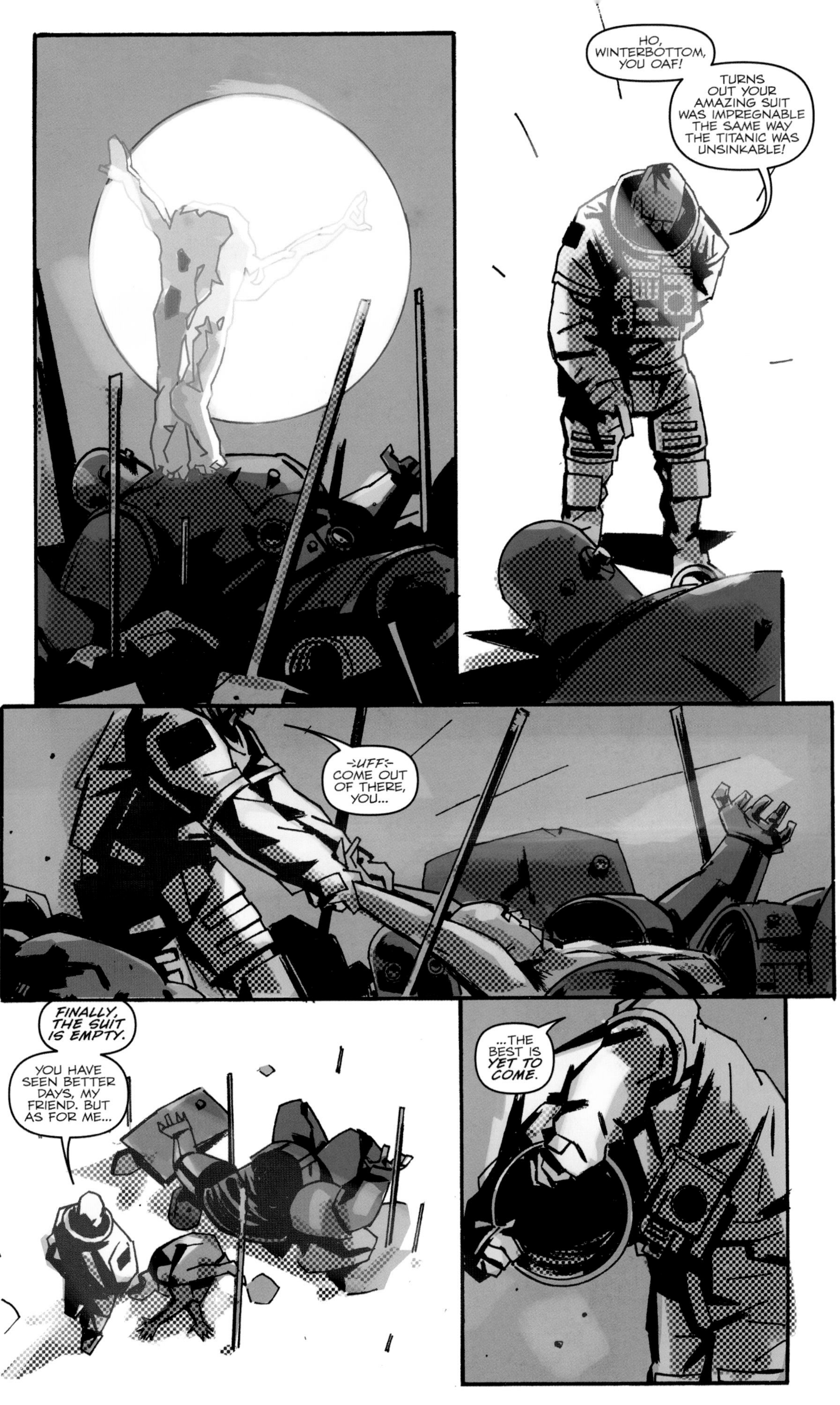
HO, WINTERBOTTOM, YOU OAF!
TURNS OUT YOUR AMAZING SUIT WAS IMPREGNABLE THE SAME WAY THE TITANIC WAS UNSINKABLE!
-UFF- COME OUT OF THERE, YOU...
FINALLY, THE SUIT IS EMPTY.
YOU HAVE SEEN BETTER DAYS, MY FRIEND. BUT AS FOR ME...
...THE BEST IS YET TO COME.

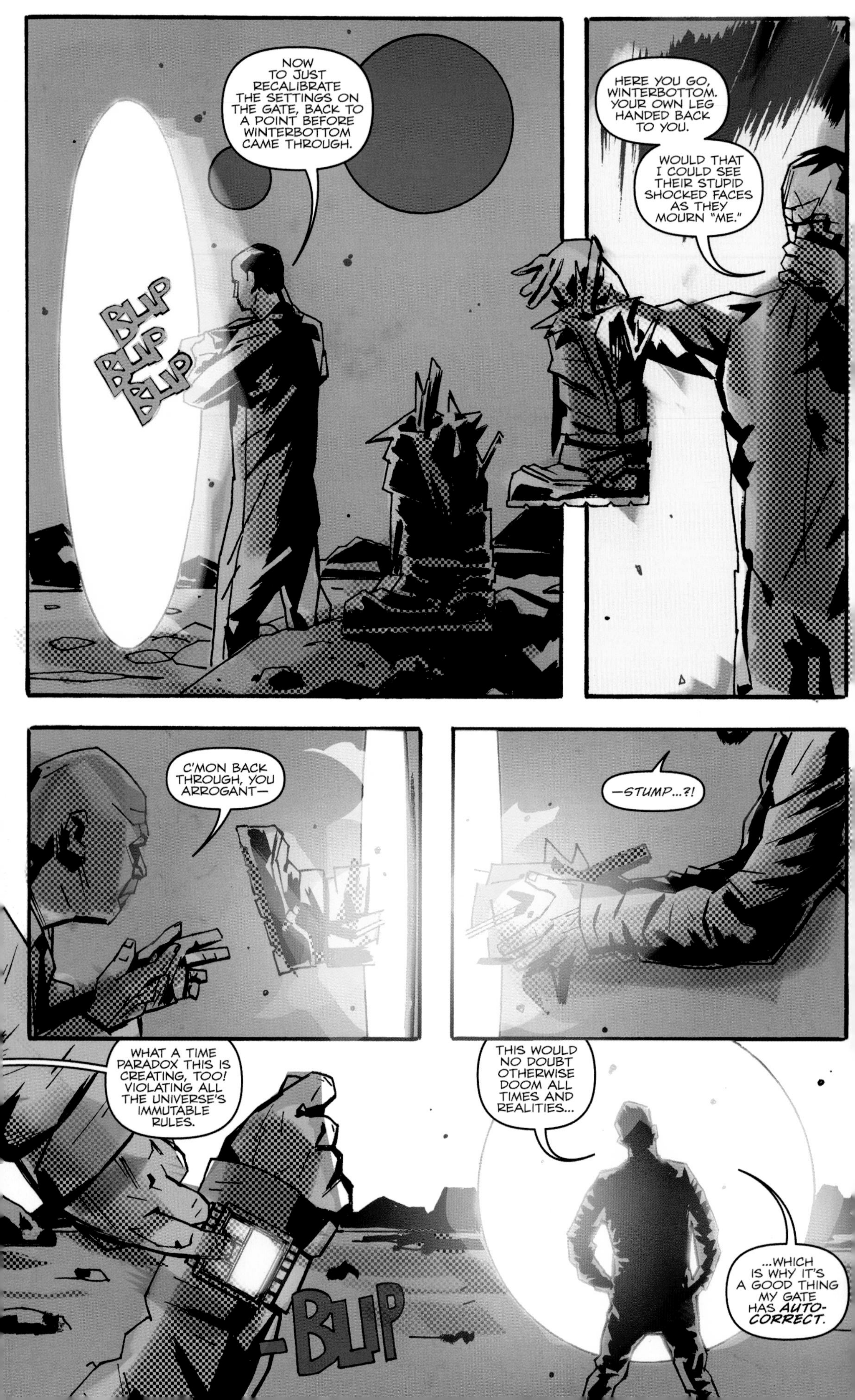
NOW TO JUST RECALIBRATE THE SETTINGS ON THE GATE, BACK TO A POINT BEFORE WINTERBOTTOM CAME THROUGH.
BLIP BLIP BLIP
HERE YOU GO, WINTERBOTTOM. YOUR OWN LEG HANDED BACK TO YOU.
WOULD THAT I COULD SEE THEIR STUPID SHOCKED FACES AS THEY MOURN "ME."
C'MON BACK THROUGH, YOU ARROGANT—
—STUMP...?!
WHAT A TIME PARADOX THIS IS CREATING, TOO! VIOLATING ALL THE UNIVERSE'S IMMUTABLE RULES.
THIS WOULD NO DOUBT OTHERWISE DOOM ALL TIMES AND REALITIES...
...WHICH IS WHY IT'S A GOOD THING MY GATE HAS ***AUTO-CORRECT***.
BLIP

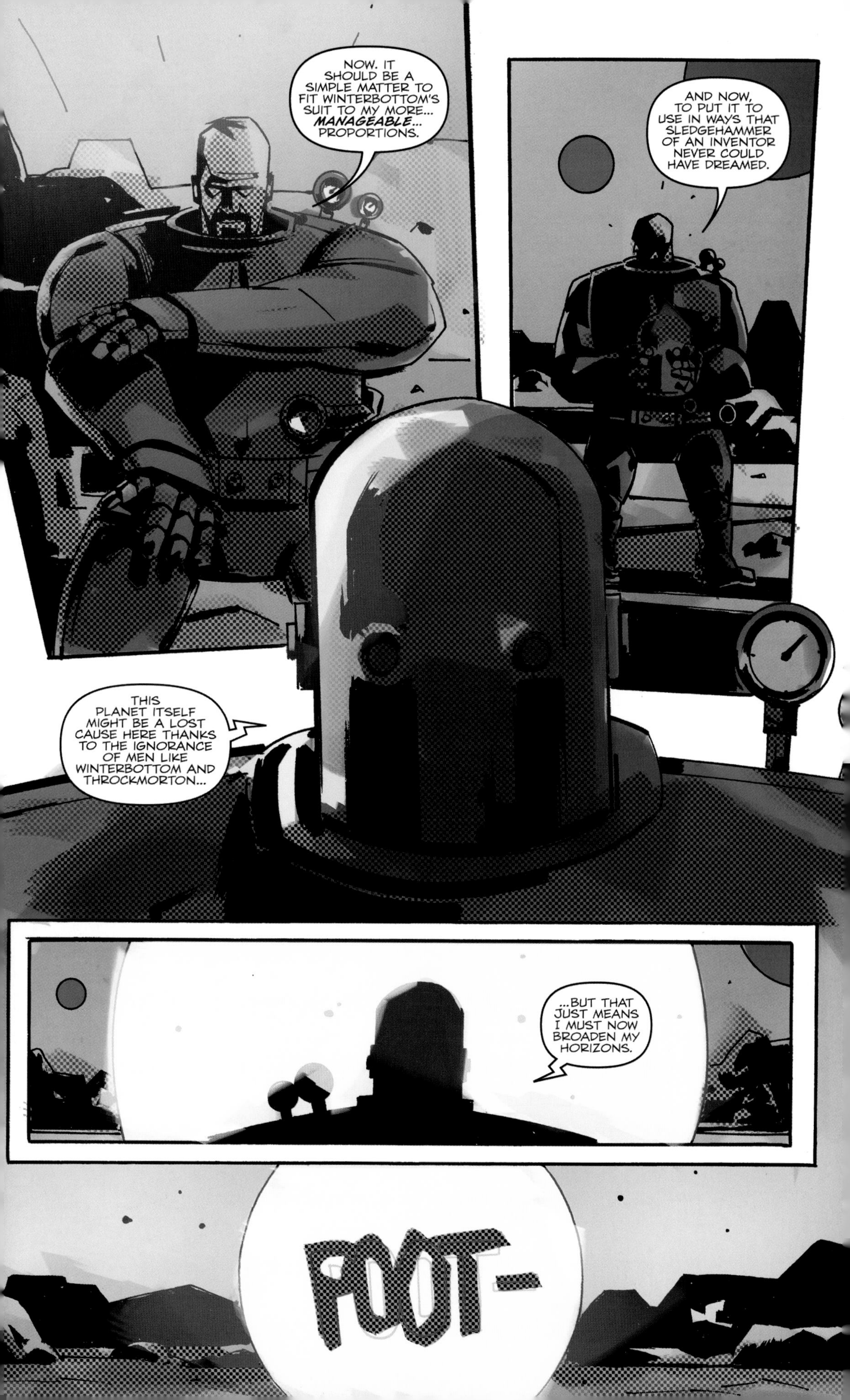
NOW. IT SHOULD BE A SIMPLE MATTER TO FIT WINTERBOTTOM'S SUIT TO MY MORE... ***MANAGEABLE***... PROPORTIONS.
AND NOW, TO PUT IT TO USE IN WAYS THAT SLEDGEHAMMER OF AN INVENTOR NEVER COULD HAVE DREAMED.
THIS PLANET ITSELF MIGHT BE A LOST CAUSE HERE THANKS TO THE IGNORANCE OF MEN LIKE WINTERBOTTOM AND THROCKMORTON...
...BUT THAT JUST MEANS I MUST NOW BROADEN MY HORIZONS.
FOOT-

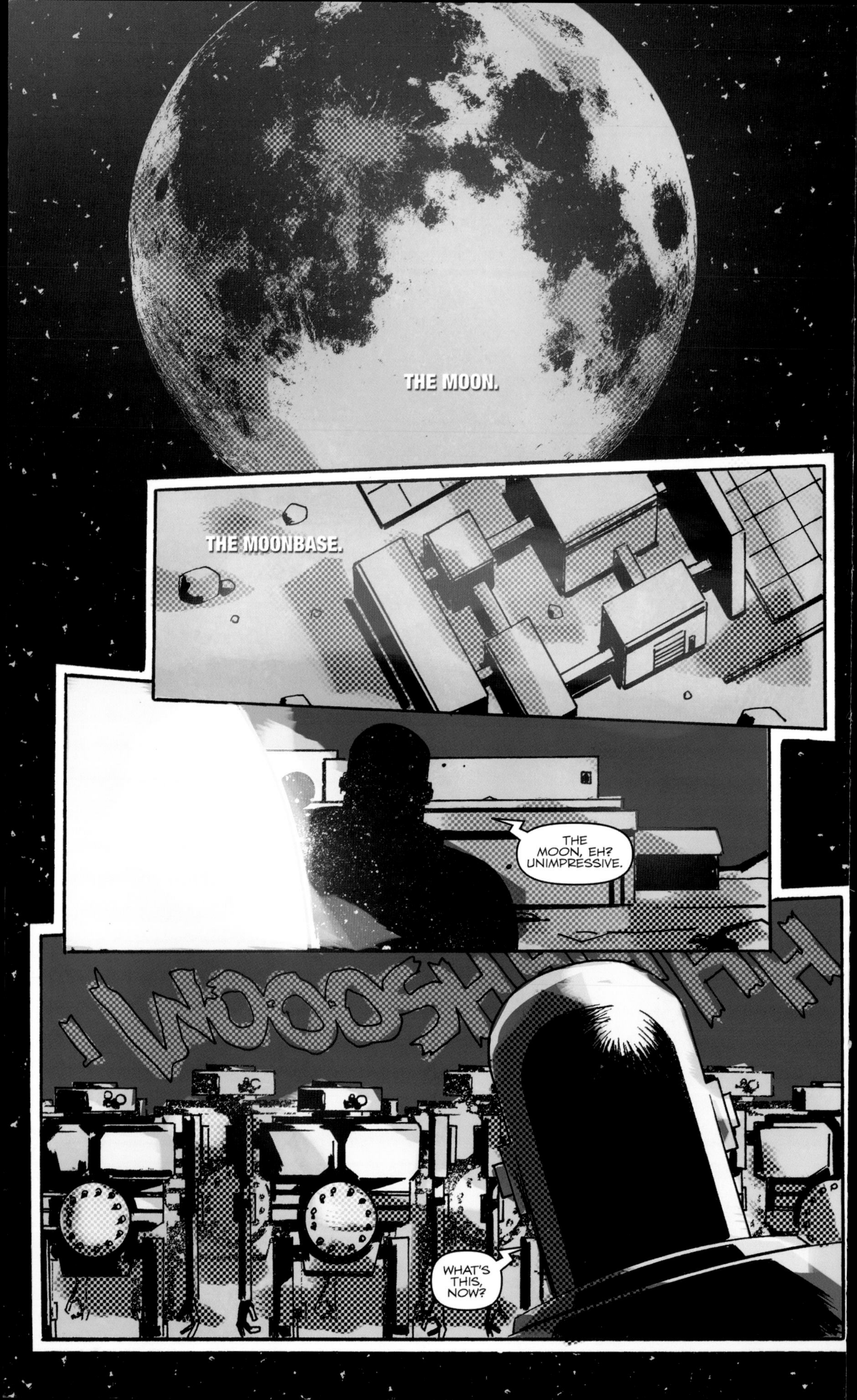
THE MOON.
THE MOONBASE.
THE MOON, EH? UNIMPRESSIVE.
WOOSHHHHHH
WHAT'S THIS, NOW?

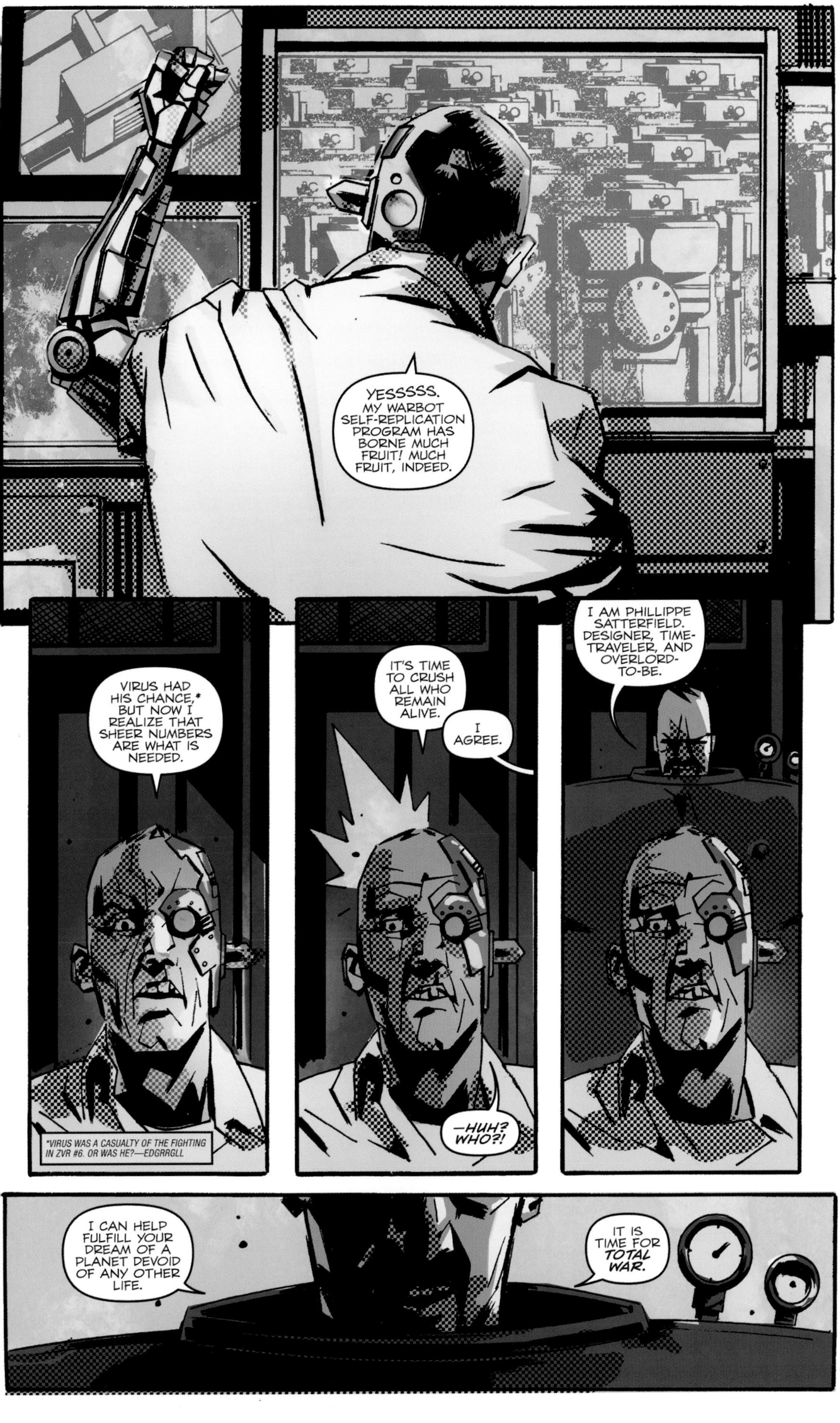
YESSSSS. MY WARBOT SELF-REPLICATION PROGRAM HAS BORNE MUCH FRUIT! MUCH FRUIT, INDEED.
VIRUS HAD HIS CHANCE,* BUT NOW I REALIZE THAT SHEER NUMBERS ARE WHAT IS NEEDED.
*VIRUS WAS A CASUALTY OF THE FIGHTING IN ZVR #6. OR WAS HE?—EDGRRGLL
IT'S TIME TO CRUSH ALL WHO REMAIN ALIVE.
I AGREE.
—HUH? WHO?!
I AM PHILLIPPE SATTERFIELD. DESIGNER, TIME-TRAVELER, AND OVERLORD-TO-BE.
I CAN HELP FULFILL YOUR DREAM OF A PLANET DEVOID OF ANY OTHER LIFE.
IT IS TIME FOR TOTAL WAR.

"THIS JUST MIGHT WORK."

OF COURSE IT'LL WORK. THESE SHIPS WERE BUILT TO CROSS OCEANS, AND THAT'S WHAT WE'RE USING IT FOR.

I CAN WIRELESSLY STEER IT, SO NO PROBLEM KEEPING OUR COURSE.

LONG AS WE'RE AWAY FROM ZOMBIES AND CRAZINESS FOR A WHILE.

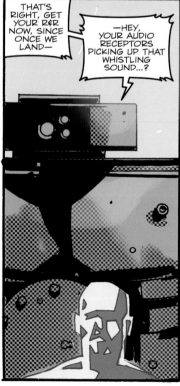

THAT'S RIGHT, GET YOUR R&R NOW, SINCE ONCE WE LAND—

—HEY, YOUR AUDIO RECEPTORS PICKING UP THAT WHISTLING SOUND...?

THEY'RE CALLED "EARS" ON HUMANS, YOU LUNK, BUT I DON'T HEAR... WAIT...

I THINK I DO HEAR SOMETHING.

OH, HOLY SHIT.

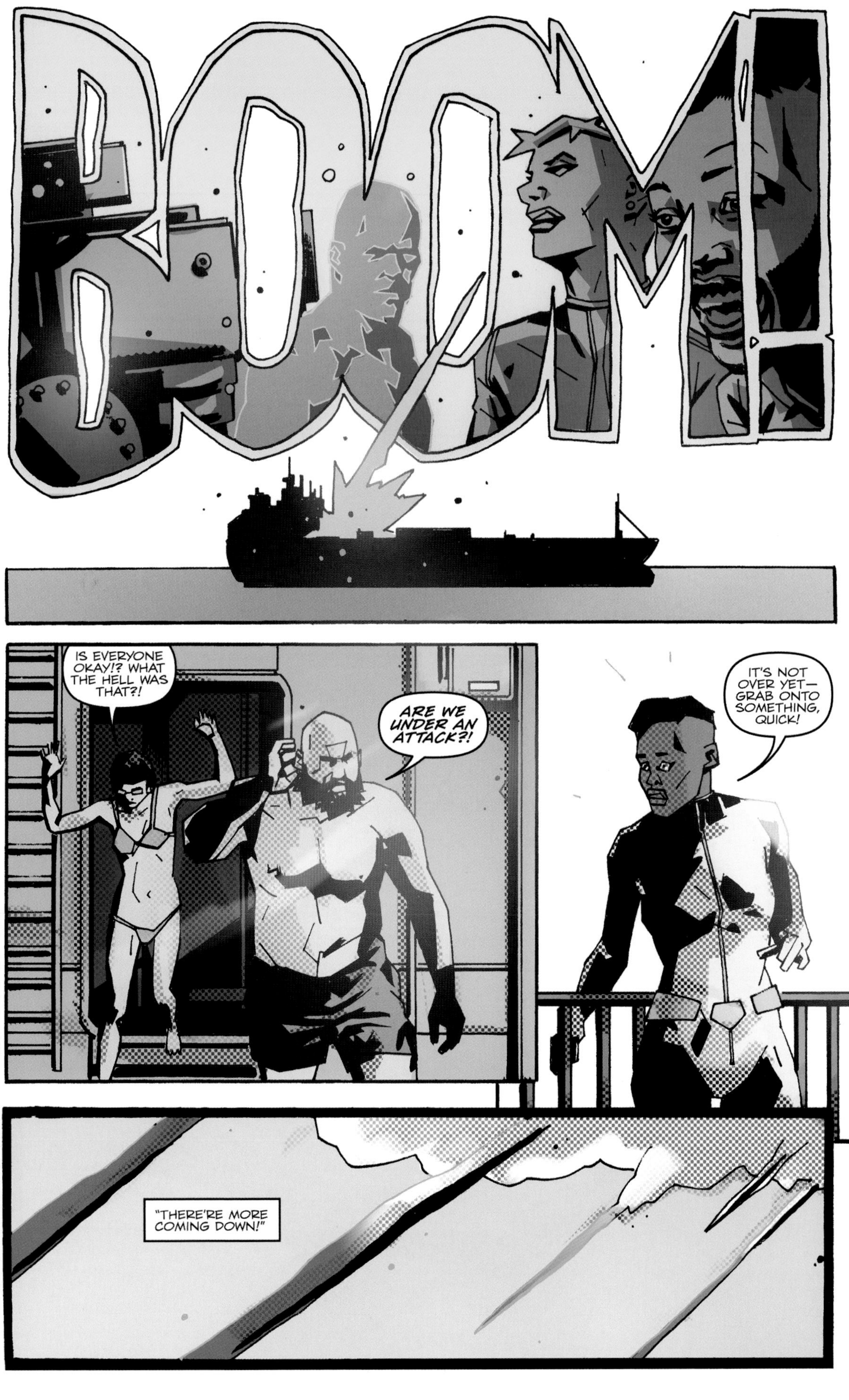
BOOM!
IS EVERYONE OKAY!? WHAT THE HELL WAS THAT?!
ARE WE UNDER AN ATTACK?!
IT'S NOT OVER YET—GRAB ONTO SOMETHING, QUICK!
"THERE'RE MORE COMING DOWN!"

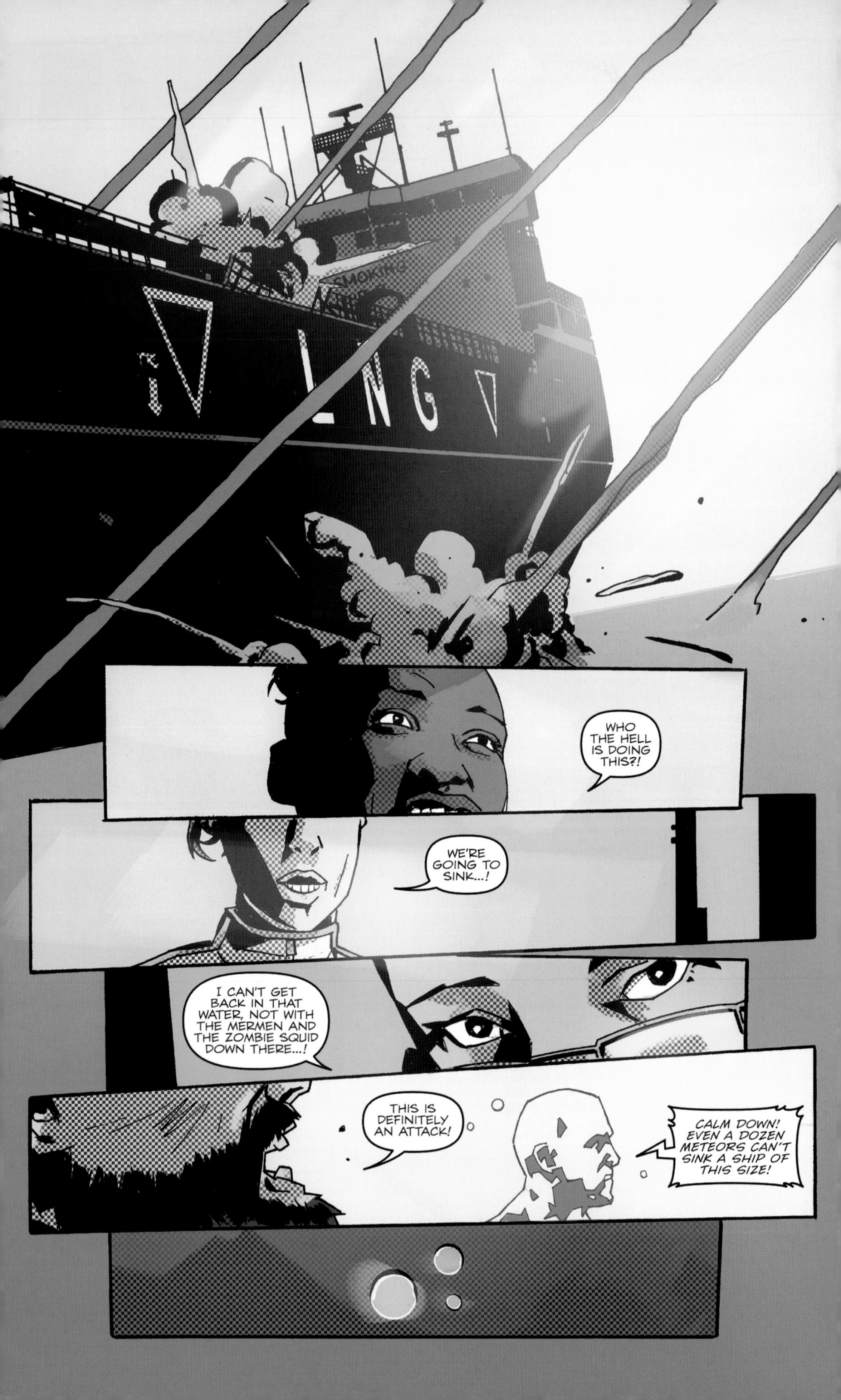
LNG
SMOKING
WHO THE HELL IS DOING THIS?!
WE'RE GOING TO SINK...!
I CAN'T GET BACK IN THAT WATER, NOT WITH THE MERMEN AND THE ZOMBIE SQUID DOWN THERE...!
THIS IS DEFINITELY AN ATTACK!
CALM DOWN! EVEN A DOZEN METEORS CAN'T SINK A SHIP OF THIS SIZE!

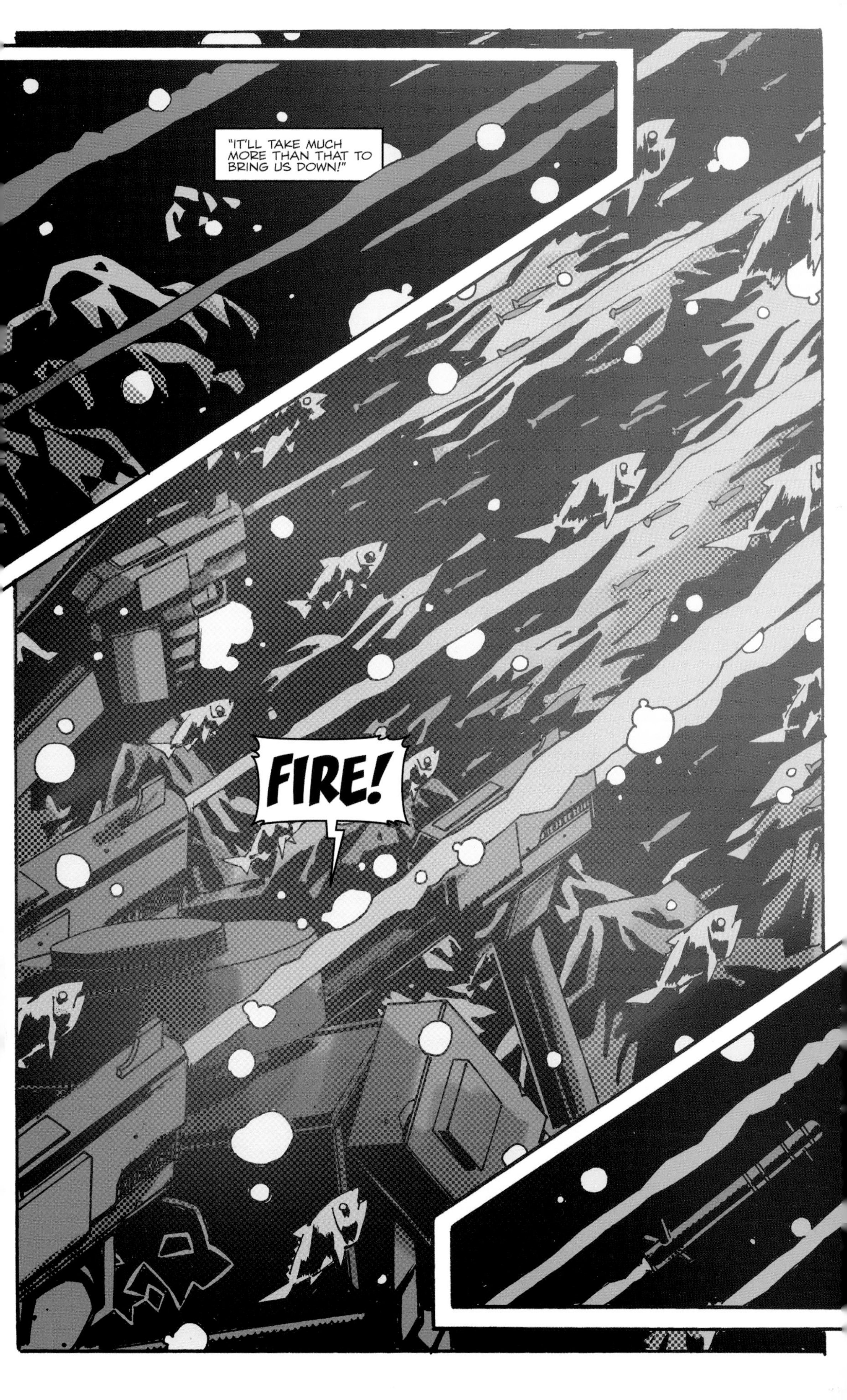
"IT'LL TAKE MUCH MORE THAN THAT TO BRING US DOWN!"
FIRE!

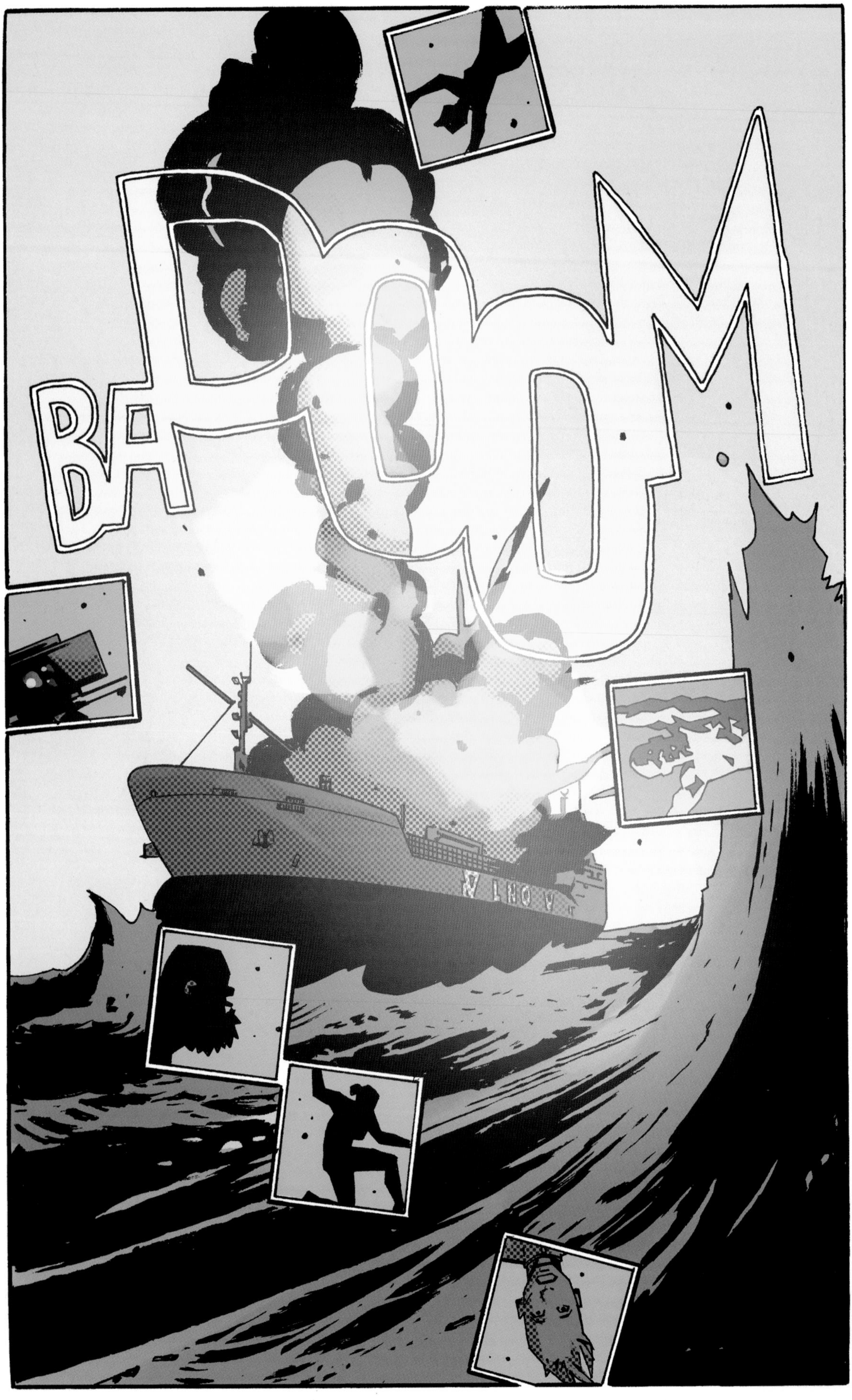
BADOOM

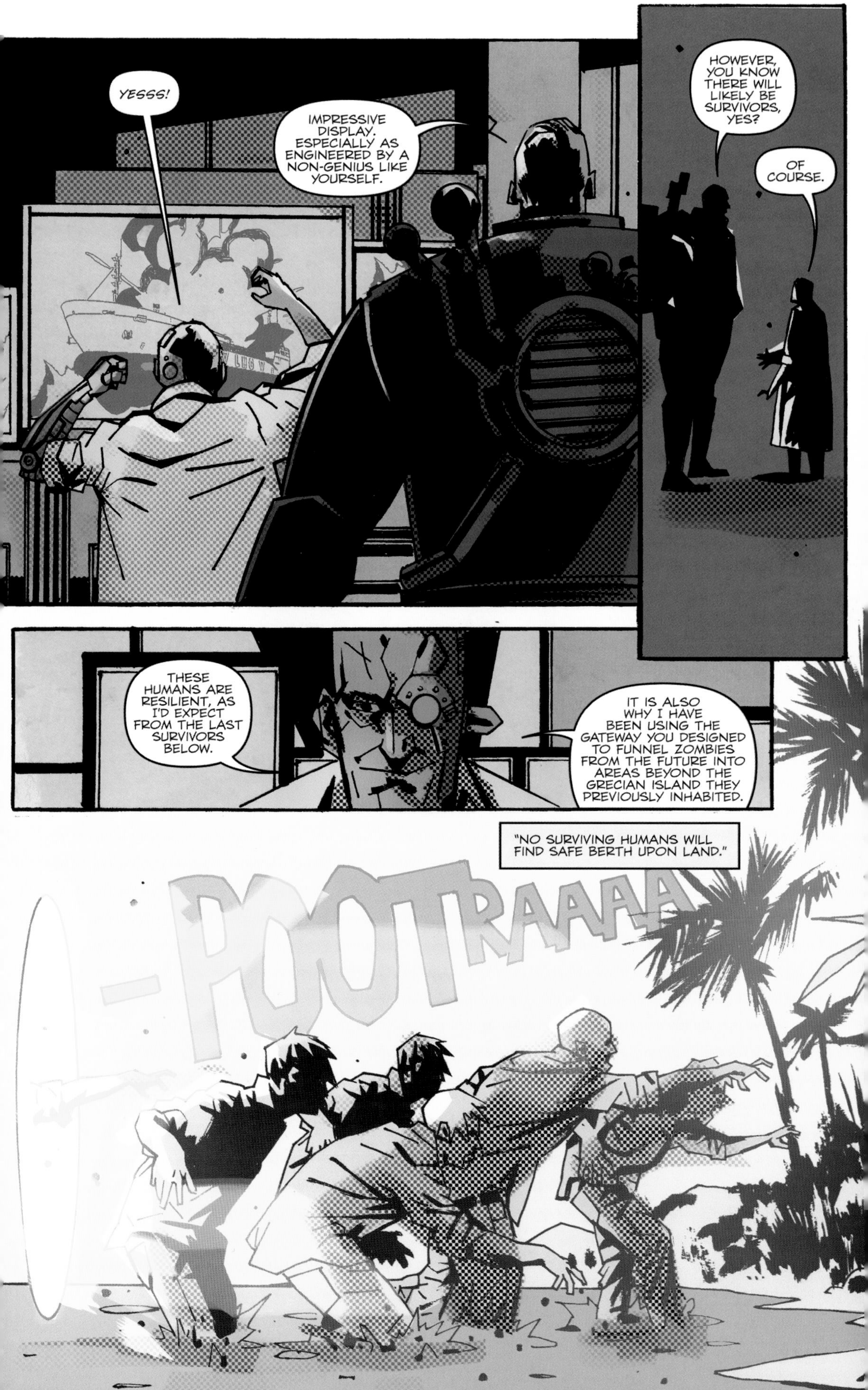
YESSS!
IMPRESSIVE DISPLAY. ESPECIALLY AS ENGINEERED BY A NON-GENIUS LIKE YOURSELF.
HOWEVER, YOU KNOW THERE WILL LIKELY BE SURVIVORS, YES?
OF COURSE.
THESE HUMANS ARE RESILIENT, AS I'D EXPECT FROM THE LAST SURVIVORS BELOW.
IT IS ALSO WHY I HAVE BEEN USING THE GATEWAY YOU DESIGNED TO FUNNEL ZOMBIES FROM THE FUTURE INTO AREAS BEYOND THE GRECIAN ISLAND THEY PREVIOUSLY INHABITED.
"NO SURVIVING HUMANS WILL FIND SAFE BERTH UPON LAND."
-POOOTRAAAA

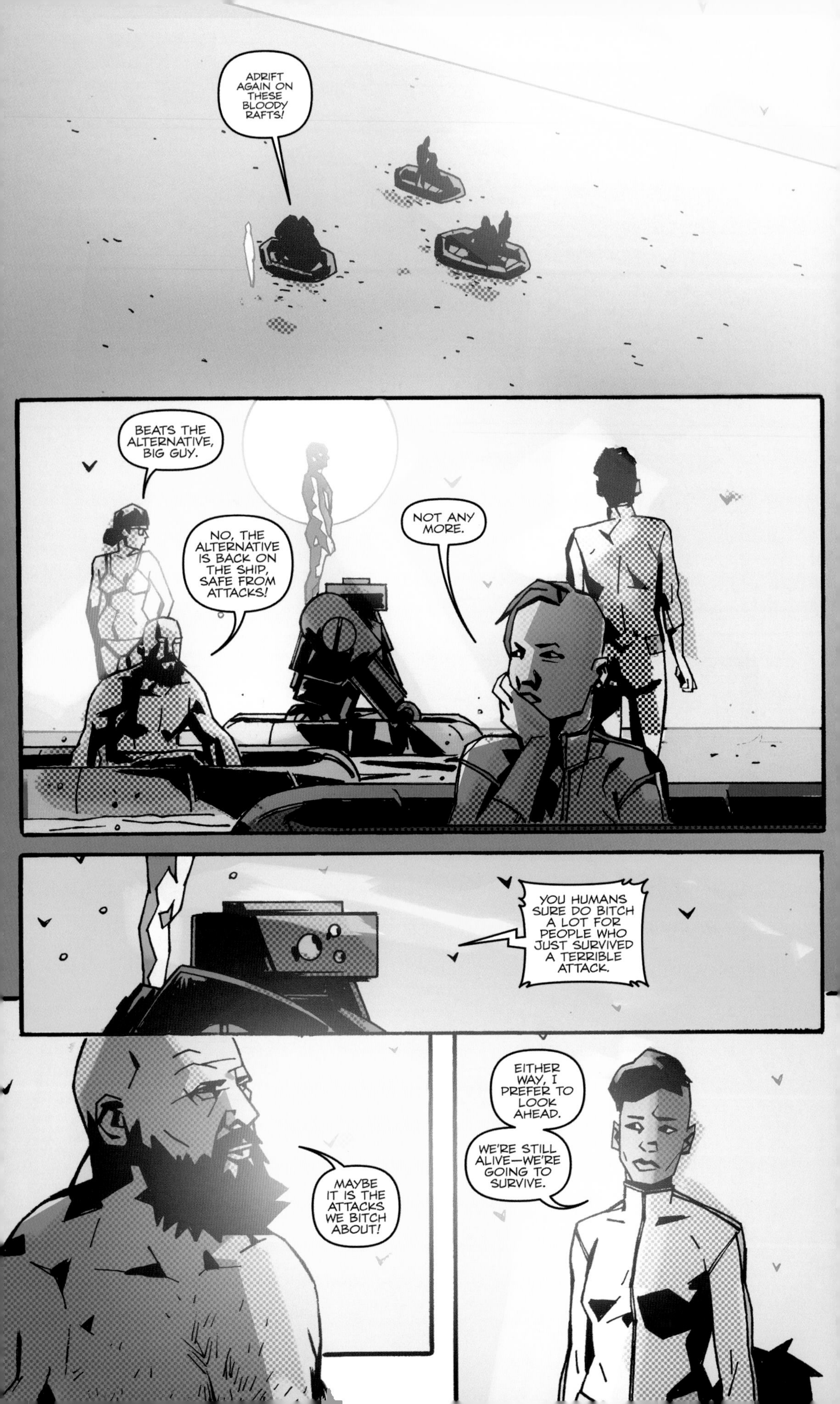

ADRIFT AGAIN ON THESE BLOODY RAFTS!
BEATS THE ALTERNATIVE, BIG GUY.
NO, THE ALTERNATIVE IS BACK ON THE SHIP, SAFE FROM ATTACKS!
NOT ANY MORE.
YOU HUMANS SURE DO BITCH A LOT FOR PEOPLE WHO JUST SURVIVED A TERRIBLE ATTACK.
MAYBE IT IS THE ATTACKS WE BITCH ABOUT!
EITHER WAY, I PREFER TO LOOK AHEAD.
WE'RE STILL ALIVE—WE'RE GOING TO SURVIVE.

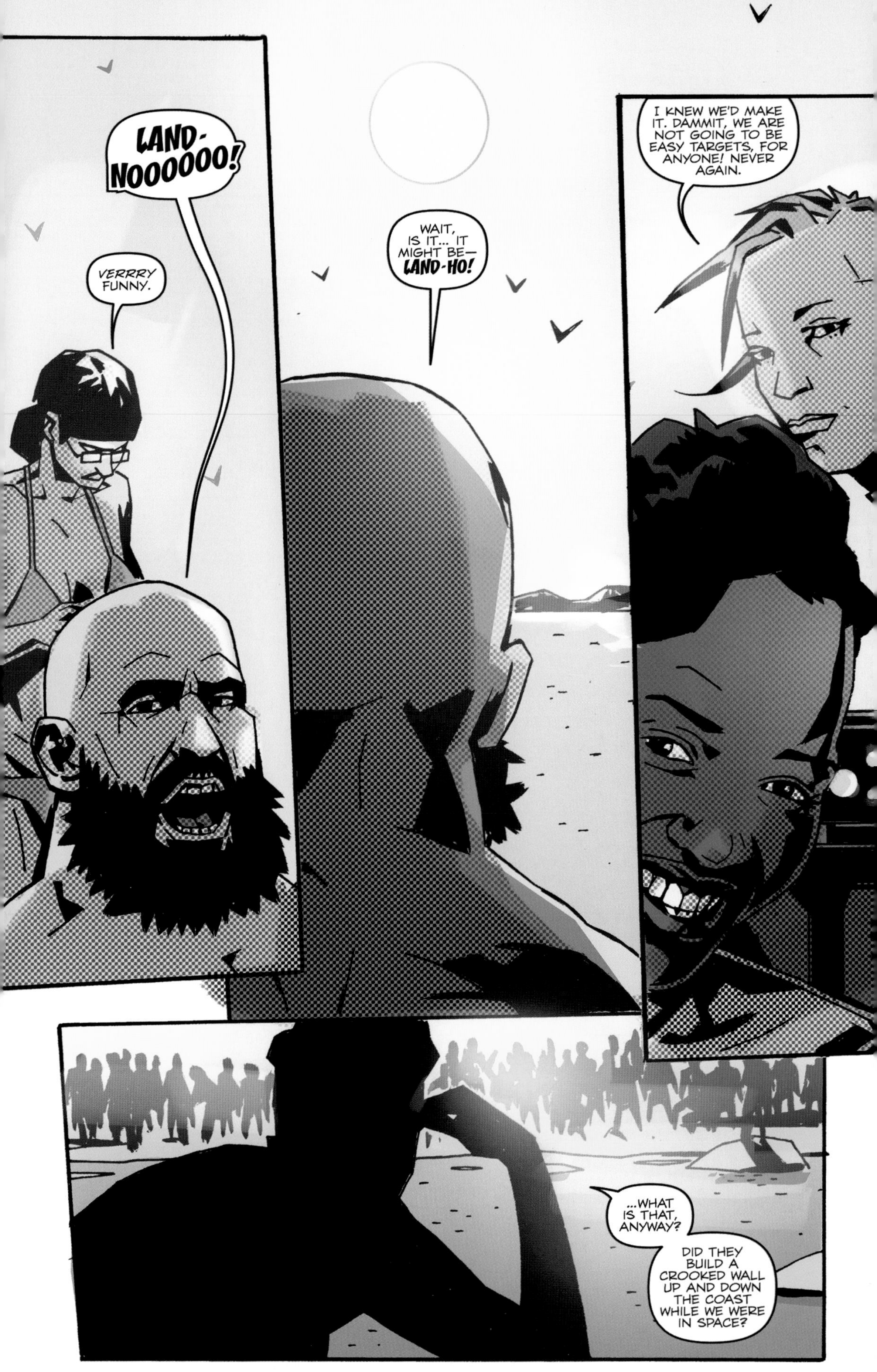
LAND-NOOOOOO!
VERRRY FUNNY.
WAIT, IS IT... IT MIGHT BE— LAND-HO!
I KNEW WE'D MAKE IT. DAMMIT, WE ARE NOT GOING TO BE EASY TARGETS, FOR ANYONE! NEVER AGAIN.
...WHAT IS THAT, ANYWAY?
DID THEY BUILD A CROOKED WALL UP AND DOWN THE COAST WHILE WE WERE IN SPACE?

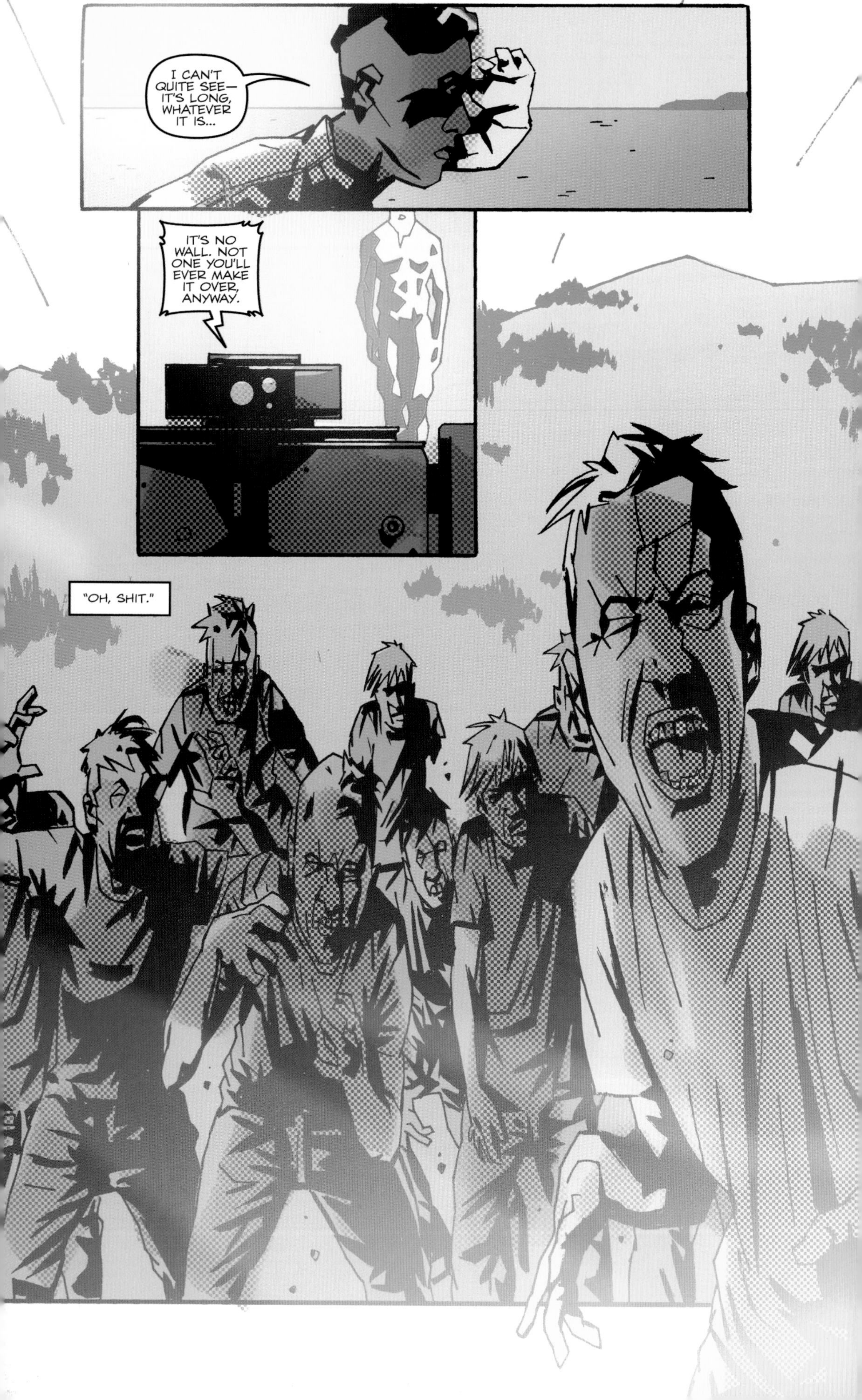
I CAN'T QUITE SEE— IT'S LONG, WHATEVER IT IS...
IT'S NO WALL. NOT ONE YOU'LL EVER MAKE IT OVER, ANYWAY.
"OH, SHIT."

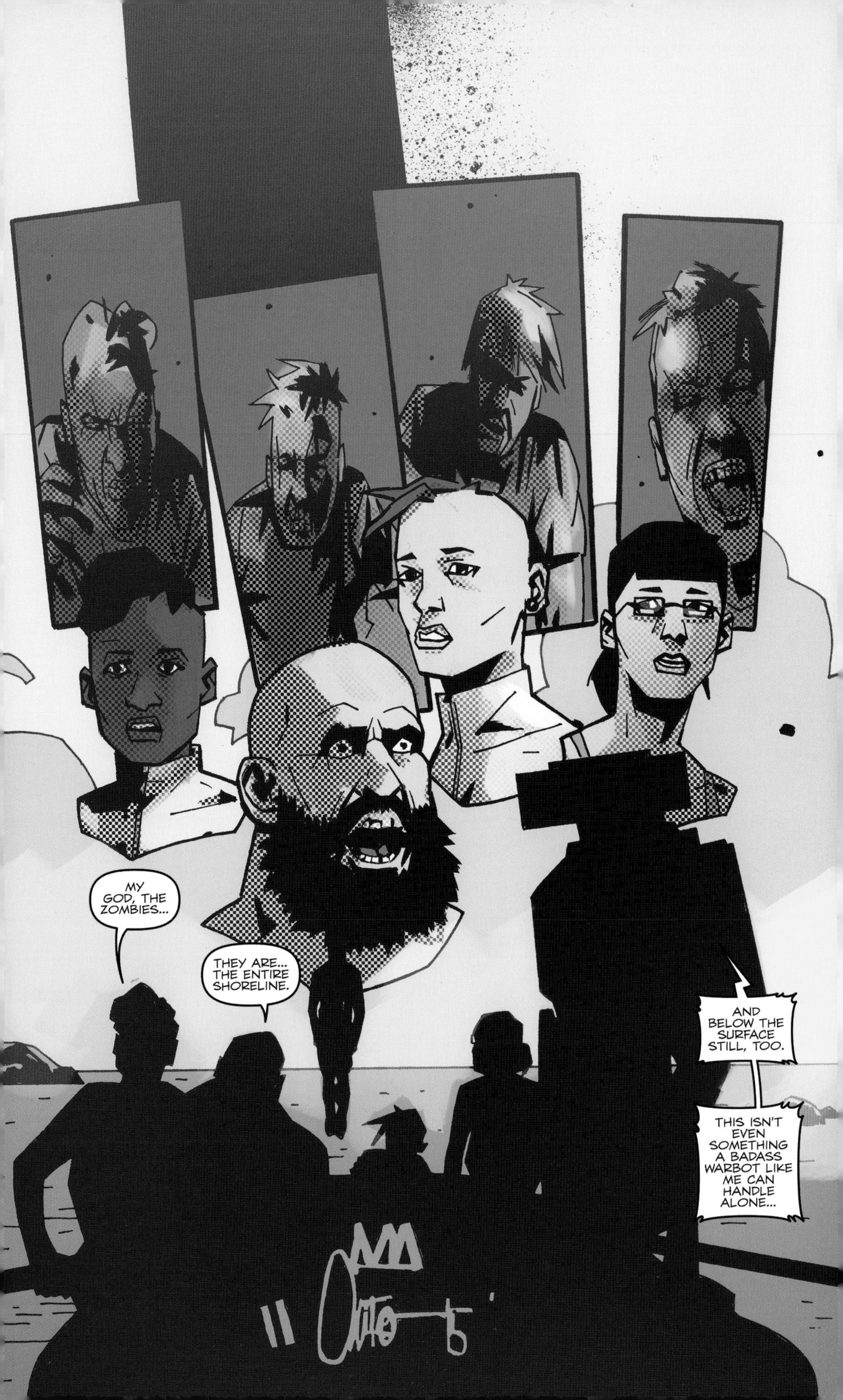
MY GOD, THE ZOMBIES...
THEY ARE... THE ENTIRE SHORELINE.
AND BELOW THE SURFACE STILL, TOO.
THIS ISN'T EVEN SOMETHING A BADASS WARBOT LIKE ME CAN HANDLE ALONE...

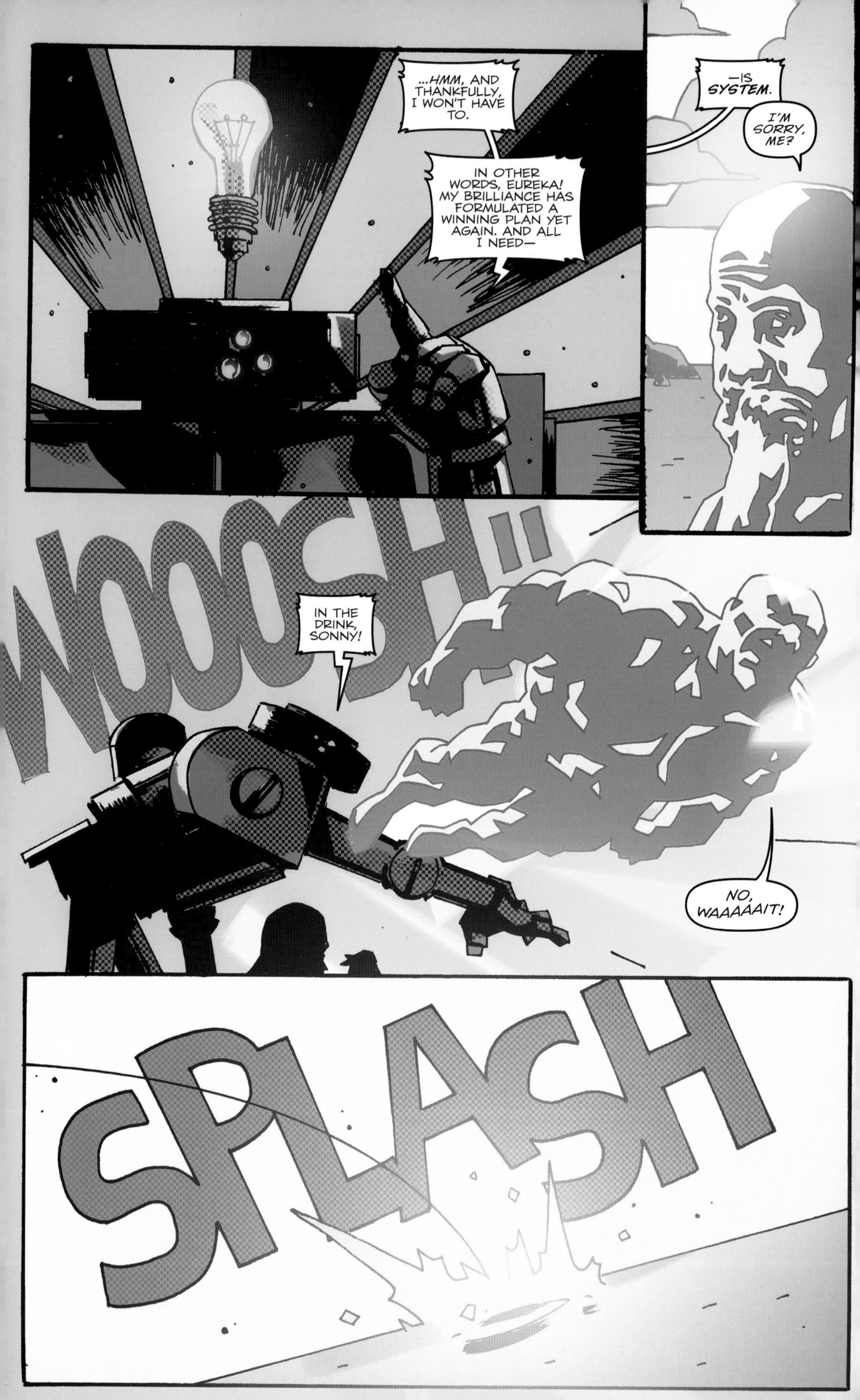
...HMM, AND THANKFULLY, I WON'T HAVE TO.
IN OTHER WORDS, EUREKA! MY BRILLIANCE HAS FORMULATED A WINNING PLAN YET AGAIN. AND ALL I NEED—
—IS SYSTEM.
I'M SORRY, ME?
WOOOSH!!
IN THE DRINK, SONNY!
NO, WAAAAAIT!
SPLASH

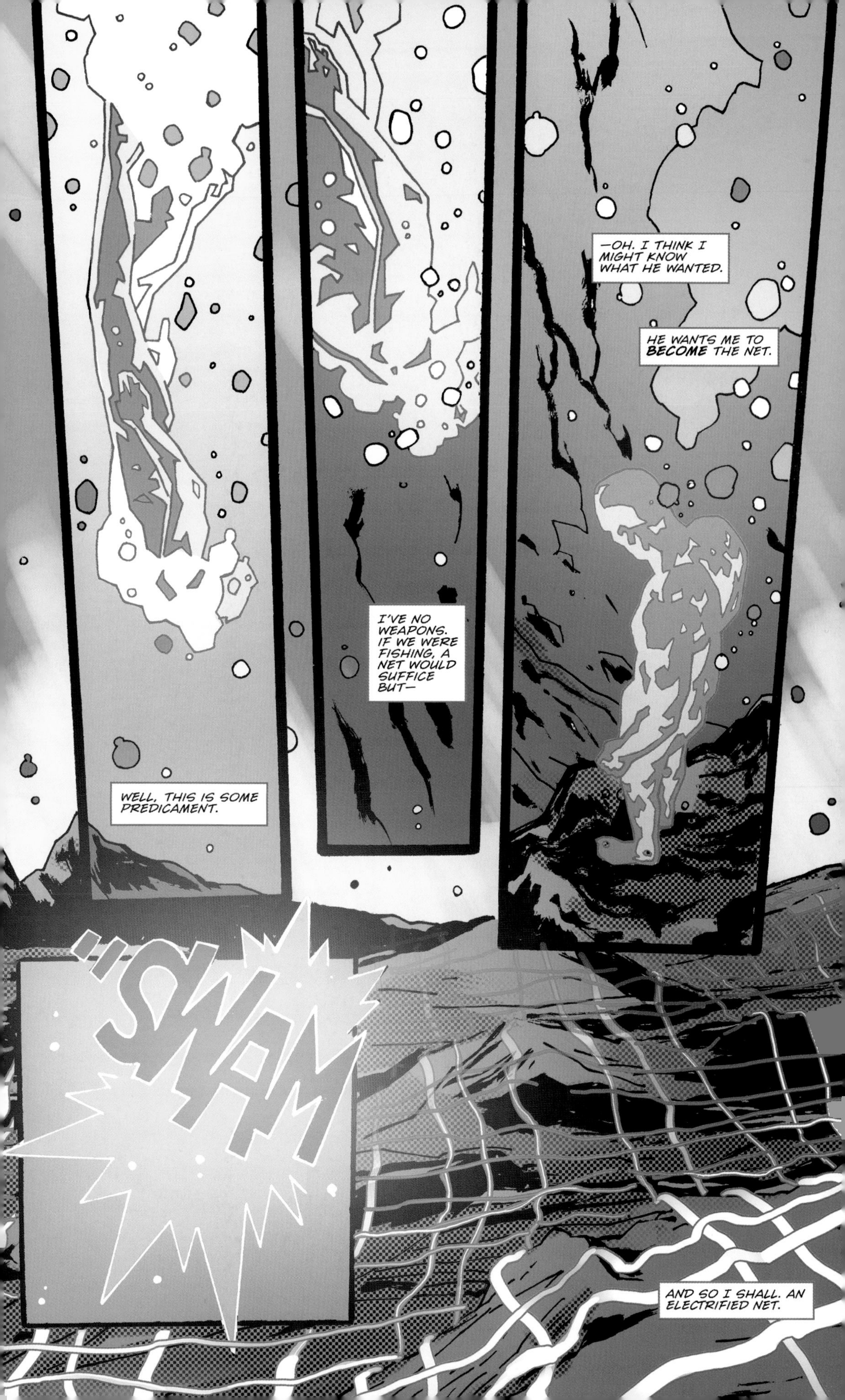
WELL, THIS IS SOME PREDICAMENT.
I'VE NO WEAPONS. IF WE WERE FISHING, A NET WOULD SUFFICE BUT—
—OH. I THINK I MIGHT KNOW WHAT HE WANTED.
HE WANTS ME TO BECOME THE NET.
SHAM
AND SO I SHALL. AN ELECTRIFIED NET.

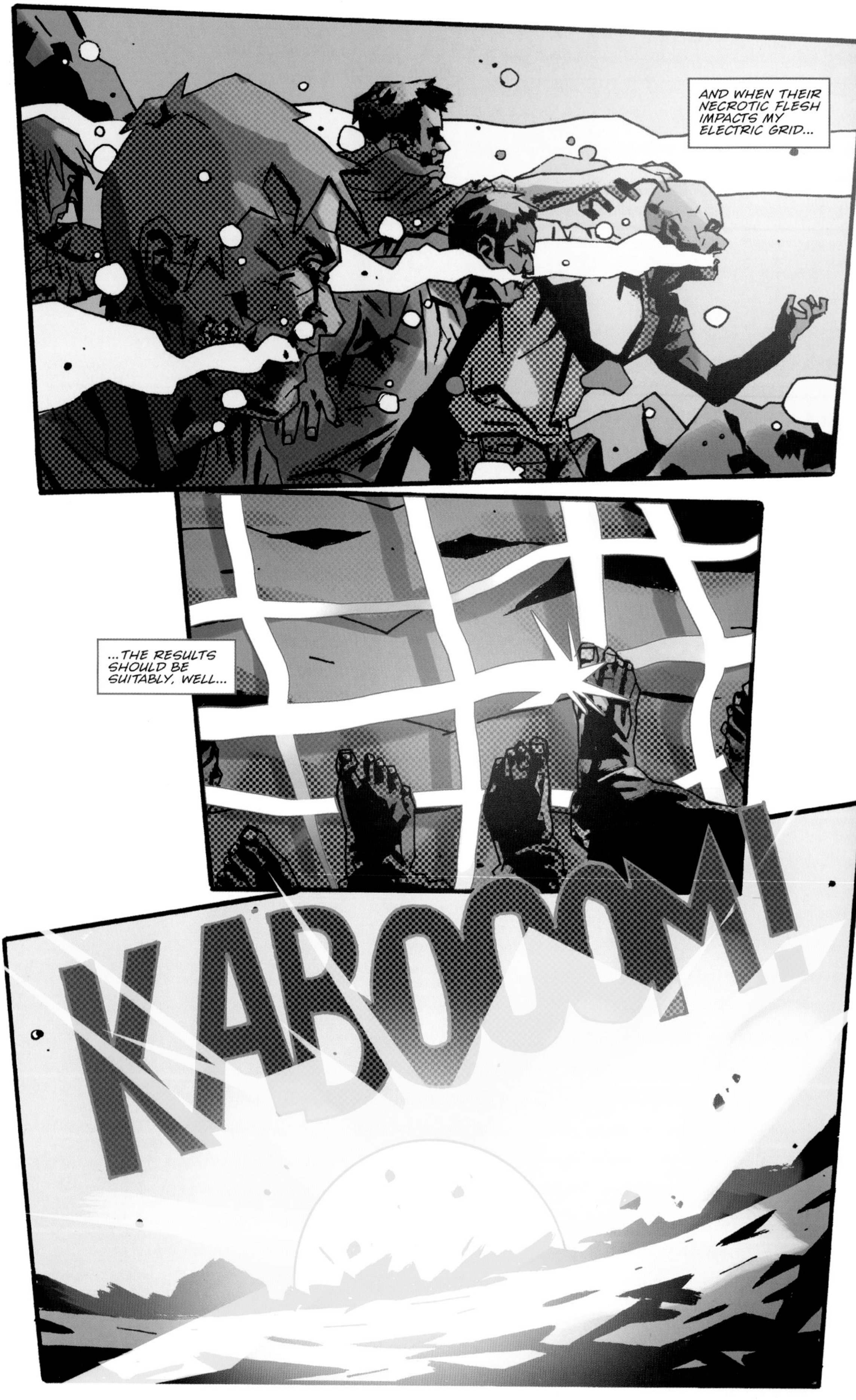
AND WHEN THEIR NECROTIC FLESH IMPACTS MY ELECTRIC GRID...
...THE RESULTS SHOULD BE SUITABLY, WELL...
KABOOOM!

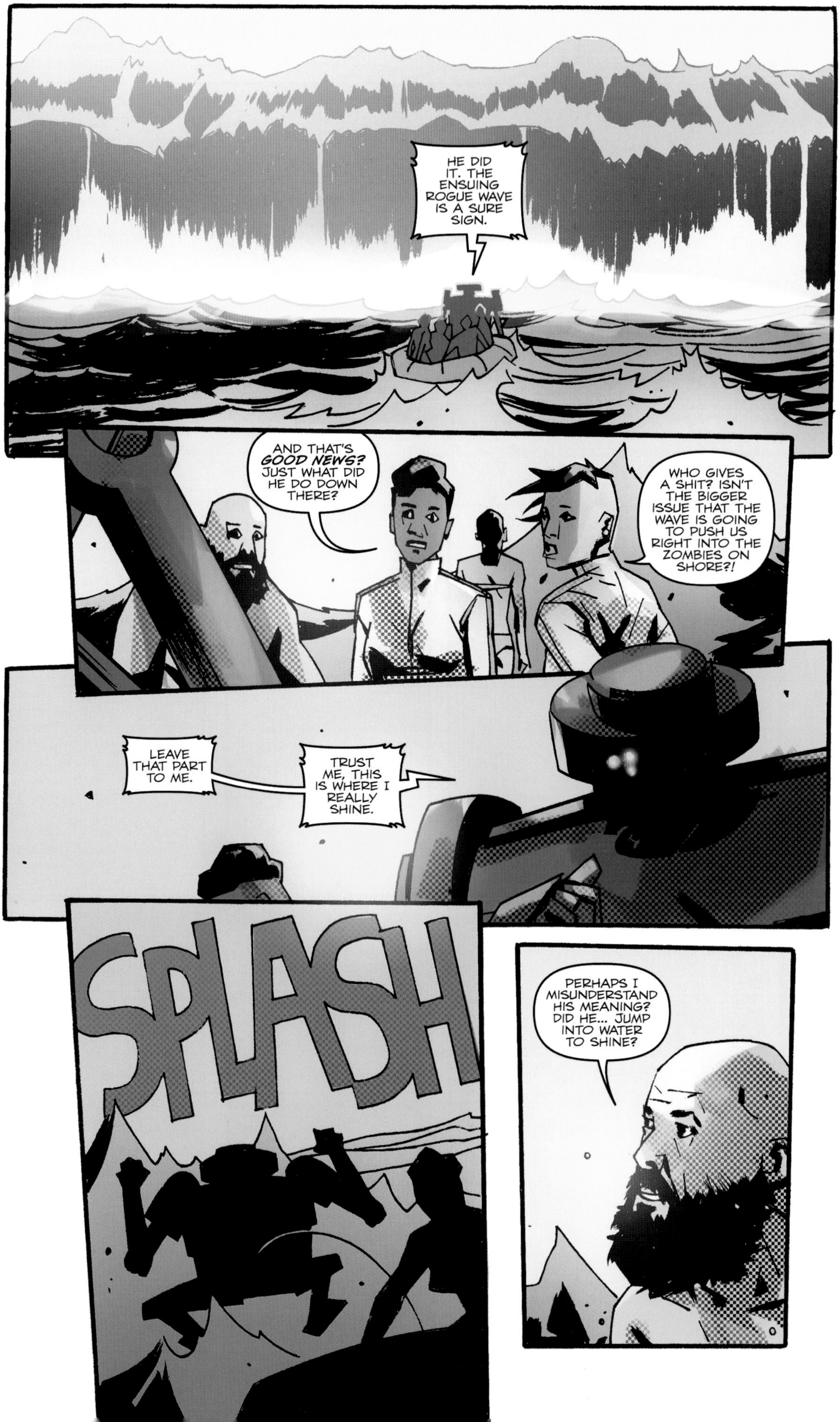

HE DID IT. THE ENSUING ROGUE WAVE IS A SURE SIGN.
AND THAT'S ***GOOD NEWS?*** JUST WHAT DID HE DO DOWN THERE?
WHO GIVES A SHIT? ISN'T THE BIGGER ISSUE THAT THE WAVE IS GOING TO PUSH US RIGHT INTO THE ZOMBIES ON SHORE?!
LEAVE THAT PART TO ME.
TRUST ME, THIS IS WHERE I REALLY SHINE.
SPLASH
PERHAPS I MISUNDERSTAND HIS MEANING? DID HE... JUMP INTO WATER TO SHINE?

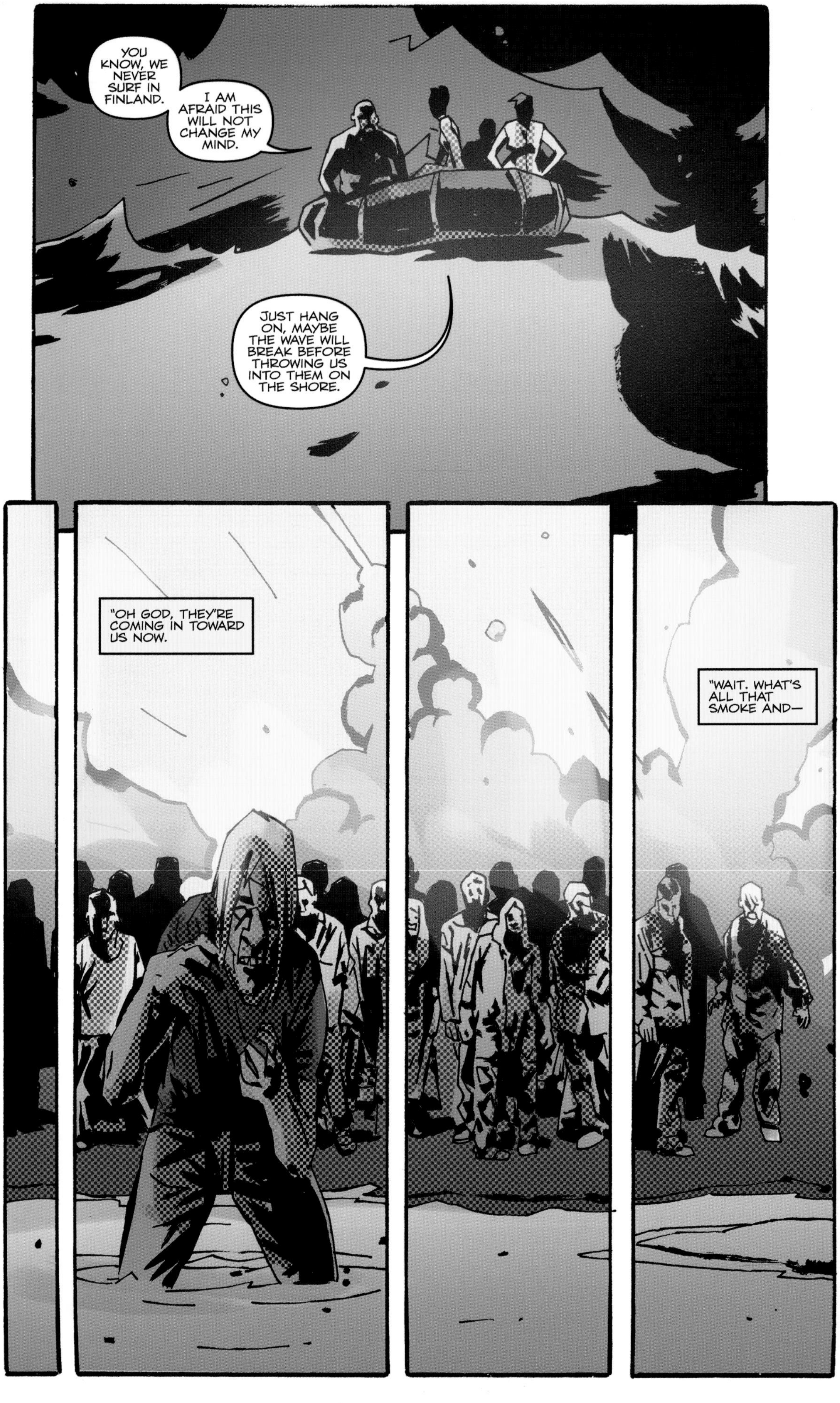
YOU KNOW, WE NEVER SURF IN FINLAND.
I AM AFRAID THIS WILL NOT CHANGE MY MIND.
JUST HANG ON, MAYBE THE WAVE WILL BREAK BEFORE THROWING US INTO THEM ON THE SHORE.
"OH GOD, THEY'RE COMING IN TOWARD US NOW.
"WAIT. WHAT'S ALL THAT SMOKE AND—

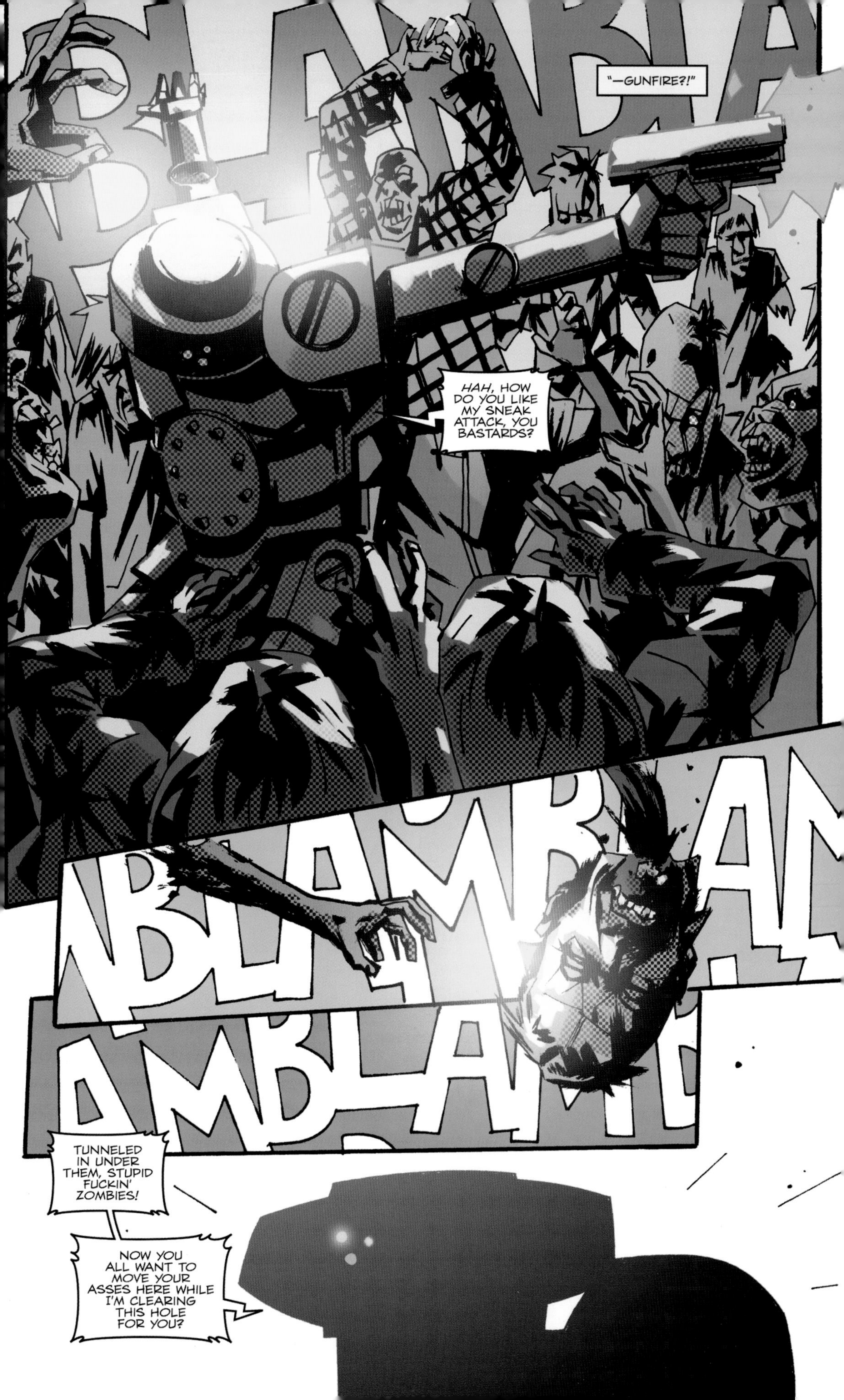
"—GUNFIRE?!"
HAH, HOW DO YOU LIKE MY SNEAK ATTACK, YOU BASTARDS?
BLAMBLAMBLAM
TUNNELED IN UNDER THEM, STUPID FUCKIN' ZOMBIES!
NOW YOU ALL WANT TO MOVE YOUR ASSES HERE WHILE I'M CLEARING THIS HOLE FOR YOU?

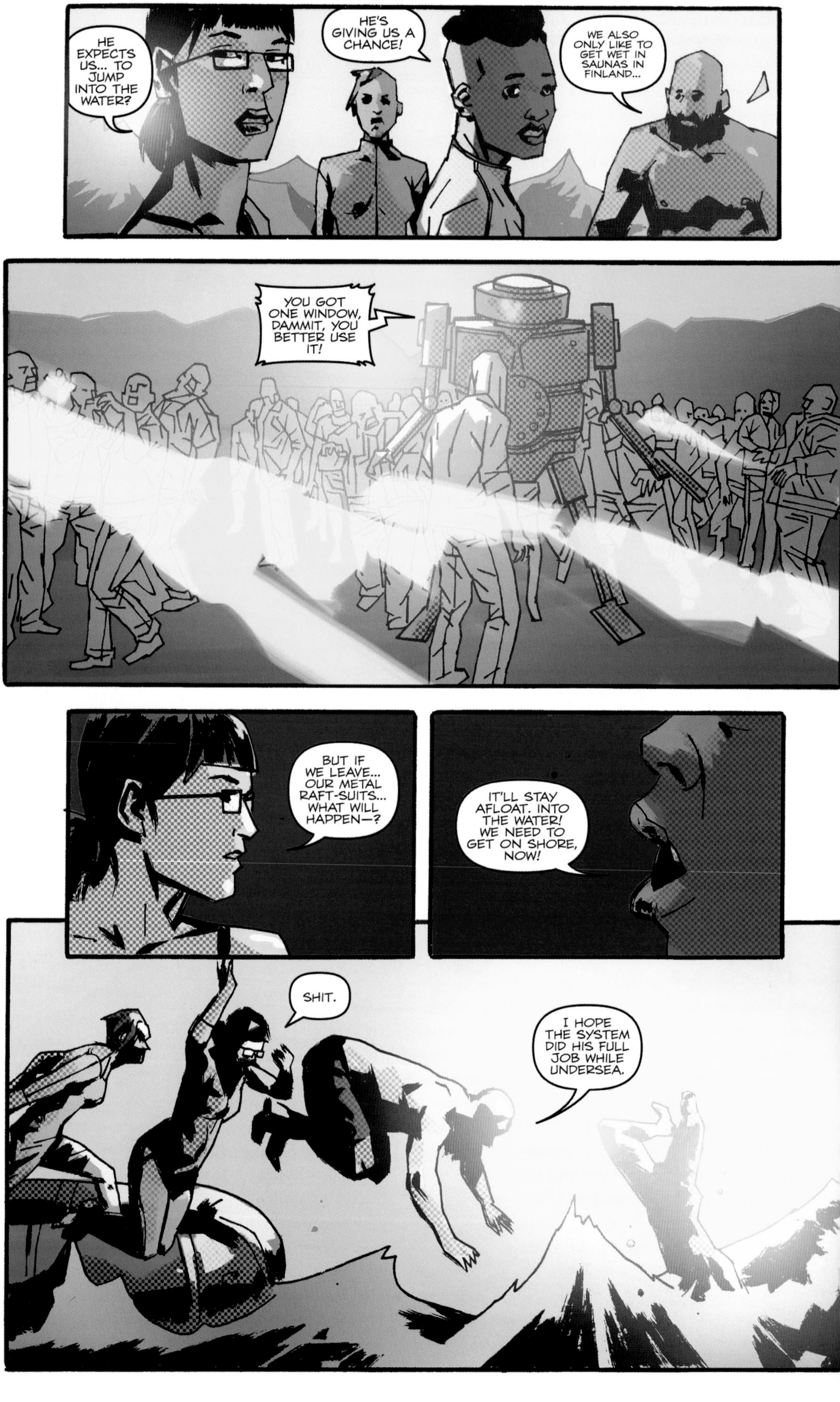
HE EXPECTS US... TO JUMP INTO THE WATER?
HE'S GIVING US A CHANCE!
WE ALSO ONLY LIKE TO GET WET IN SAUNAS IN FINLAND...
YOU GOT ONE WINDOW, DAMMIT, YOU BETTER USE IT!
BUT IF WE LEAVE... OUR METAL RAFT-SUITS... WHAT WILL HAPPEN—?
IT'LL STAY AFLOAT. INTO THE WATER! WE NEED TO GET ON SHORE, NOW!
SHIT.
I HOPE THE SYSTEM DID HIS FULL JOB WHILE UNDERSEA.

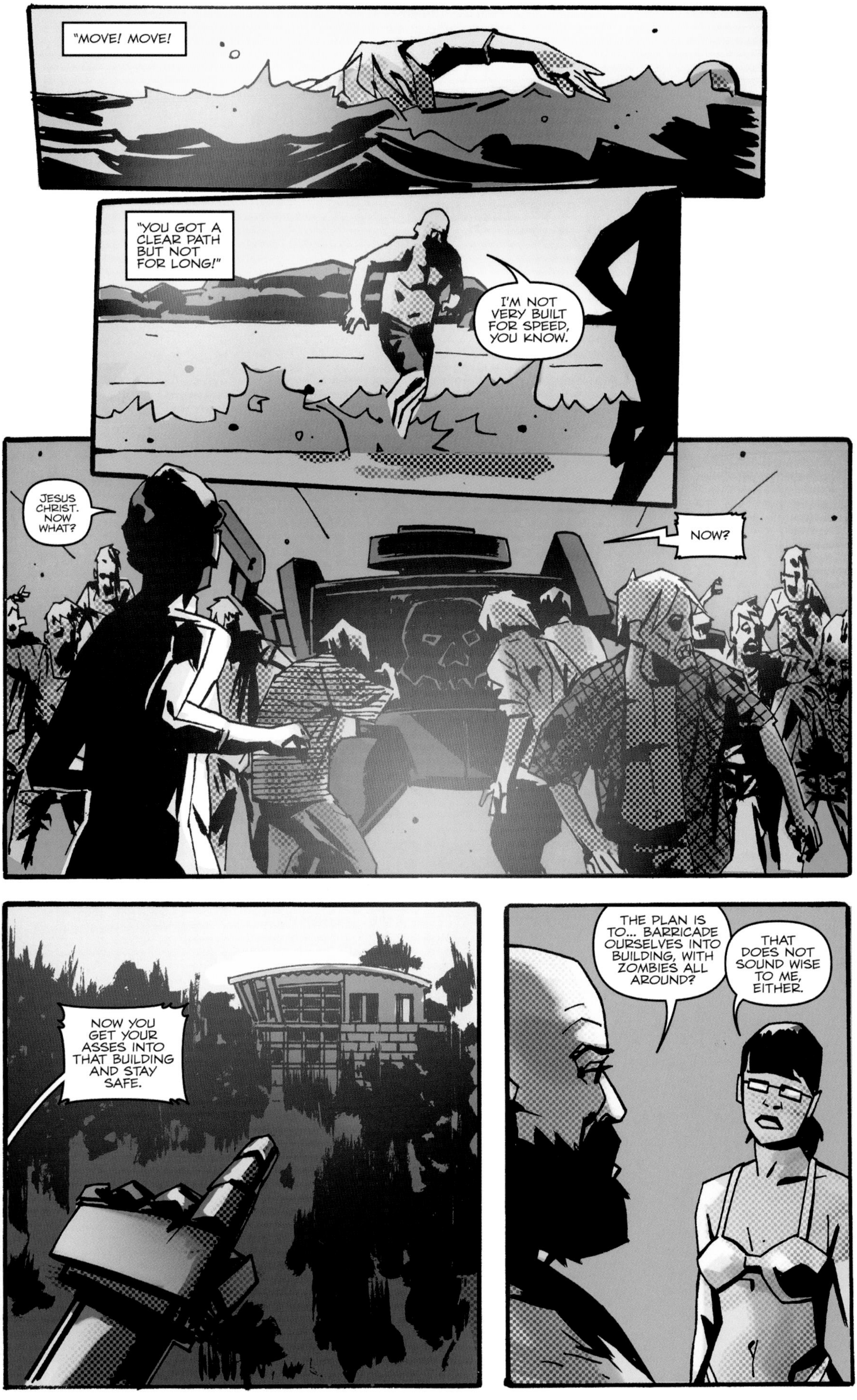
"MOVE! MOVE!
"YOU GOT A CLEAR PATH BUT NOT FOR LONG!"
I'M NOT VERY BUILT FOR SPEED, YOU KNOW.
JESUS CHRIST. NOW WHAT?
NOW?
NOW YOU GET YOUR ASSES INTO THAT BUILDING AND STAY SAFE.
THE PLAN IS TO... BARRICADE OURSELVES INTO BUILDING, WITH ZOMBIES ALL AROUND?
THAT DOES NOT SOUND WISE TO ME, EITHER.

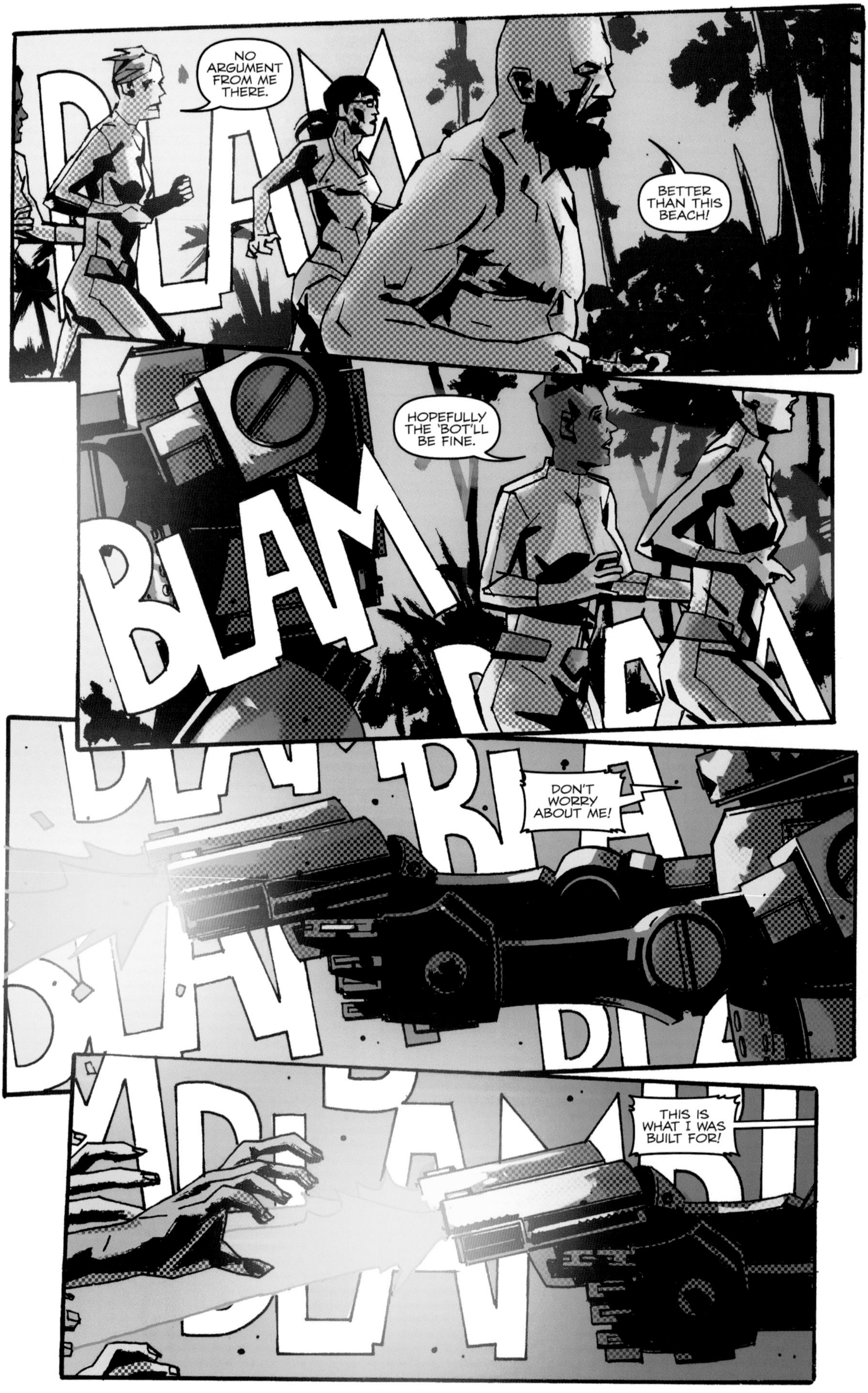

NO ARGUMENT FROM ME THERE.
BLAM
BETTER THAN THIS BEACH!
HOPEFULLY THE 'BOT'LL BE FINE.
BLAM
DON'T WORRY ABOUT ME!
THIS IS WHAT I WAS BUILT FOR!

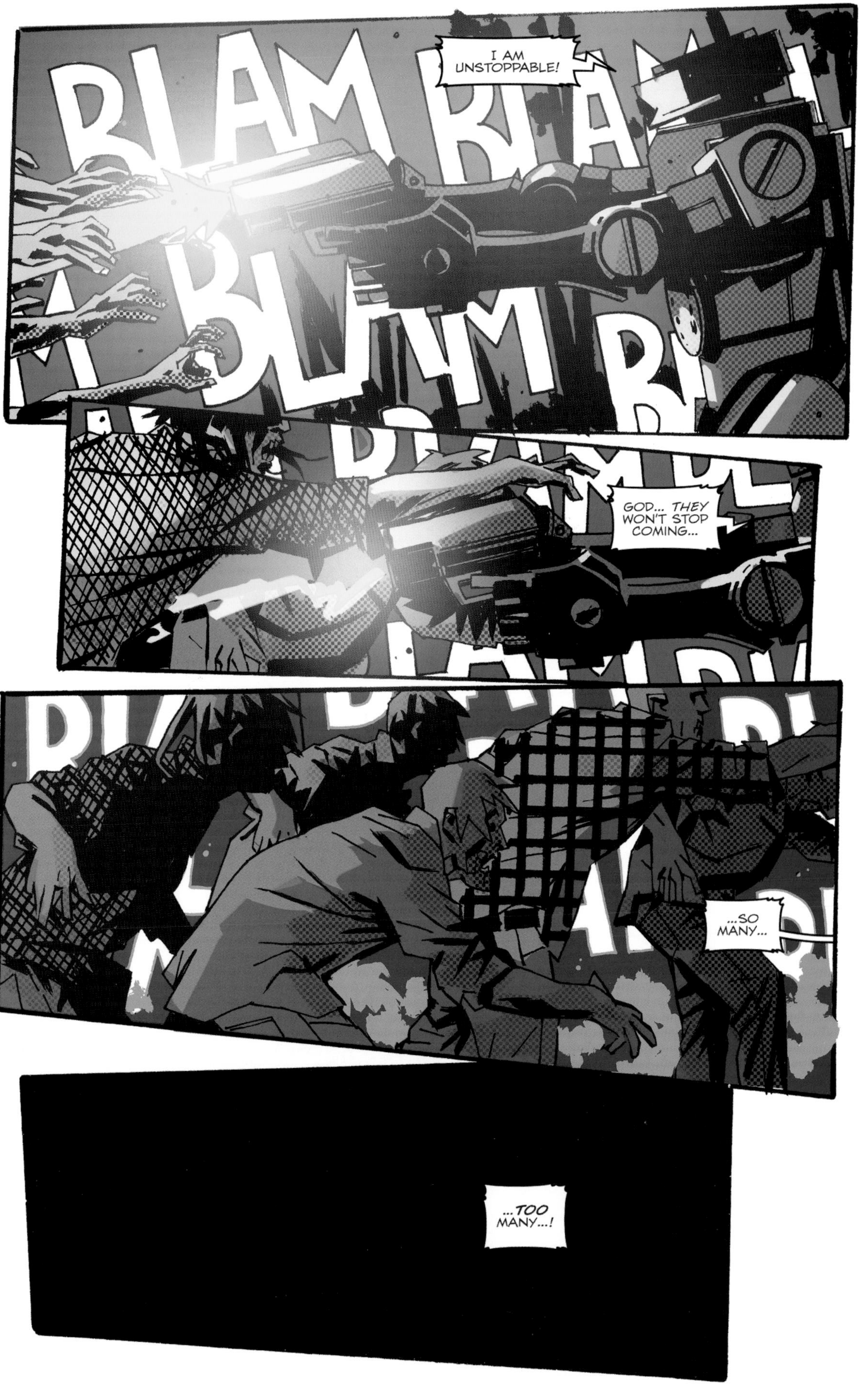
BLAM
I AM UNSTOPPABLE!
GOD... THEY WON'T STOP COMING...
...SO MANY...
...TOO MANY...!

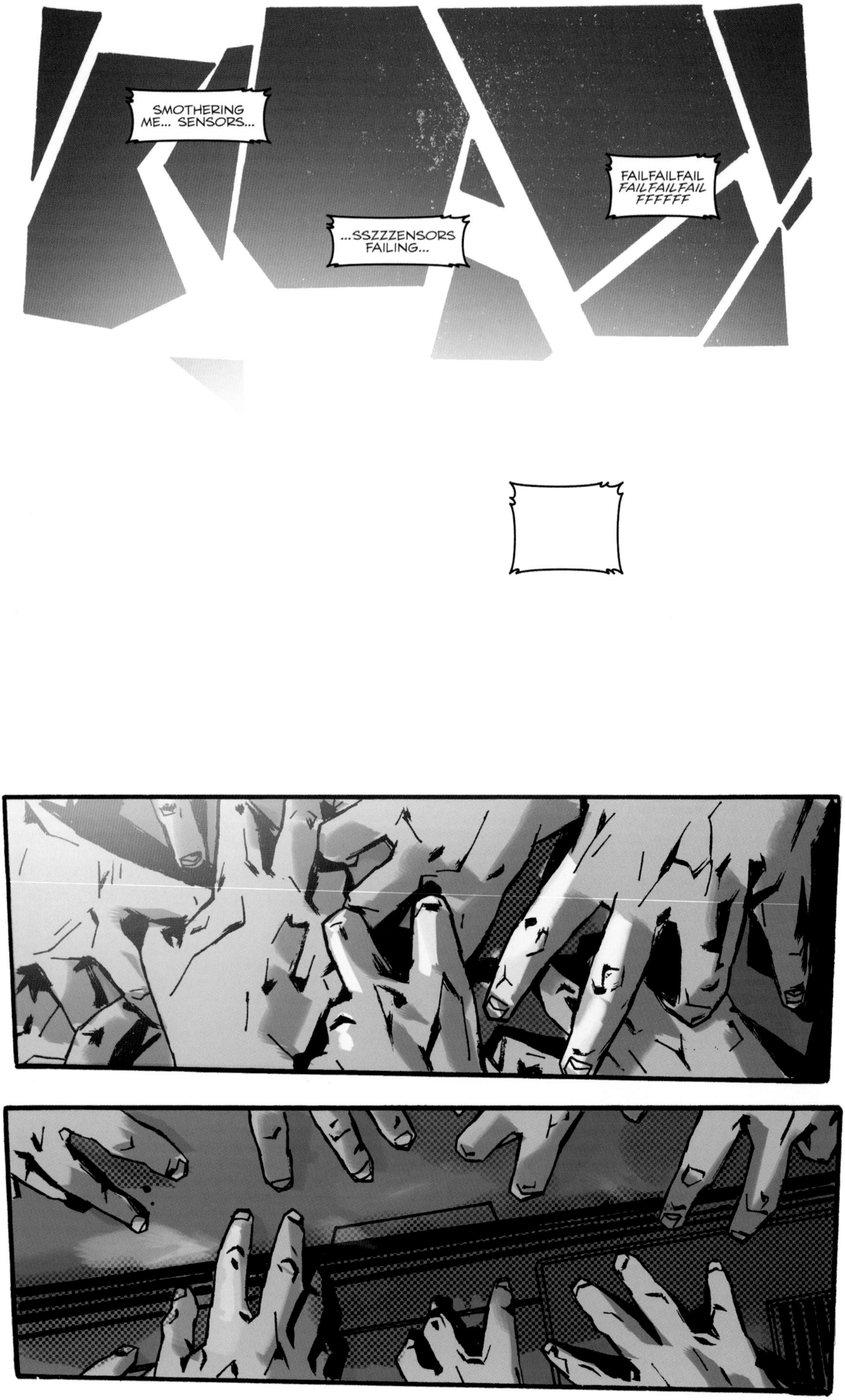
SMOTHERING ME... SENSORS...
...SSZZZENSORS FAILING...
FAILFAILFAIL FAILFAILFAIL FFFFFF

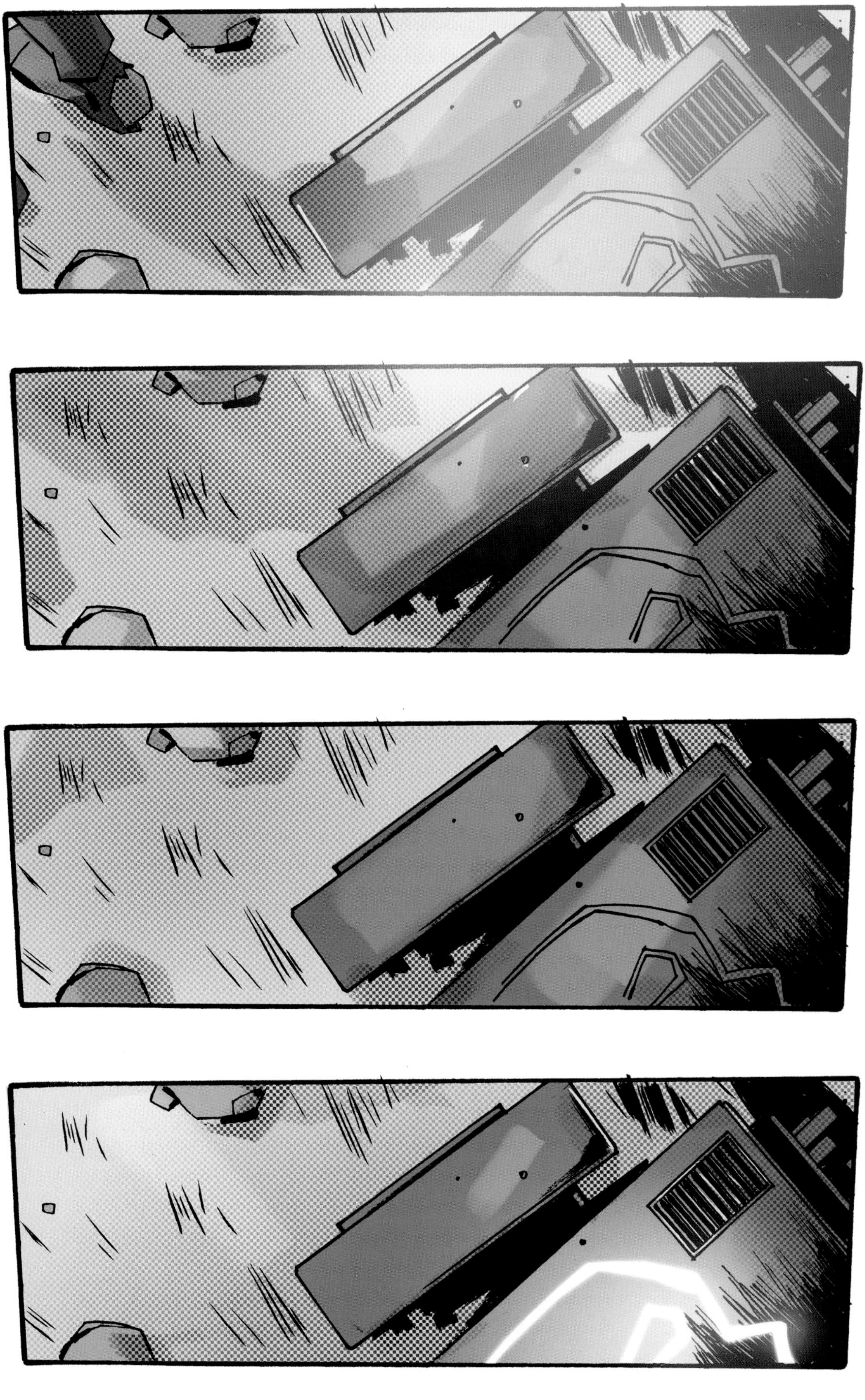

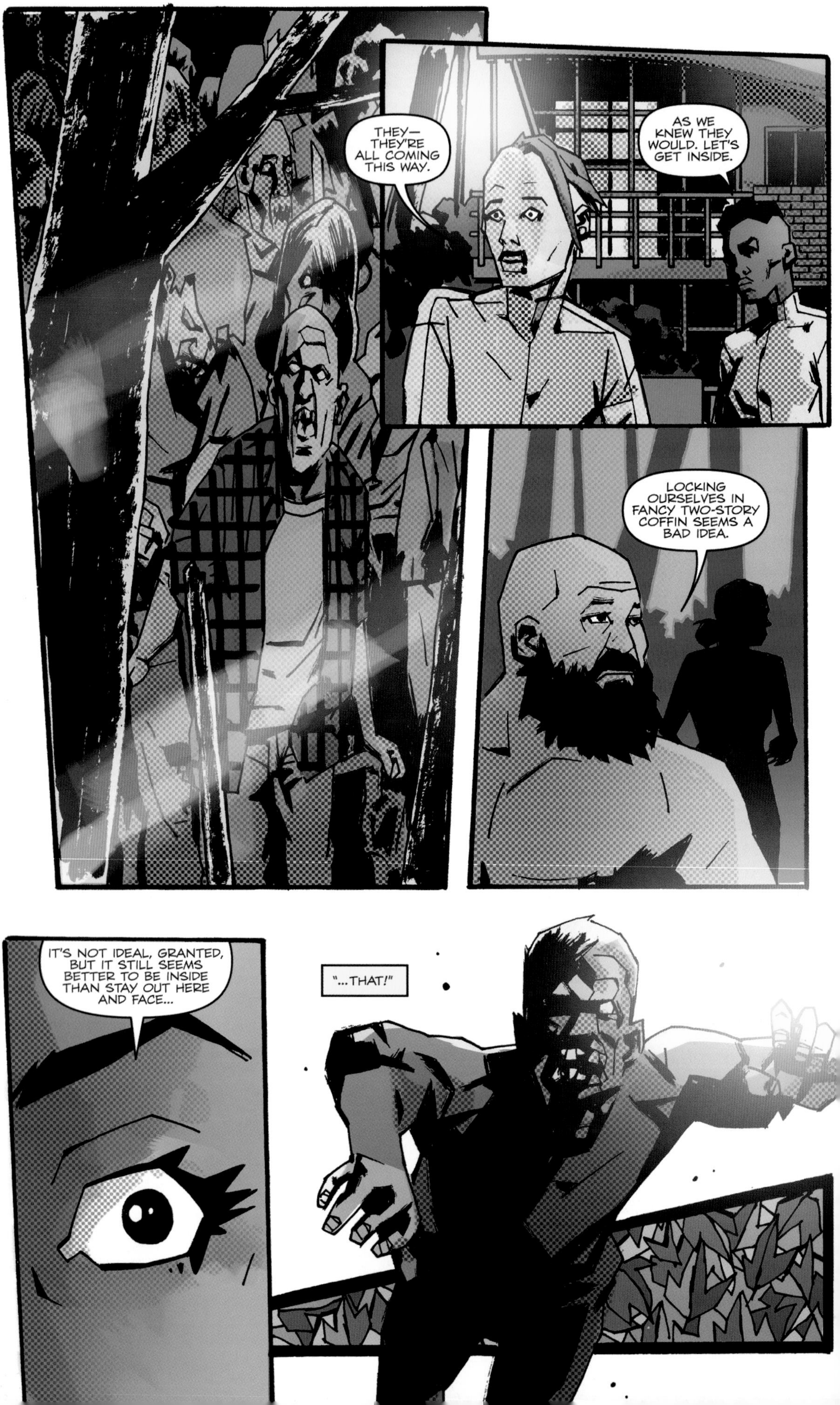
THEY— THEY'RE ALL COMING THIS WAY.
AS WE KNEW THEY WOULD. LET'S GET INSIDE.
LOCKING OURSELVES IN FANCY TWO-STORY COFFIN SEEMS A BAD IDEA.
IT'S NOT IDEAL, GRANTED, BUT IT STILL SEEMS BETTER TO BE INSIDE THAN STAY OUT HERE AND FACE...
"...THAT!"

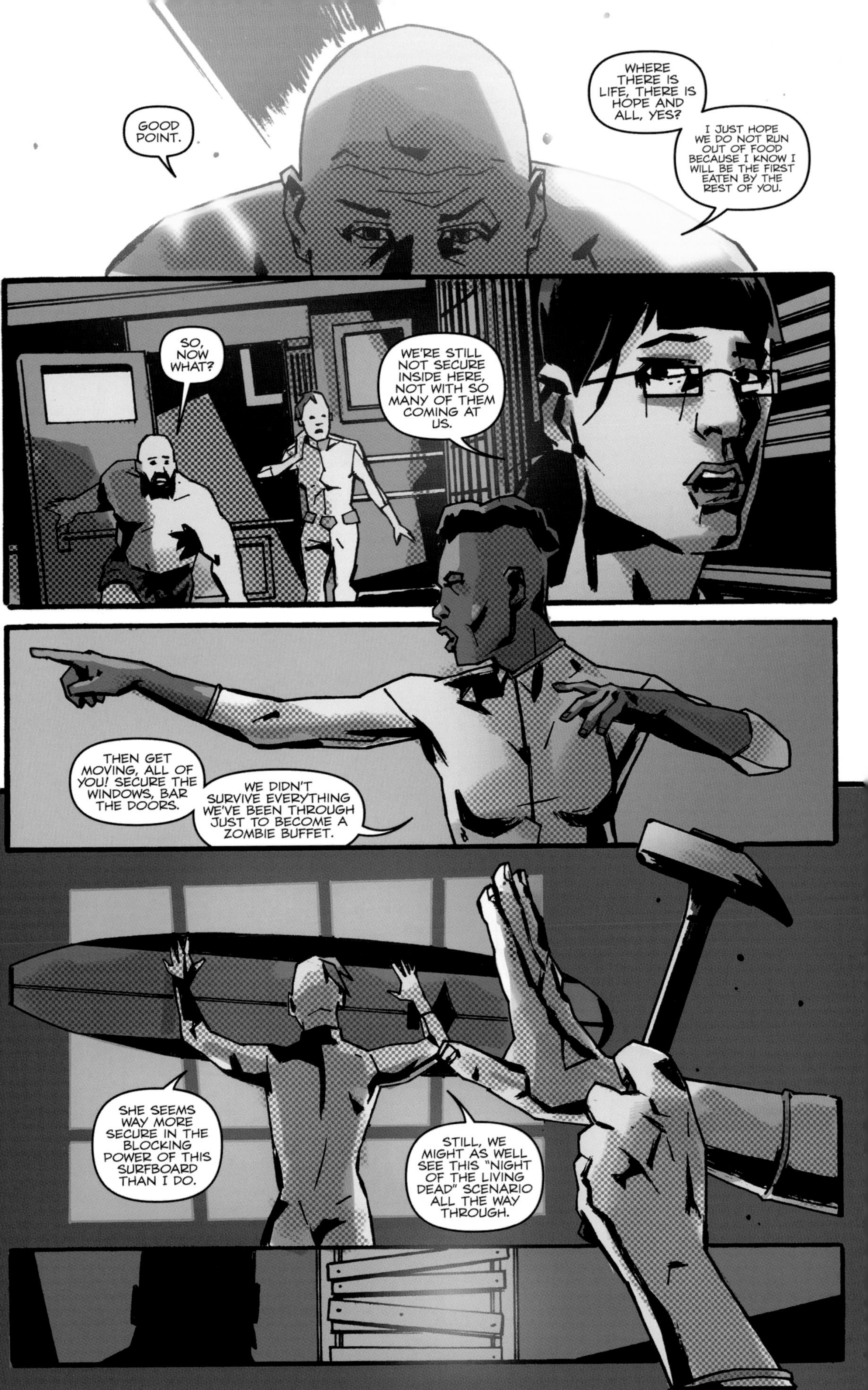
GOOD POINT.
WHERE THERE IS LIFE, THERE IS HOPE AND ALL, YES?
I JUST HOPE WE DO NOT RUN OUT OF FOOD BECAUSE I KNOW I WILL BE THE FIRST EATEN BY THE REST OF YOU.
SO, NOW WHAT?
WE'RE STILL NOT SECURE INSIDE HERE, NOT WITH SO MANY OF THEM COMING AT US.
THEN GET MOVING, ALL OF YOU! SECURE THE WINDOWS, BAR THE DOORS.
WE DIDN'T SURVIVE EVERYTHING WE'VE BEEN THROUGH JUST TO BECOME A ZOMBIE BUFFET.
SHE SEEMS WAY MORE SECURE IN THE BLOCKING POWER OF THIS SURFBOARD THAN I DO.
STILL, WE MIGHT AS WELL SEE THIS "NIGHT OF THE LIVING DEAD" SCENARIO ALL THE WAY THROUGH.

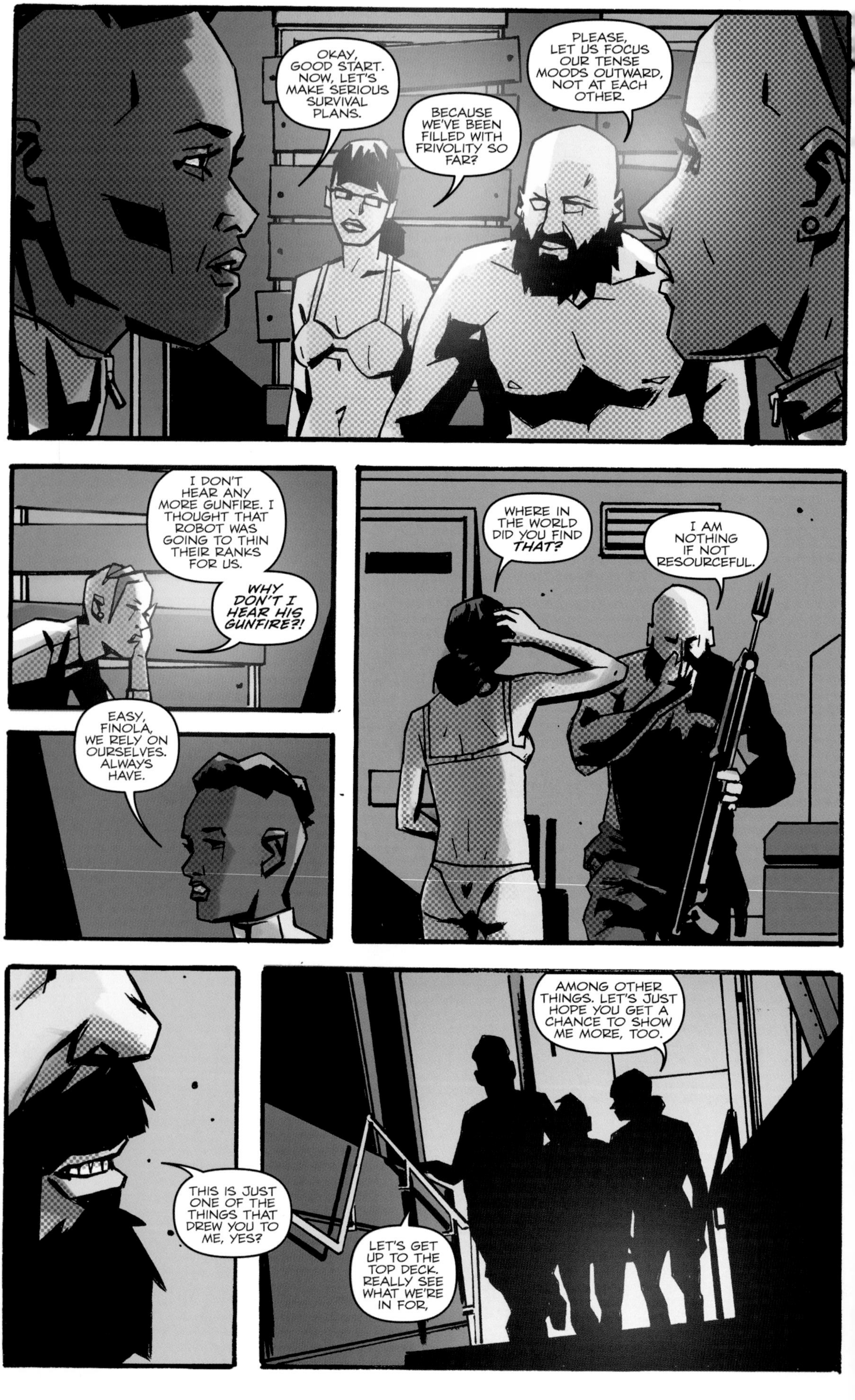
OKAY, GOOD START. NOW, LET'S MAKE SERIOUS SURVIVAL PLANS.
BECAUSE WE'VE BEEN FILLED WITH FRIVOLITY SO FAR?
PLEASE, LET US FOCUS OUR TENSE MOODS OUTWARD, NOT AT EACH OTHER.
I DON'T HEAR ANY MORE GUNFIRE. I THOUGHT THAT ROBOT WAS GOING TO THIN THEIR RANKS FOR US.
WHY DON'T I HEAR HIS GUNFIRE?!
EASY, FINOLA, WE RELY ON OURSELVES. ALWAYS HAVE.
WHERE IN THE WORLD DID YOU FIND THAT?
I AM NOTHING IF NOT RESOURCEFUL.
THIS IS JUST ONE OF THE THINGS THAT DREW YOU TO ME, YES?
AMONG OTHER THINGS. LET'S JUST HOPE YOU GET A CHANCE TO SHOW ME MORE, TOO.
LET'S GET UP TO THE TOP DECK. REALLY SEE WHAT WE'RE IN FOR,

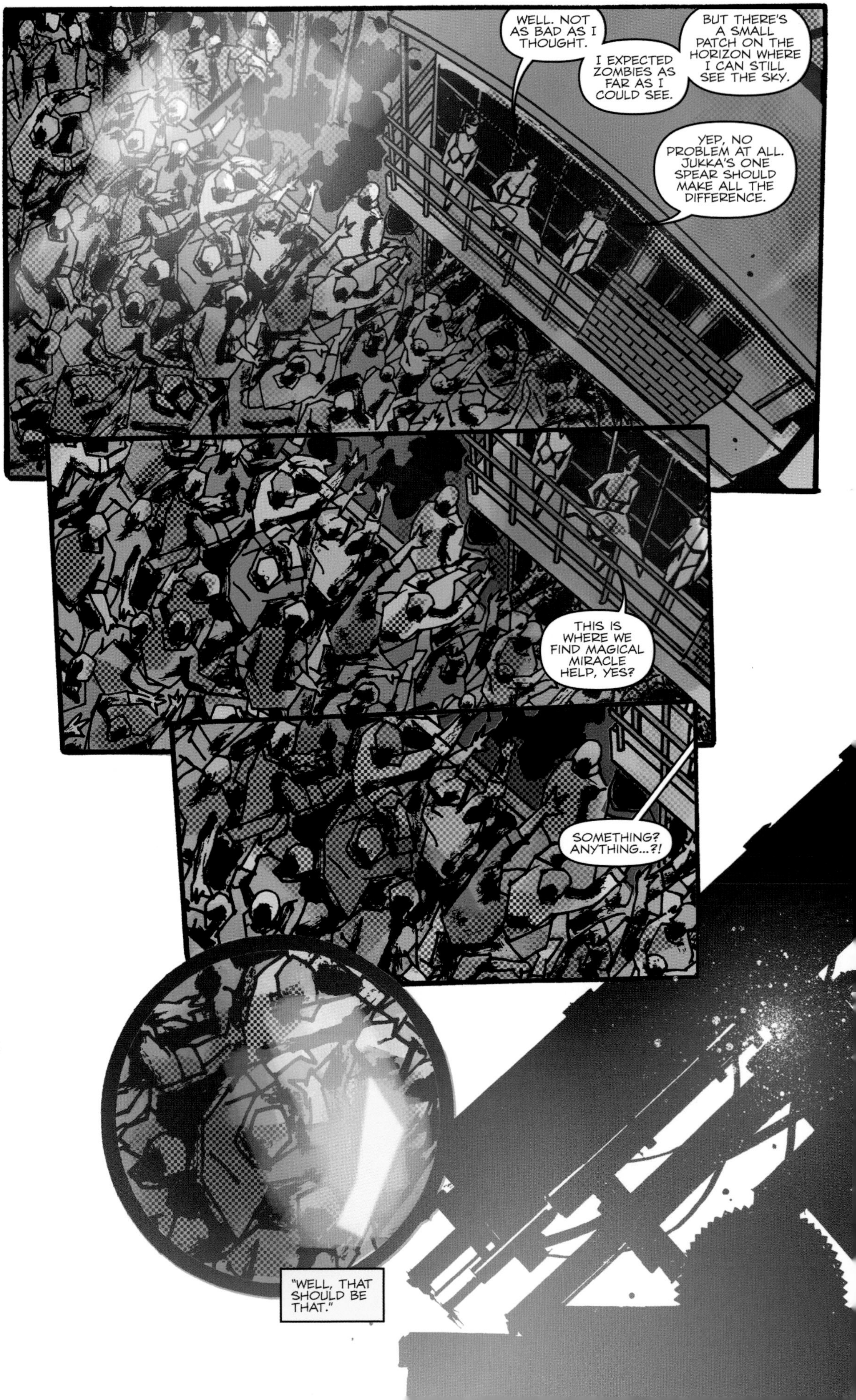
WELL. NOT AS BAD AS I THOUGHT.
I EXPECTED ZOMBIES AS FAR AS I COULD SEE.
BUT THERE'S A SMALL PATCH ON THE HORIZON WHERE I CAN STILL SEE THE SKY.
YEP, NO PROBLEM AT ALL. JUKKA'S ONE SPEAR SHOULD MAKE ALL THE DIFFERENCE.
THIS IS WHERE WE FIND MAGICAL MIRACLE HELP, YES?
SOMETHING? ANYTHING...?!
"WELL, THAT SHOULD BE THAT."

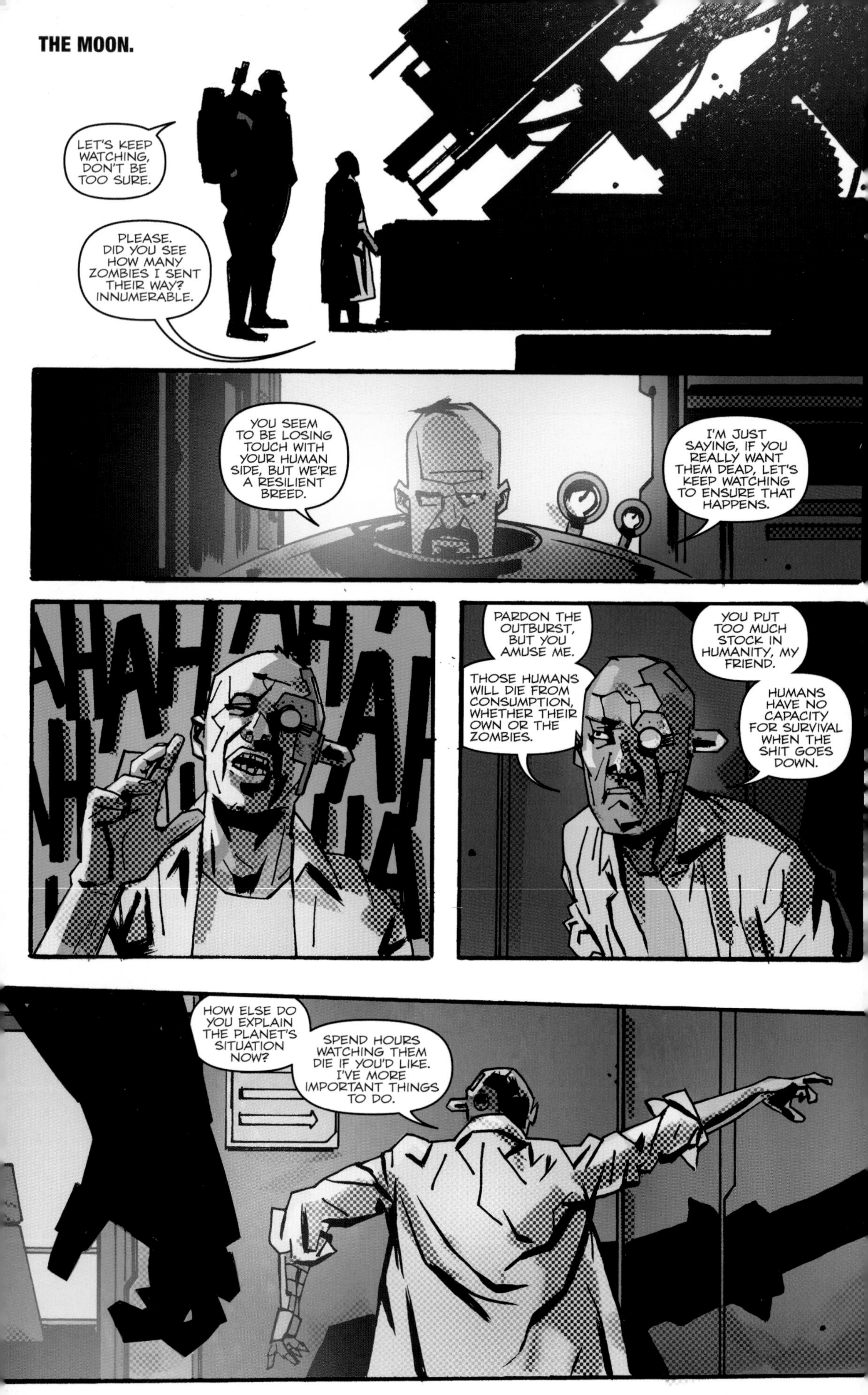
THE MOON.
LET'S KEEP WATCHING, DON'T BE TOO SURE.
PLEASE. DID YOU SEE HOW MANY ZOMBIES I SENT THEIR WAY? INNUMERABLE.
YOU SEEM TO BE LOSING TOUCH WITH YOUR HUMAN SIDE, BUT WE'RE A RESILIENT BREED.
I'M JUST SAYING, IF YOU REALLY WANT THEM DEAD, LET'S KEEP WATCHING TO ENSURE THAT HAPPENS.
PARDON THE OUTBURST, BUT YOU AMUSE ME.
THOSE HUMANS WILL DIE FROM CONSUMPTION, WHETHER THEIR OWN OR THE ZOMBIES.
YOU PUT TOO MUCH STOCK IN HUMANITY, MY FRIEND.
HUMANS HAVE NO CAPACITY FOR SURVIVAL WHEN THE SHIT GOES DOWN.
HOW ELSE DO YOU EXPLAIN THE PLANET'S SITUATION NOW?
SPEND HOURS WATCHING THEM DIE IF YOU'D LIKE. I'VE MORE IMPORTANT THINGS TO DO.

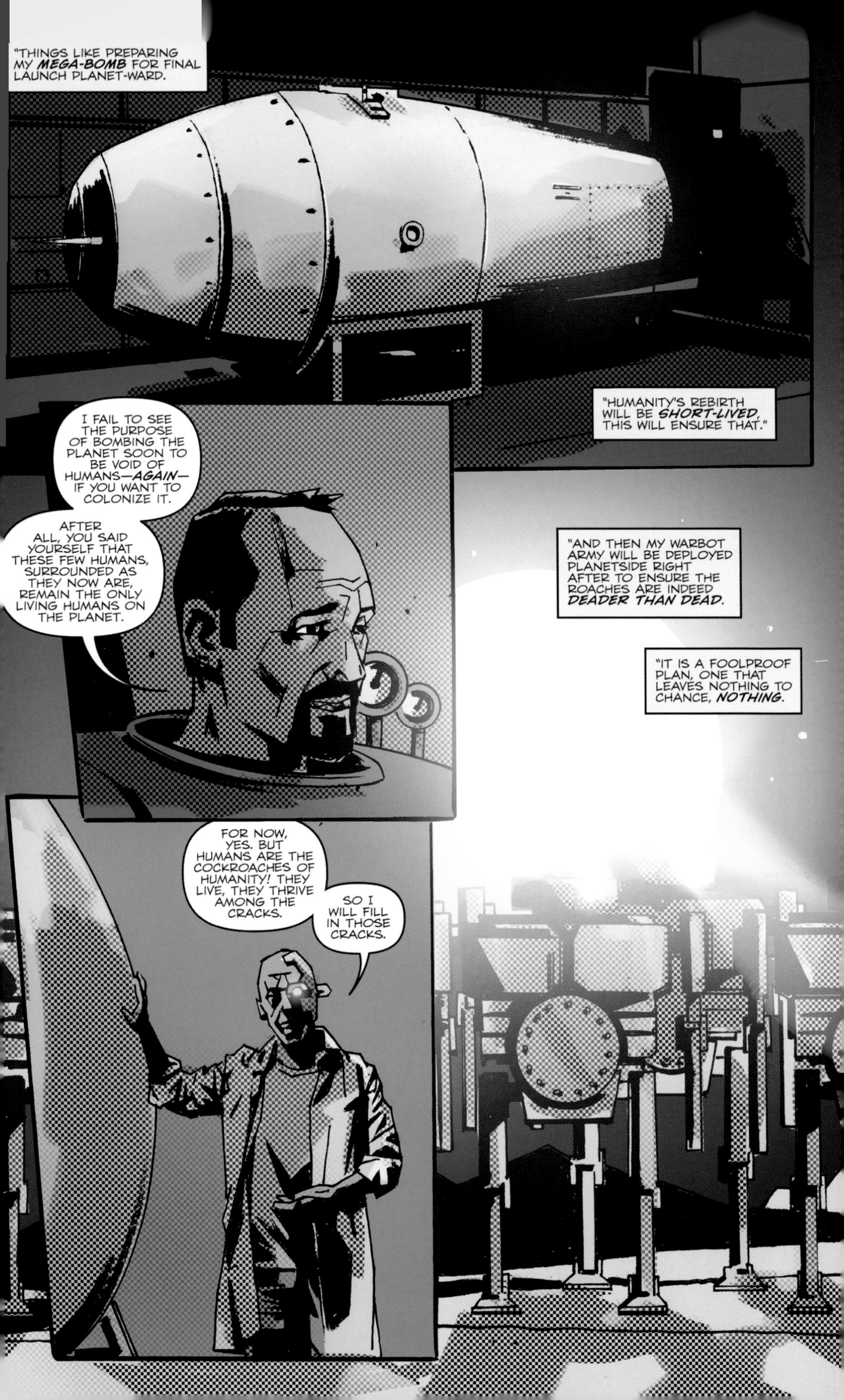
"THINGS LIKE PREPARING MY MEGA-BOMB FOR FINAL LAUNCH PLANET-WARD.
"HUMANITY'S REBIRTH WILL BE SHORT-LIVED, THIS WILL ENSURE THAT."
I FAIL TO SEE THE PURPOSE OF BOMBING THE PLANET SOON TO BE VOID OF HUMANS—AGAIN—IF YOU WANT TO COLONIZE IT.
AFTER ALL, YOU SAID YOURSELF THAT THESE FEW HUMANS, SURROUNDED AS THEY NOW ARE, REMAIN THE ONLY LIVING HUMANS ON THE PLANET.
"AND THEN MY WARBOT ARMY WILL BE DEPLOYED PLANETSIDE RIGHT AFTER TO ENSURE THE ROACHES ARE INDEED DEADER THAN DEAD.
"IT IS A FOOLPROOF PLAN, ONE THAT LEAVES NOTHING TO CHANCE, NOTHING.
FOR NOW, YES. BUT HUMANS ARE THE COCKROACHES OF HUMANITY! THEY LIVE, THEY THRIVE AMONG THE CRACKS.
SO I WILL FILL IN THOSE CRACKS.

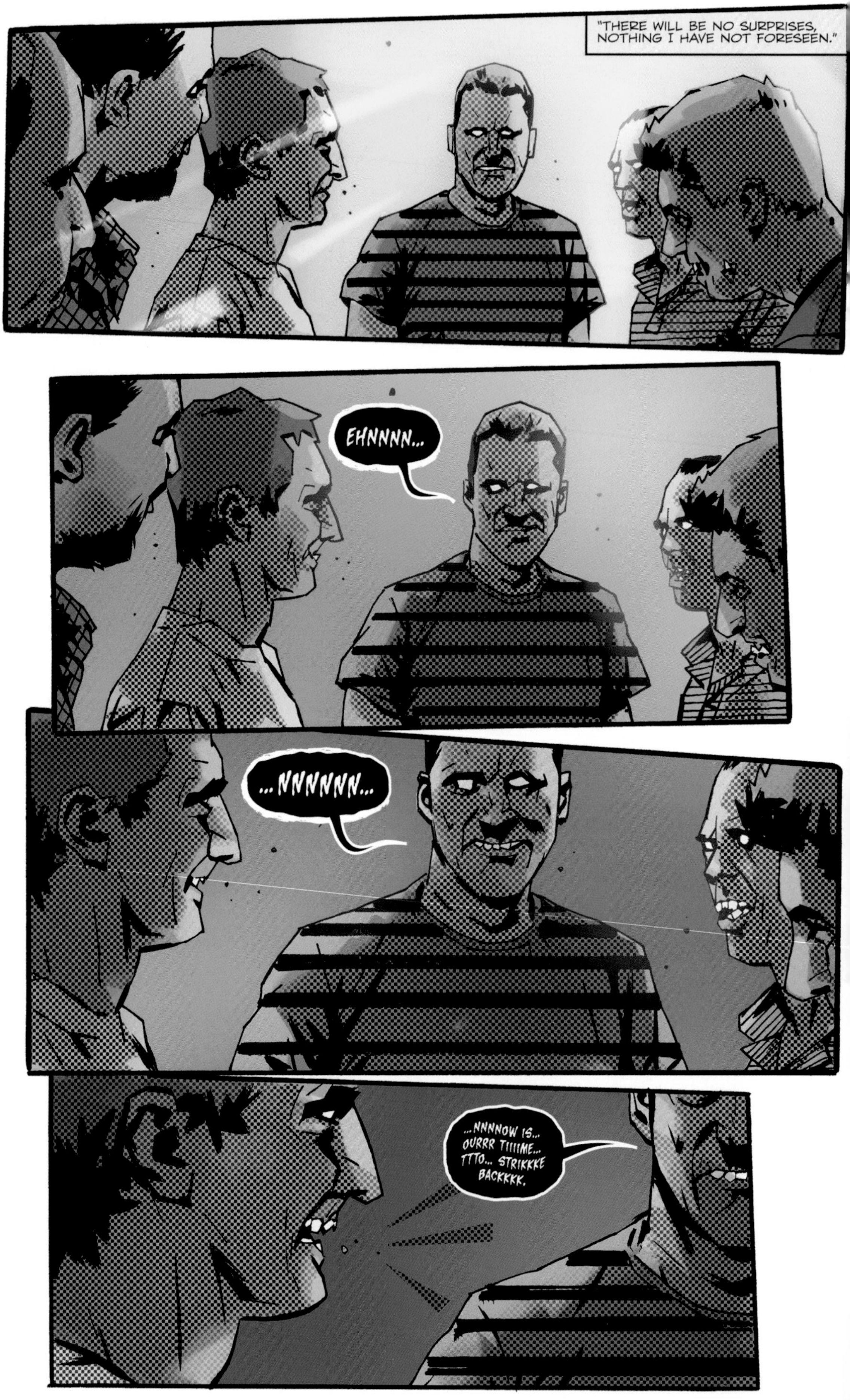
"THERE WILL BE NO SURPRISES, NOTHING I HAVE NOT FORESEEN."
EHNNNN...
...NNNNNN...
...NNNNOW IS... OURRR TIIIIME... TTTO... STRIKKKE BACKKKK.

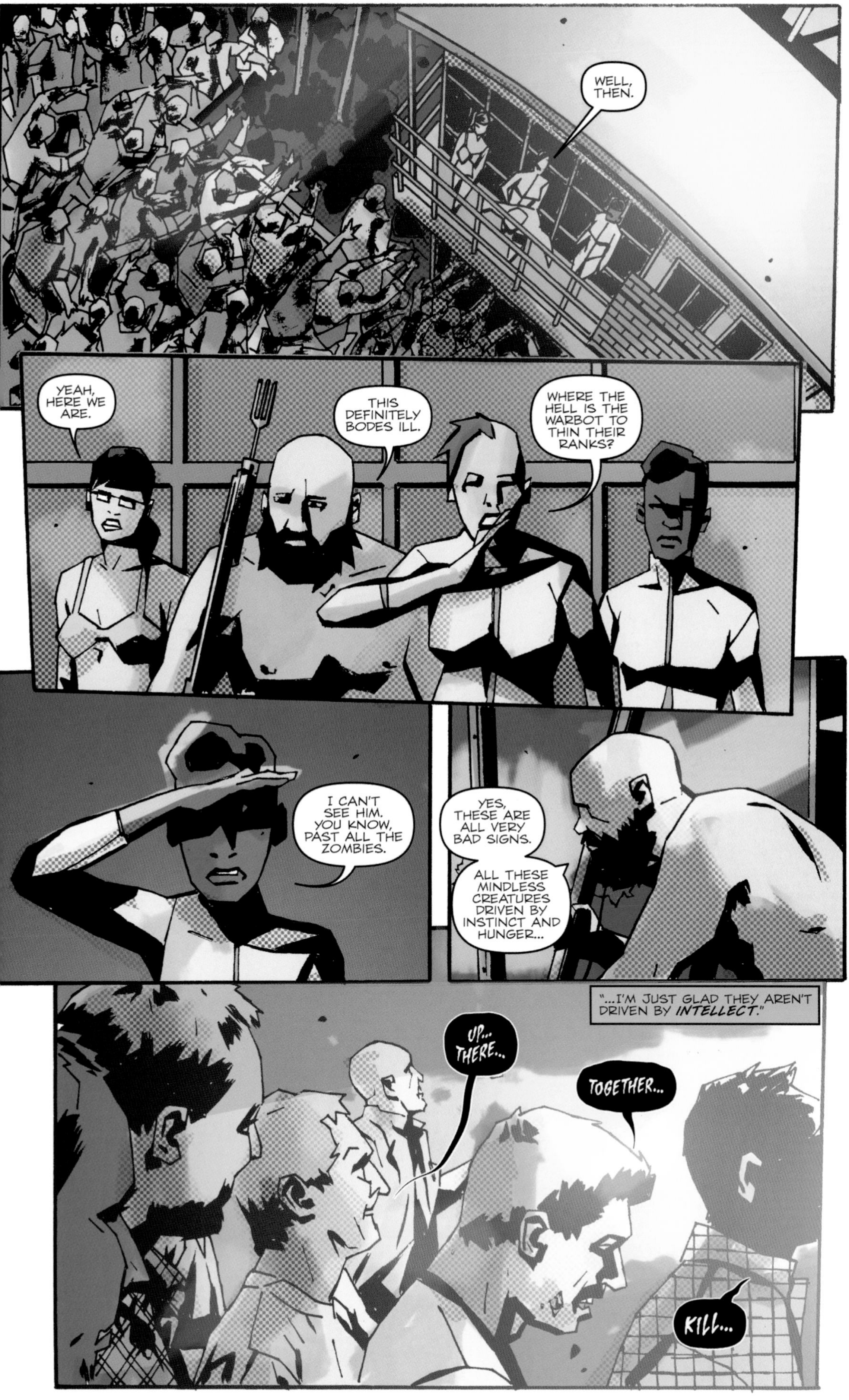

WELL, THEN.
YEAH, HERE WE ARE.
THIS DEFINITELY BODES ILL.
WHERE THE HELL IS THE WARBOT TO THIN THEIR RANKS?
I CAN'T SEE HIM. YOU KNOW, PAST ALL THE ZOMBIES.
YES, THESE ARE ALL VERY BAD SIGNS.
ALL THESE MINDLESS CREATURES DRIVEN BY INSTINCT AND HUNGER...
"...I'M JUST GLAD THEY AREN'T DRIVEN BY *INTELLECT*."
UP... THERE...
TOGETHER...
KILL...

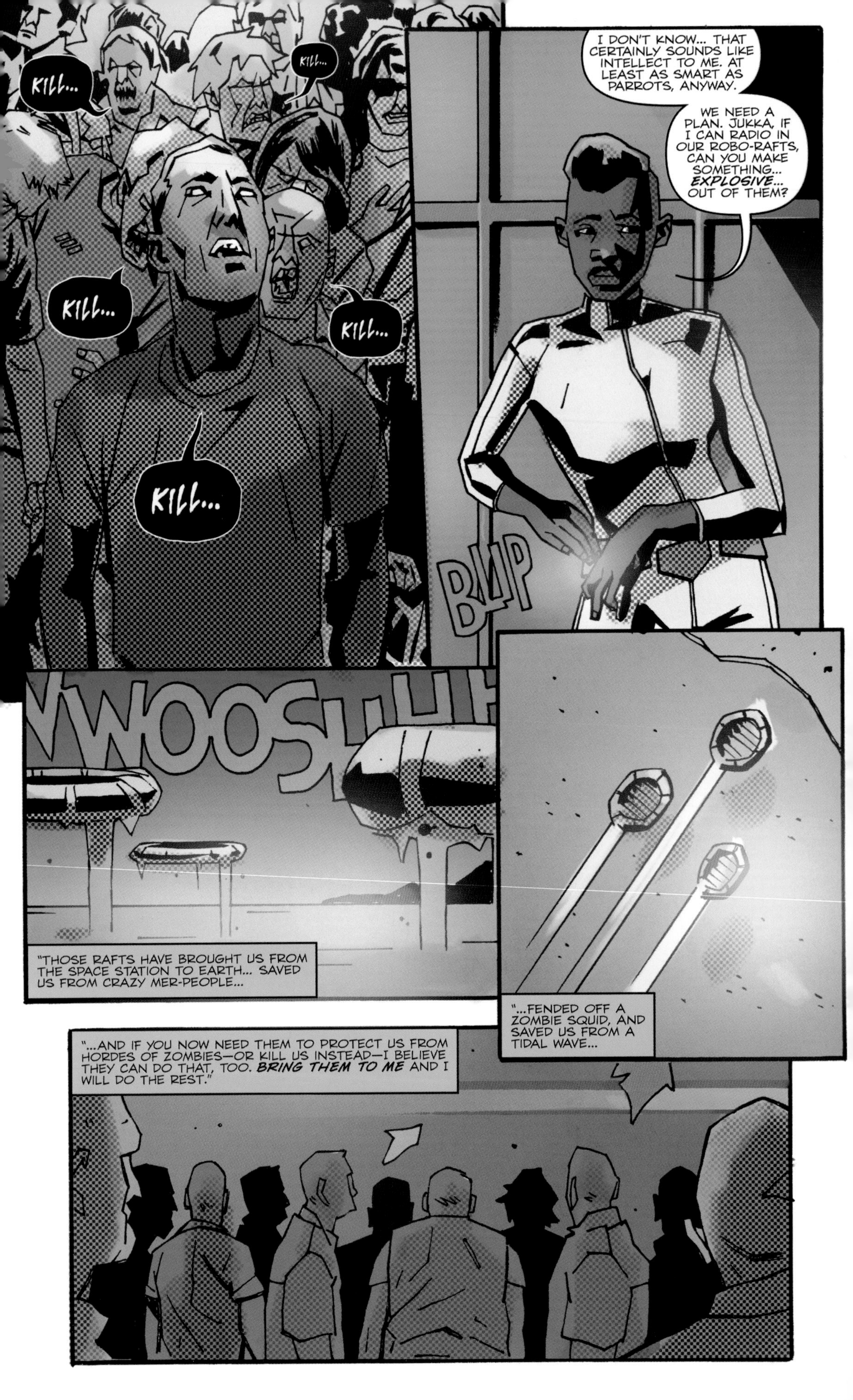
KILL...
KILL...
KILL...
KILL...
KILL...
I DON'T KNOW... THAT CERTAINLY SOUNDS LIKE INTELLECT TO ME. AT LEAST AS SMART AS PARROTS, ANYWAY.
WE NEED A PLAN. JUKKA, IF I CAN RADIO IN OUR ROBO-RAFTS, CAN YOU MAKE SOMETHING... *EXPLOSIVE*... OUT OF THEM?
BLIP
WWOOSHHH
"THOSE RAFTS HAVE BROUGHT US FROM THE SPACE STATION TO EARTH... SAVED US FROM CRAZY MER-PEOPLE...
"...FENDED OFF A ZOMBIE SQUID, AND SAVED US FROM A TIDAL WAVE...
"...AND IF YOU NOW NEED THEM TO PROTECT US FROM HORDES OF ZOMBIES—OR KILL US INSTEAD—I BELIEVE THEY CAN DO THAT, TOO. *BRING THEM TO ME* AND I WILL DO THE REST."

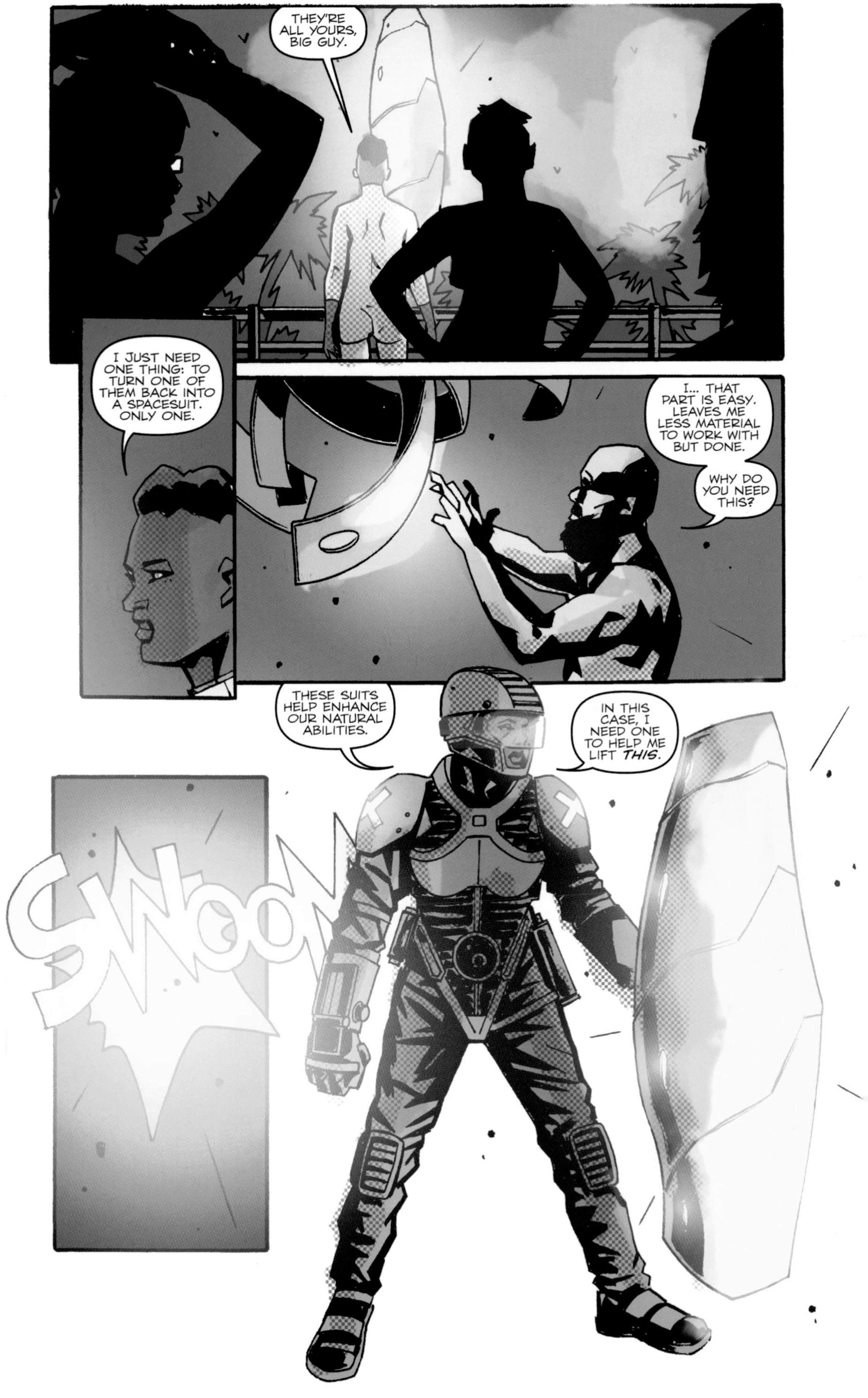
THEY'RE ALL YOURS, BIG GUY.
I JUST NEED ONE THING: TO TURN ONE OF THEM BACK INTO A SPACESUIT. ONLY ONE.
I... THAT PART IS EASY. LEAVES ME LESS MATERIAL TO WORK WITH BUT DONE.
WHY DO YOU NEED THIS?
THESE SUITS HELP ENHANCE OUR NATURAL ABILITIES.
IN THIS CASE, I NEED ONE TO HELP ME LIFT THIS.
SWOOM

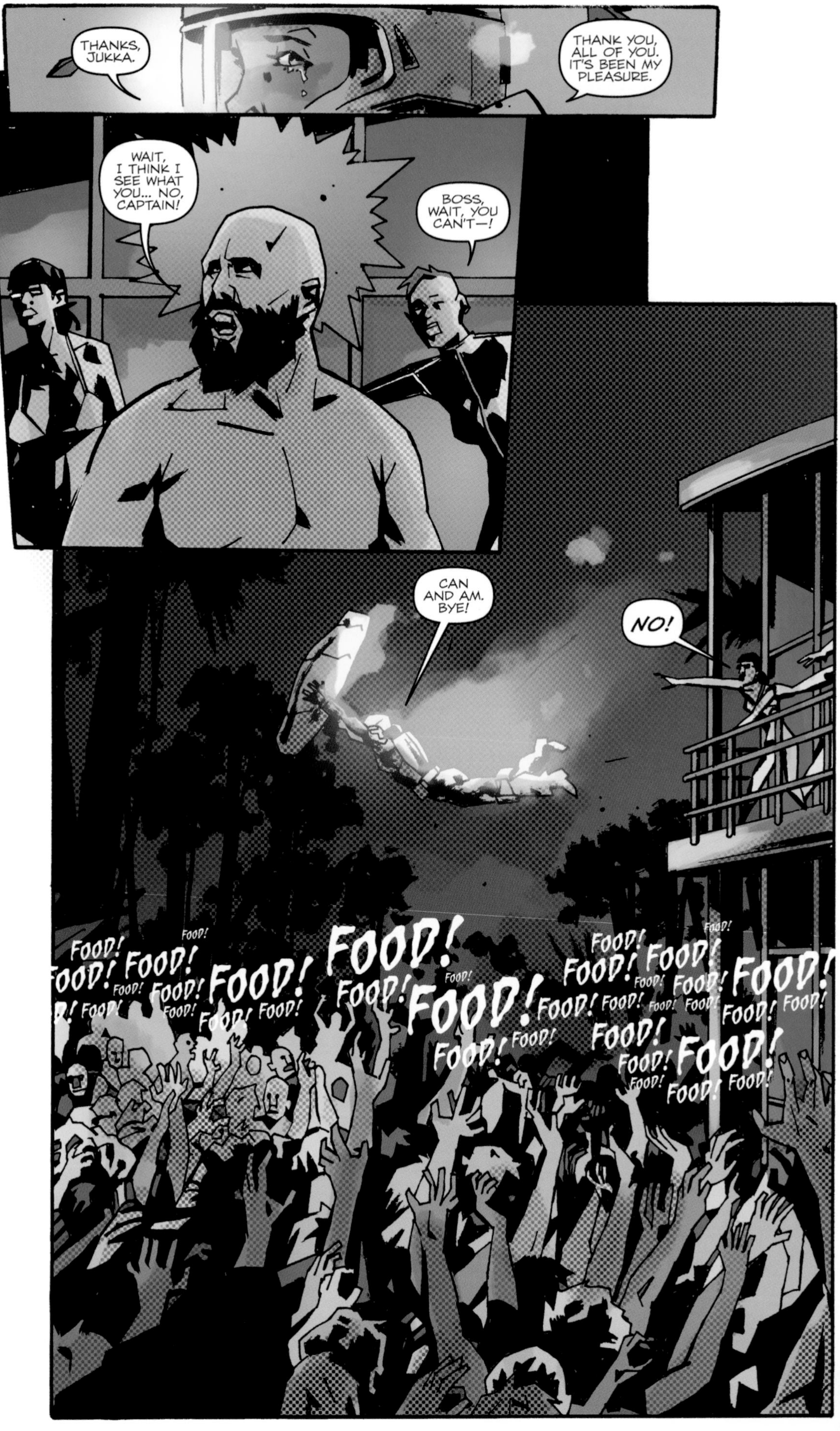
THANKS, JUKKA.
THANK YOU, ALL OF YOU. IT'S BEEN MY PLEASURE.
WAIT, I THINK I SEE WHAT YOU... NO, CAPTAIN!
BOSS, WAIT, YOU CAN'T—!
CAN AND AM. BYE!
NO!
FOOD! FOOD! FOOD! FOOD! FOOD! FOOD! FOOD! FOOD!
FOOD! FOOD! FOOD! FOOD! FOOD! FOOD! FOOD! FOOD! FOOD!
FOOD! FOOD! FOOD! FOOD! FOOD! FOOD! FOOD! FOOD! FOOD! FOOD!
FOOD! FOOD! FOOD! FOOD! FOOD! FOOD! FOOD! FOOD!

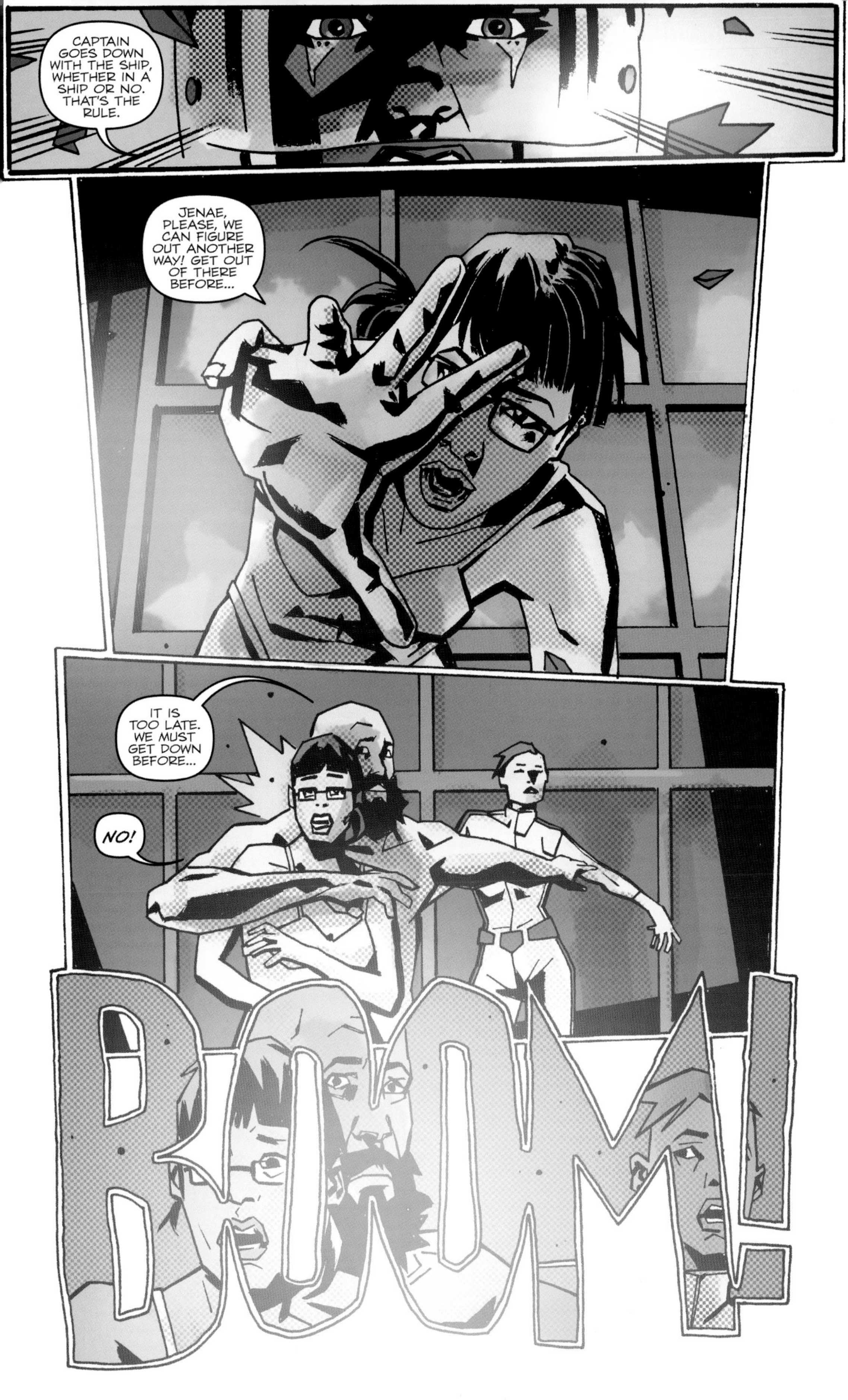
CAPTAIN GOES DOWN WITH THE SHIP, WHETHER IN A SHIP OR NO. THAT'S THE RULE.
JENAE, PLEASE, WE CAN FIGURE OUT ANOTHER WAY! GET OUT OF THERE BEFORE...
IT IS TOO LATE. WE MUST GET DOWN BEFORE...
NO!
BOOOM!

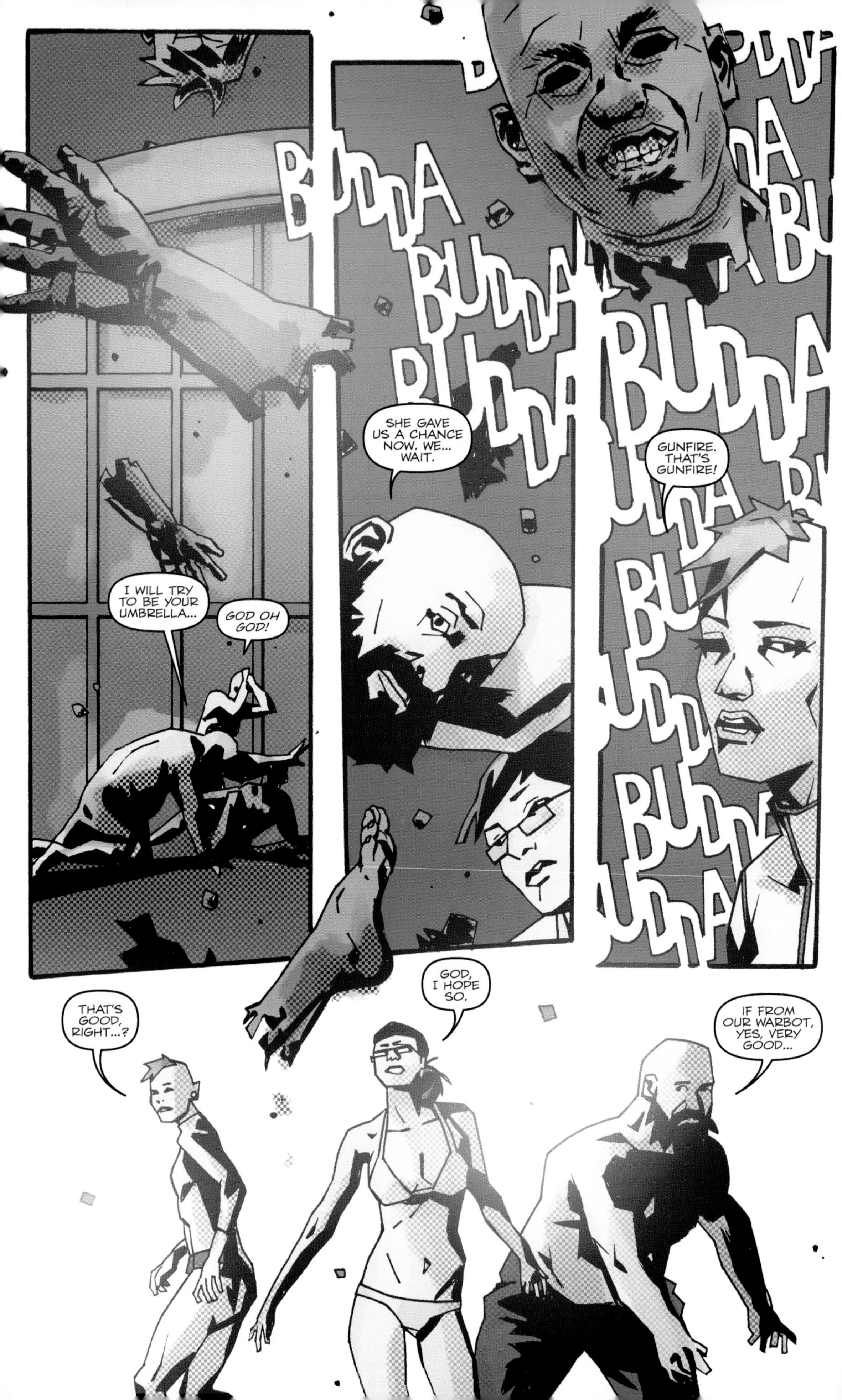
I WILL TRY TO BE YOUR UMBRELLA...
GOD OH GOD!
BUDDA BUDDA BUDDA
SHE GAVE US A CHANCE NOW. WE... WAIT.
BUDDA BUDDA
GUNFIRE. THAT'S GUNFIRE!
BUDDA BUDDA BUDDA
THAT'S GOOD, RIGHT...?
GOD, I HOPE SO.
IF FROM OUR WARBOT, YES, VERY GOOD...

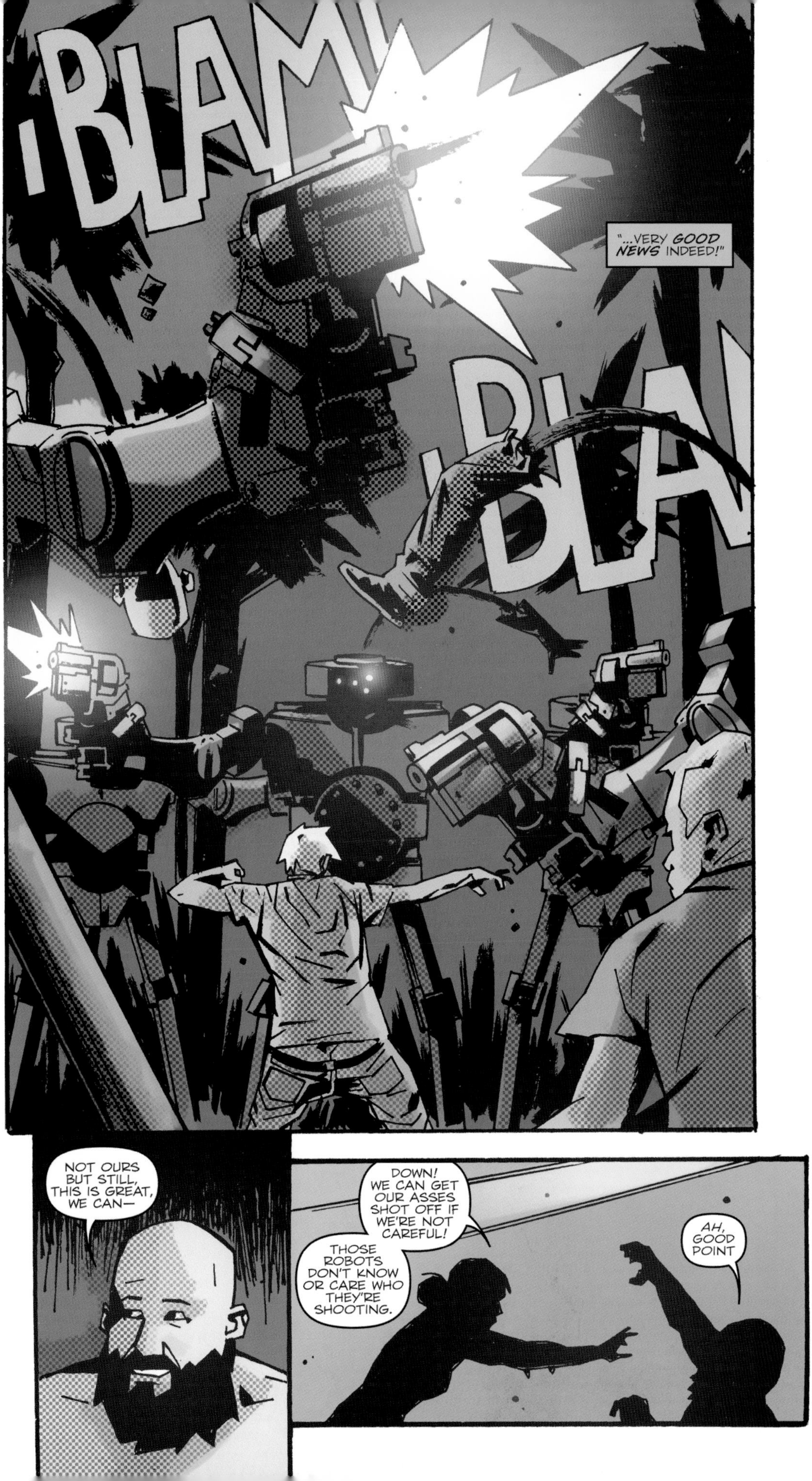

BLAM!
"...VERY GOOD NEWS INDEED!"
BLA
NOT OURS BUT STILL, THIS IS GREAT, WE CAN—
DOWN! WE CAN GET OUR ASSES SHOT OFF IF WE'RE NOT CAREFUL!
THOSE ROBOTS DON'T KNOW OR CARE WHO THEY'RE SHOOTING.
AH, GOOD POINT

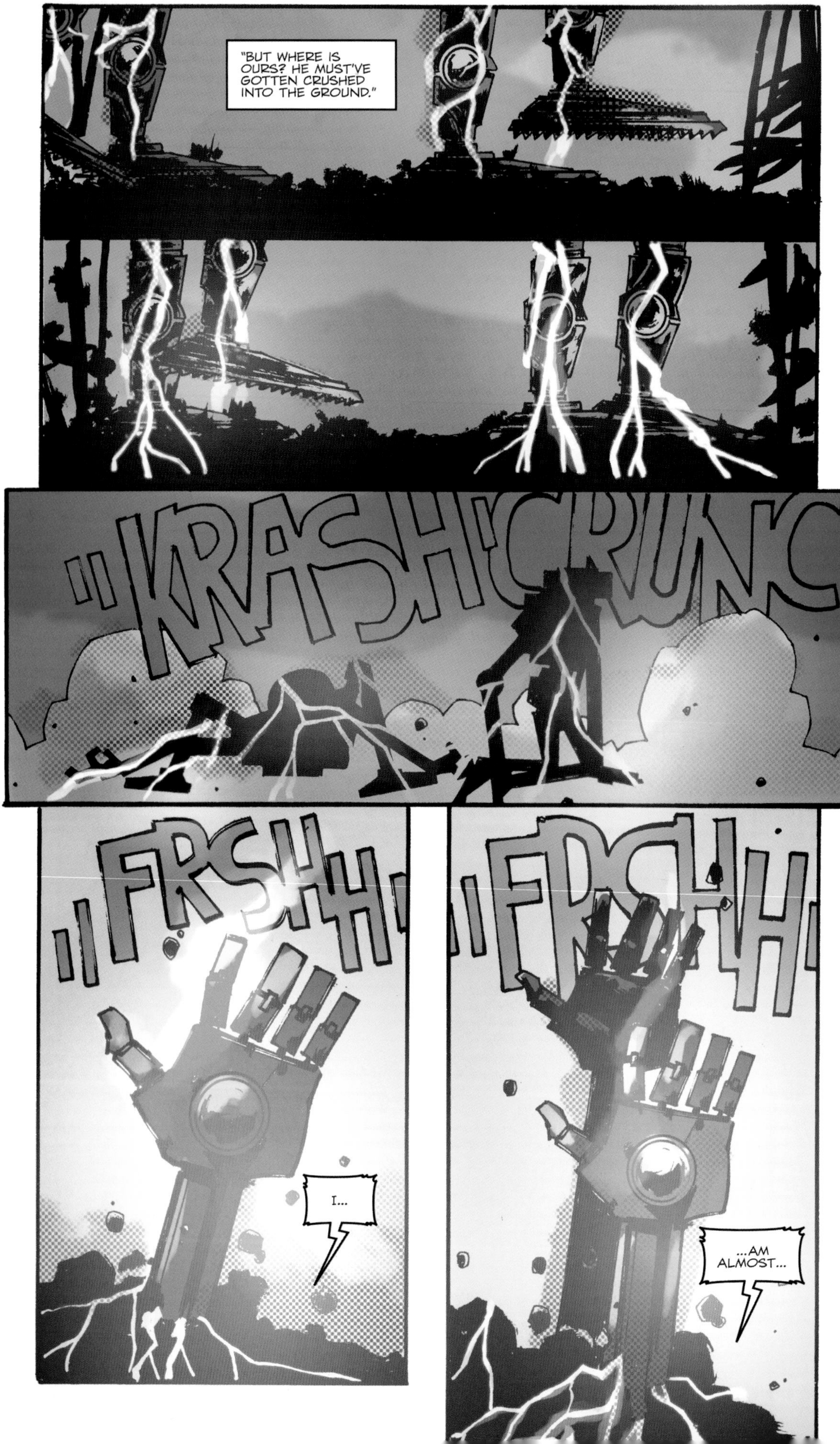
"BUT WHERE IS OURS? HE MUST'VE GOTTEN CRUSHED INTO THE GROUND."
KRASH!CRUNC
FRSHH
FRSHH
I...
...AM ALMOST...

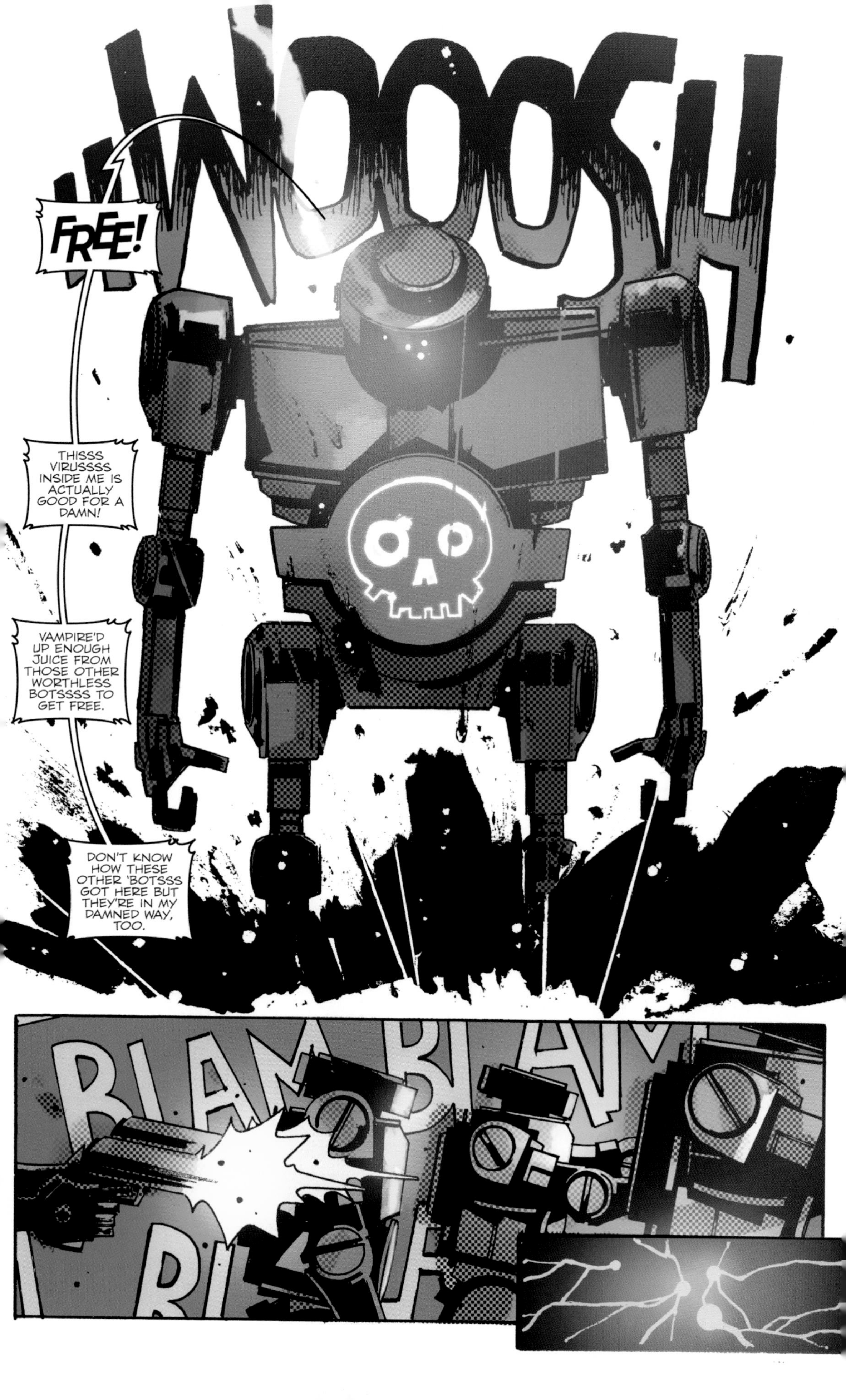
WOOOSH
FREE!
THISSS VIRUSSSS INSIDE ME IS ACTUALLY GOOD FOR A DAMN!
VAMPIRE'D UP ENOUGH JUICE FROM THOSE OTHER WORTHLESS BOTSSSS TO GET FREE.
DON'T KNOW HOW THESE OTHER 'BOTSSS GOT HERE BUT THEY'RE IN MY DAMNED WAY, TOO.
BLAM BLAM

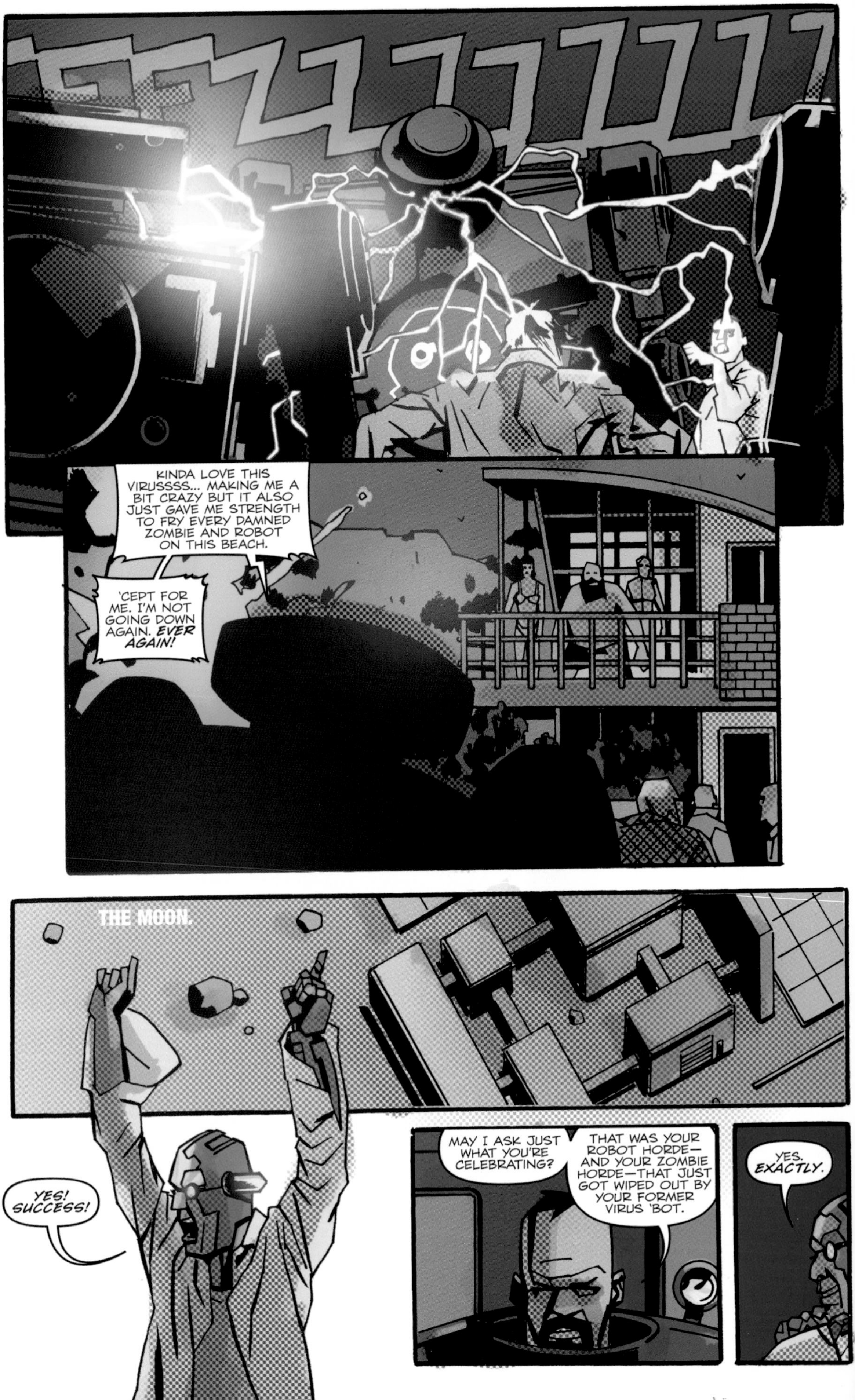
ZZZZZZZZZZZ
KINDA LOVE THIS VIRUSSSS... MAKING ME A BIT CRAZY BUT IT ALSO JUST GAVE ME STRENGTH TO FRY EVERY DAMNED ZOMBIE AND ROBOT ON THIS BEACH.
'CEPT FOR ME. I'M NOT GOING DOWN AGAIN. EVER AGAIN!
THE MOON.
YES! SUCCESS!
MAY I ASK JUST WHAT YOU'RE CELEBRATING?
THAT WAS YOUR ROBOT HORDE—AND YOUR ZOMBIE HORDE—THAT JUST GOT WIPED OUT BY YOUR FORMER VIRUS 'BOT.
YES. EXACTLY.

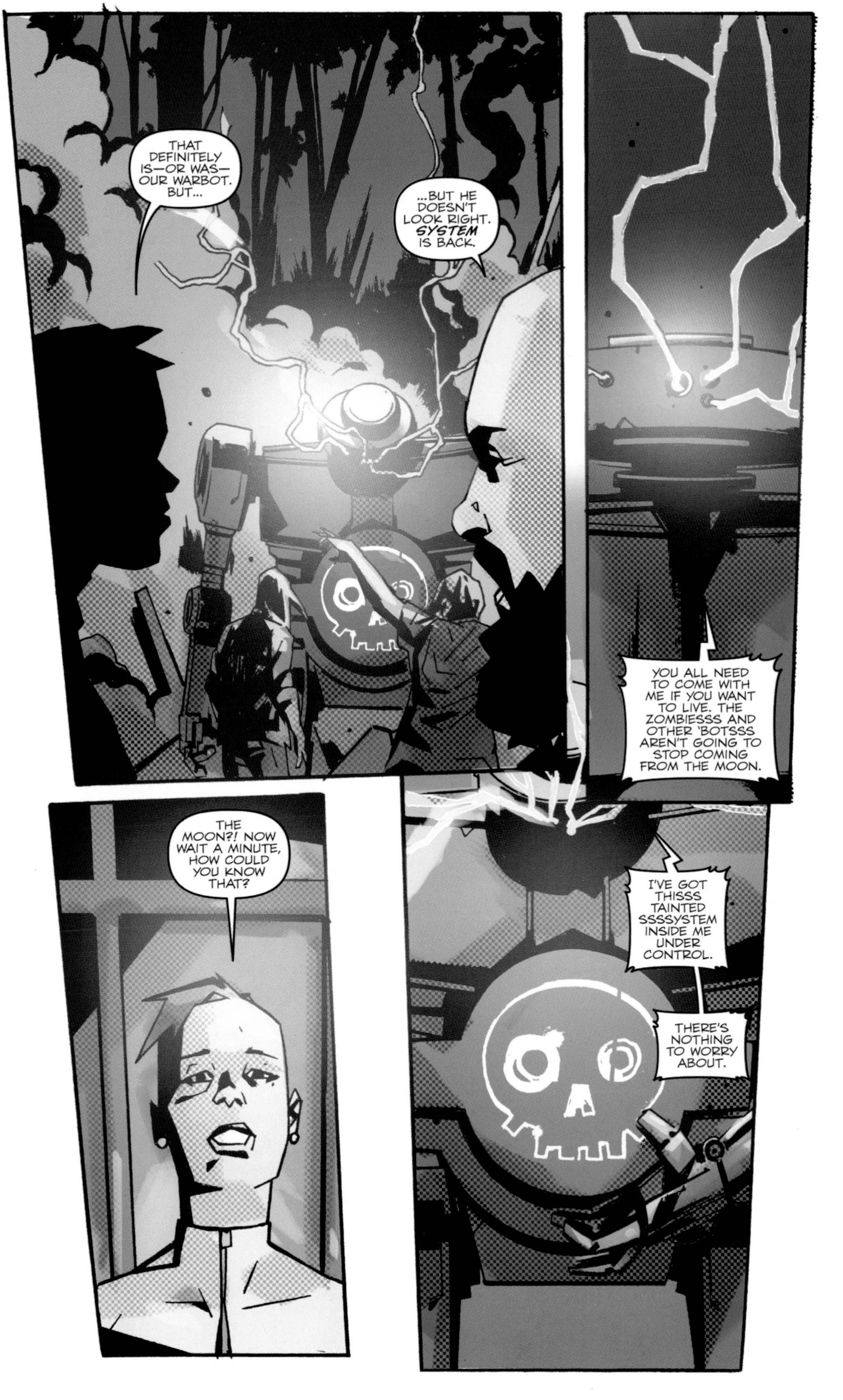

THAT DEFINITELY IS—OR WAS—OUR WARBOT. BUT...
...BUT HE DOESN'T LOOK RIGHT. SYSTEM IS BACK.
YOU ALL NEED TO COME WITH ME IF YOU WANT TO LIVE. THE ZOMBIESSS AND OTHER 'BOTSSS AREN'T GOING TO STOP COMING FROM THE MOON.
THE MOON?! NOW WAIT A MINUTE, HOW COULD YOU KNOW THAT?
I'VE GOT THISSS TAINTED SSSSYSTEM INSIDE ME UNDER CONTROL.
THERE'S NOTHING TO WORRY ABOUT.

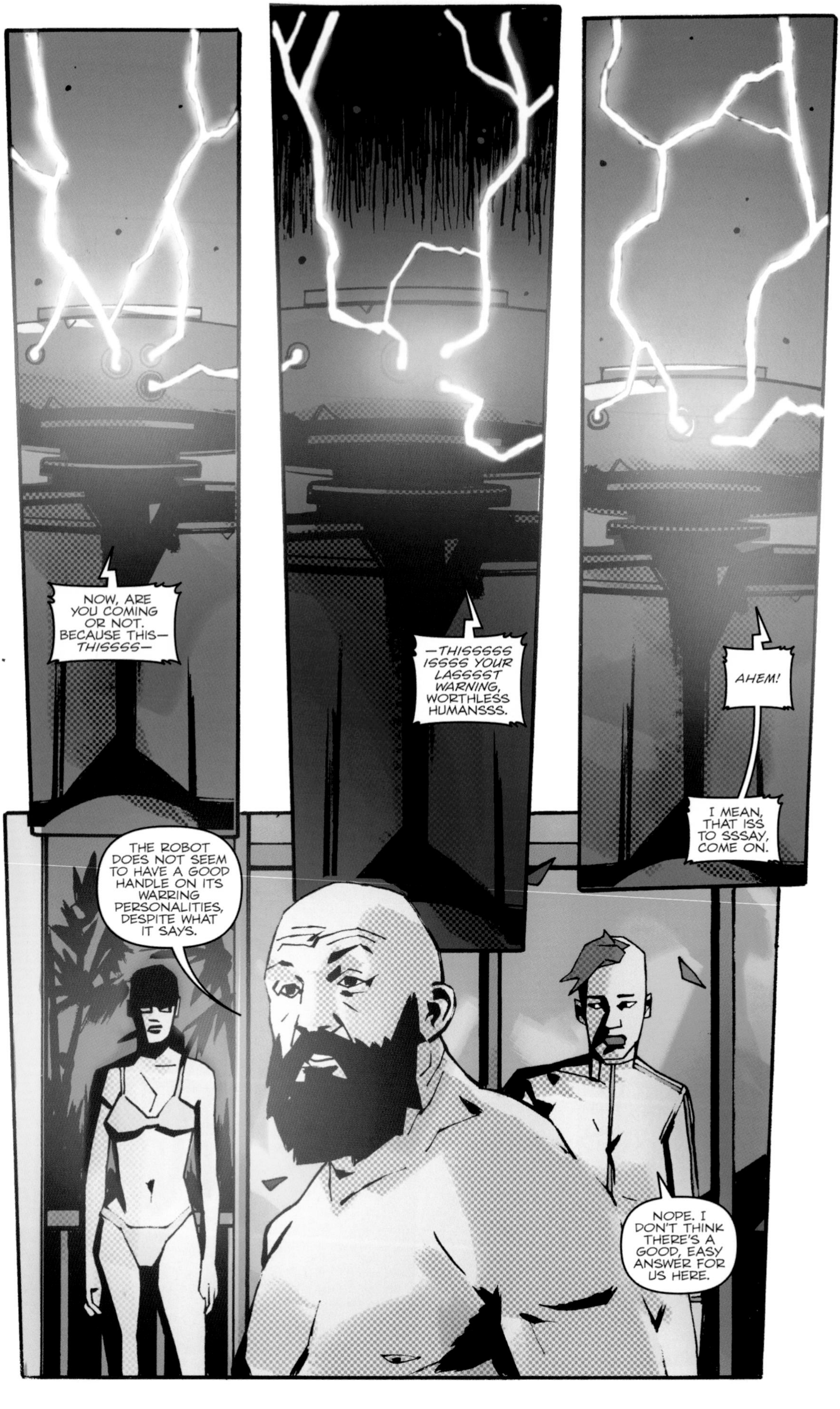
NOW, ARE YOU COMING OR NOT. BECAUSE THIS— *THISSSS—*
—THISSSSS ISSSS YOUR LASSSST WARNING, WORTHLESS HUMANSSS.
AHEM!
I MEAN, THAT ISS TO SSSAY, COME ON.
THE ROBOT DOES NOT SEEM TO HAVE A GOOD HANDLE ON ITS WARRING PERSONALITIES, DESPITE WHAT IT SAYS.
NOPE. I DON'T THINK THERE'S A GOOD, EASY ANSWER FOR US HERE.

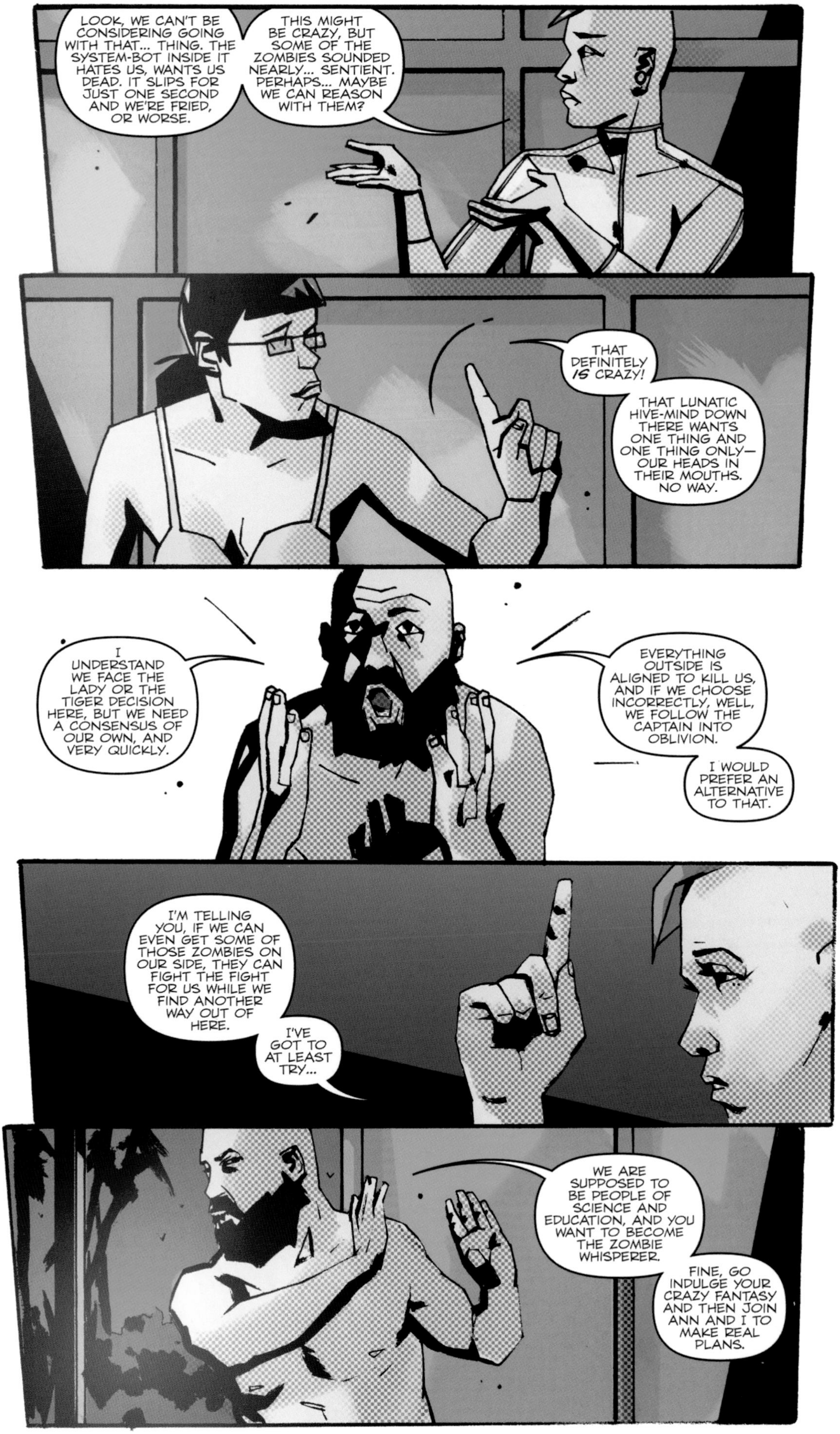
LOOK, WE CAN'T BE CONSIDERING GOING WITH THAT... THING. THE SYSTEM-BOT INSIDE IT HATES US, WANTS US DEAD. IT SLIPS FOR JUST ONE SECOND AND WE'RE FRIED, OR WORSE.
THIS MIGHT BE CRAZY, BUT SOME OF THE ZOMBIES SOUNDED NEARLY... SENTIENT. PERHAPS... MAYBE WE CAN REASON WITH THEM?
THAT DEFINITELY *IS* CRAZY!
THAT LUNATIC HIVE-MIND DOWN THERE WANTS ONE THING AND ONE THING ONLY— OUR HEADS IN THEIR MOUTHS. NO WAY.
I UNDERSTAND WE FACE THE LADY OR THE TIGER DECISION HERE, BUT WE NEED A CONSENSUS OF OUR OWN, AND VERY QUICKLY.
EVERYTHING OUTSIDE IS ALIGNED TO KILL US, AND IF WE CHOOSE INCORRECTLY, WELL, WE FOLLOW THE CAPTAIN INTO OBLIVION.
I WOULD PREFER AN ALTERNATIVE TO THAT.
I'M TELLING YOU, IF WE CAN EVEN GET SOME OF THOSE ZOMBIES ON OUR SIDE, THEY CAN FIGHT THE FIGHT FOR US WHILE WE FIND ANOTHER WAY OUT OF HERE.
I'VE GOT TO AT LEAST TRY...
WE ARE SUPPOSED TO BE PEOPLE OF SCIENCE AND EDUCATION, AND YOU WANT TO BECOME THE ZOMBIE WHISPERER.
FINE, GO INDULGE YOUR CRAZY FANTASY AND THEN JOIN ANN AND I TO MAKE REAL PLANS.

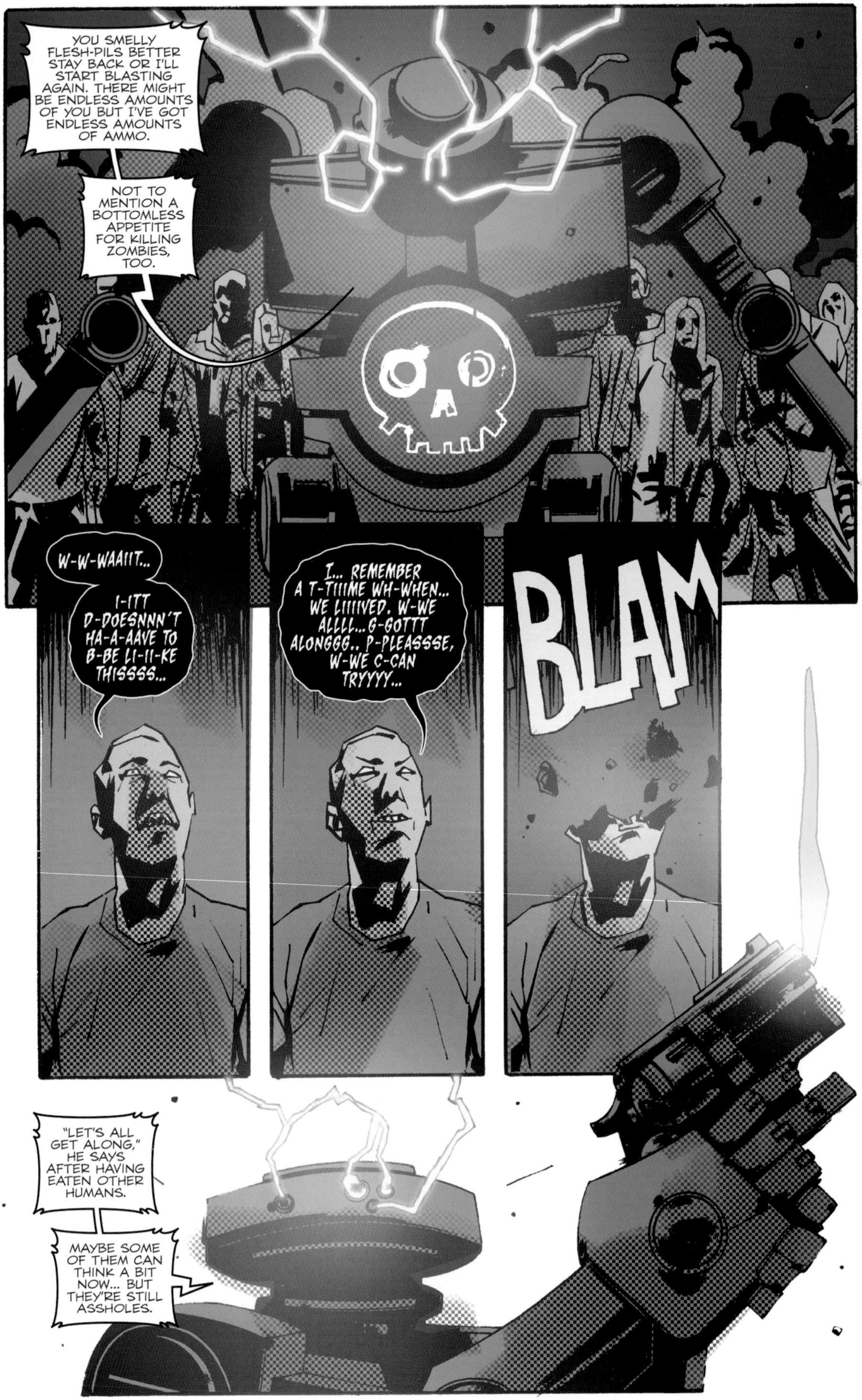
YOU SMELLY FLESH-PILS BETTER STAY BACK OR I'LL START BLASTING AGAIN. THERE MIGHT BE ENDLESS AMOUNTS OF YOU BUT I'VE GOT ENDLESS AMOUNTS OF AMMO.
NOT TO MENTION A BOTTOMLESS APPETITE FOR KILLING ZOMBIES, TOO.
W-W-WAAIIT...
I-ITT D-DOESNNN'T HA-A-AAVE TO B-BE LI-II-KE THISSSS...
I... REMEMBER A T-TIIIME WH-WHEN... WE LIIIIVED. W-WE ALLLL... G-GOTTT ALONGGG.. P-PLEASSSE, W-WE C-CAN TRYYYY...
BLAM
"LET'S ALL GET ALONG," HE SAYS AFTER HAVING EATEN OTHER HUMANS.
MAYBE SOME OF THEM CAN THINK A BIT NOW... BUT THEY'RE STILL ASSHOLES.

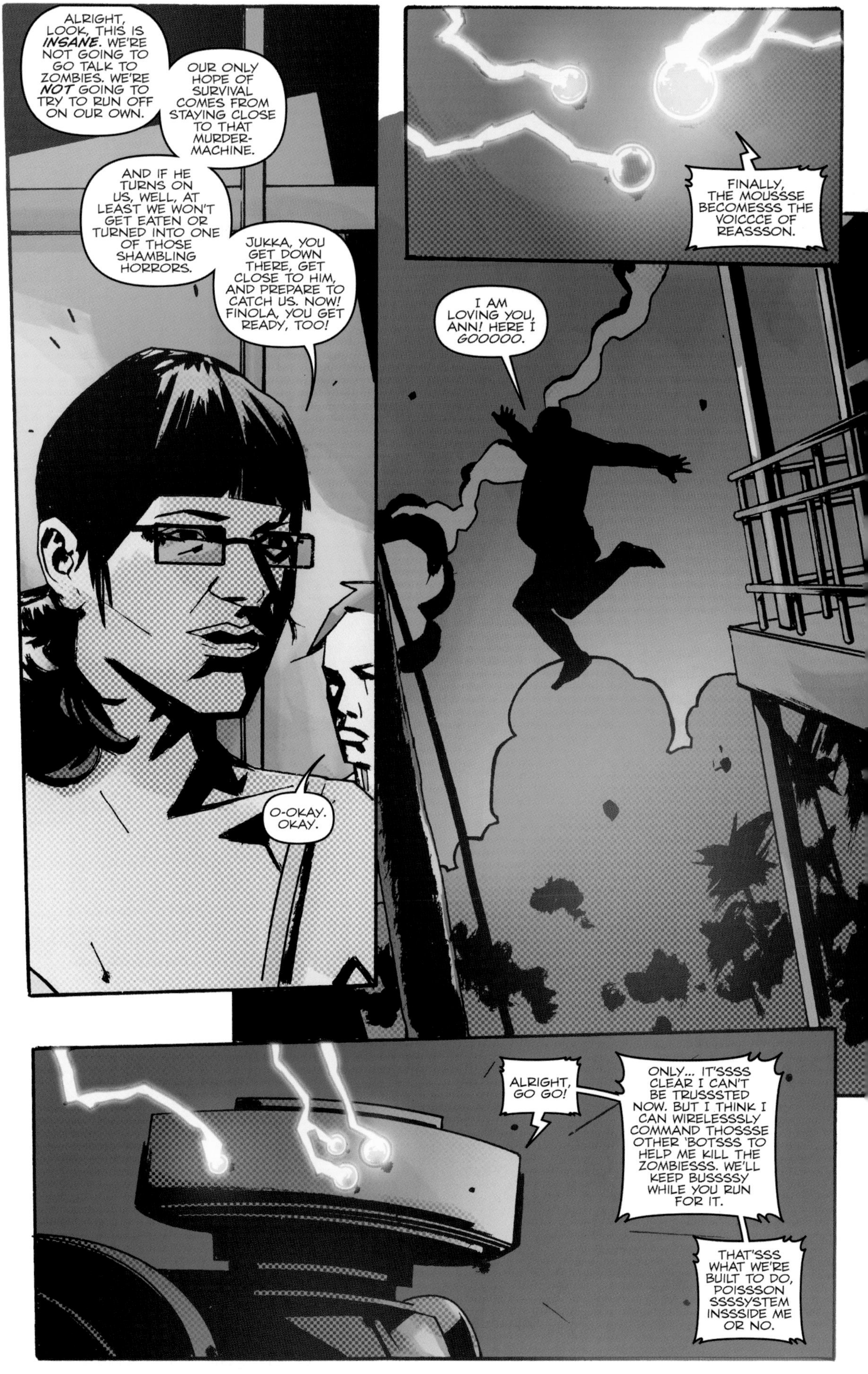

ALRIGHT, LOOK, THIS IS *INSANE*. WE'RE NOT GOING TO GO TALK TO ZOMBIES. WE'RE *NOT* GOING TO TRY TO RUN OFF ON OUR OWN.
OUR ONLY HOPE OF SURVIVAL COMES FROM STAYING CLOSE TO THAT MURDER-MACHINE.
AND IF HE TURNS ON US, WELL, AT LEAST WE WON'T GET EATEN OR TURNED INTO ONE OF THOSE SHAMBLING HORRORS.
JUKKA, YOU GET DOWN THERE, GET CLOSE TO HIM, AND PREPARE TO CATCH US. NOW! FINOLA, YOU GET READY, TOO!
O-OKAY. OKAY.
FINALLY, THE MOUSSSE BECOMESSS THE VOICCCE OF REASSSON.
I AM LOVING YOU, ANN! HERE I *GOOOOO*.
ALRIGHT, GO GO!
ONLY... IT'SSSS CLEAR I CAN'T BE TRUSSSTED NOW. BUT I THINK I CAN WIRELESSSLY COMMAND THOSSSE OTHER 'BOTSSS TO HELP ME KILL THE ZOMBIESSS. WE'LL KEEP BUSSSSY WHILE YOU RUN FOR IT.
THAT'SSS WHAT WE'RE BUILT TO DO, POISSSON SSSSYSTEM INSSSIDE ME OR NO.

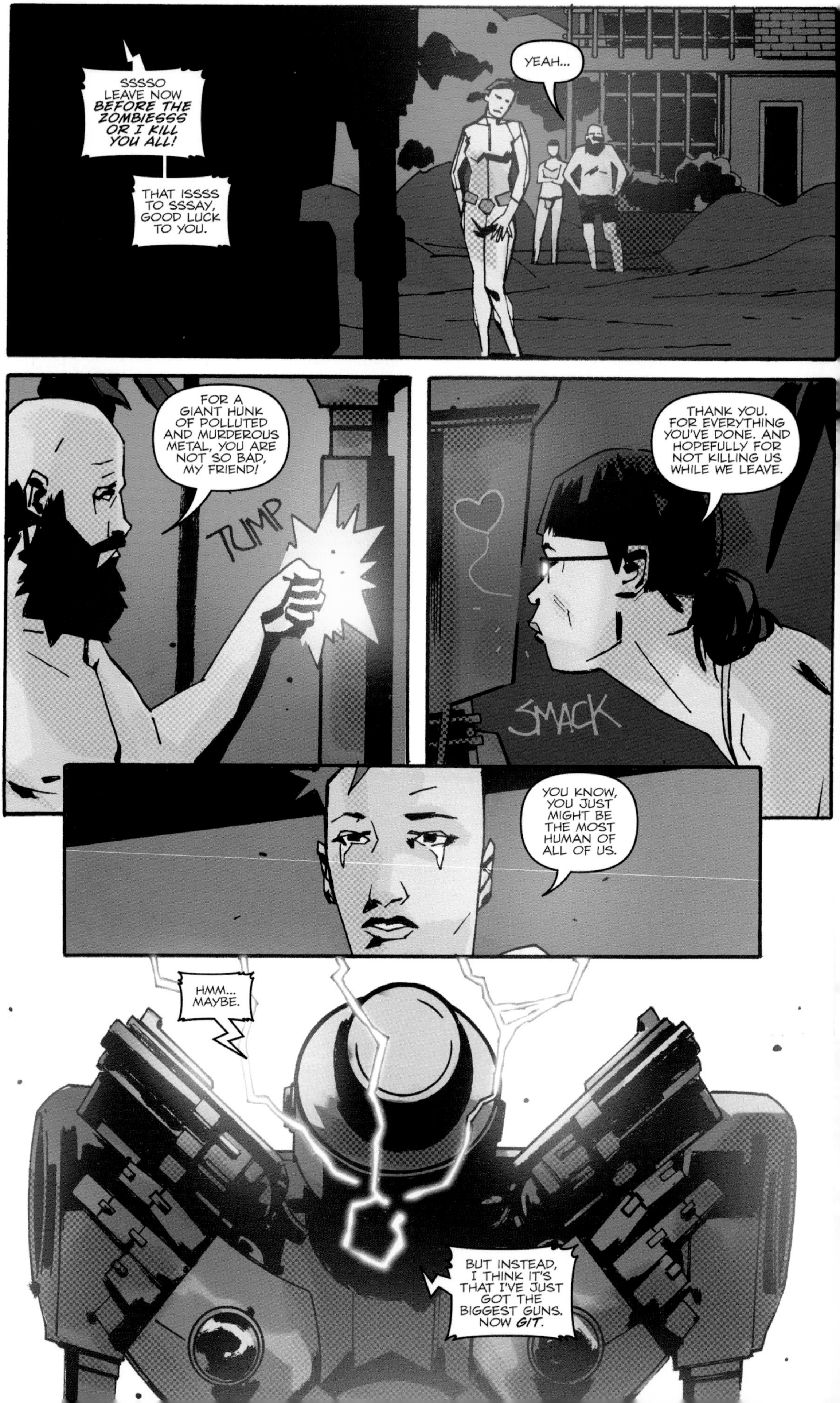
SSSSO LEAVE NOW BEFORE THE ZOMBIESSS OR I KILL YOU ALL!
THAT ISSSS TO SSSAY, GOOD LUCK TO YOU.
YEAH...
FOR A GIANT HUNK OF POLLUTED AND MURDEROUS METAL, YOU ARE NOT SO BAD, MY FRIEND!
TUMP
THANK YOU. FOR EVERYTHING YOU'VE DONE. AND HOPEFULLY FOR NOT KILLING US WHILE WE LEAVE.
SMACK
YOU KNOW, YOU JUST MIGHT BE THE MOST HUMAN OF ALL OF US.
HMM... MAYBE.
BUT INSTEAD, I THINK IT'S THAT I'VE JUST GOT THE BIGGEST GUNS. NOW GIT.

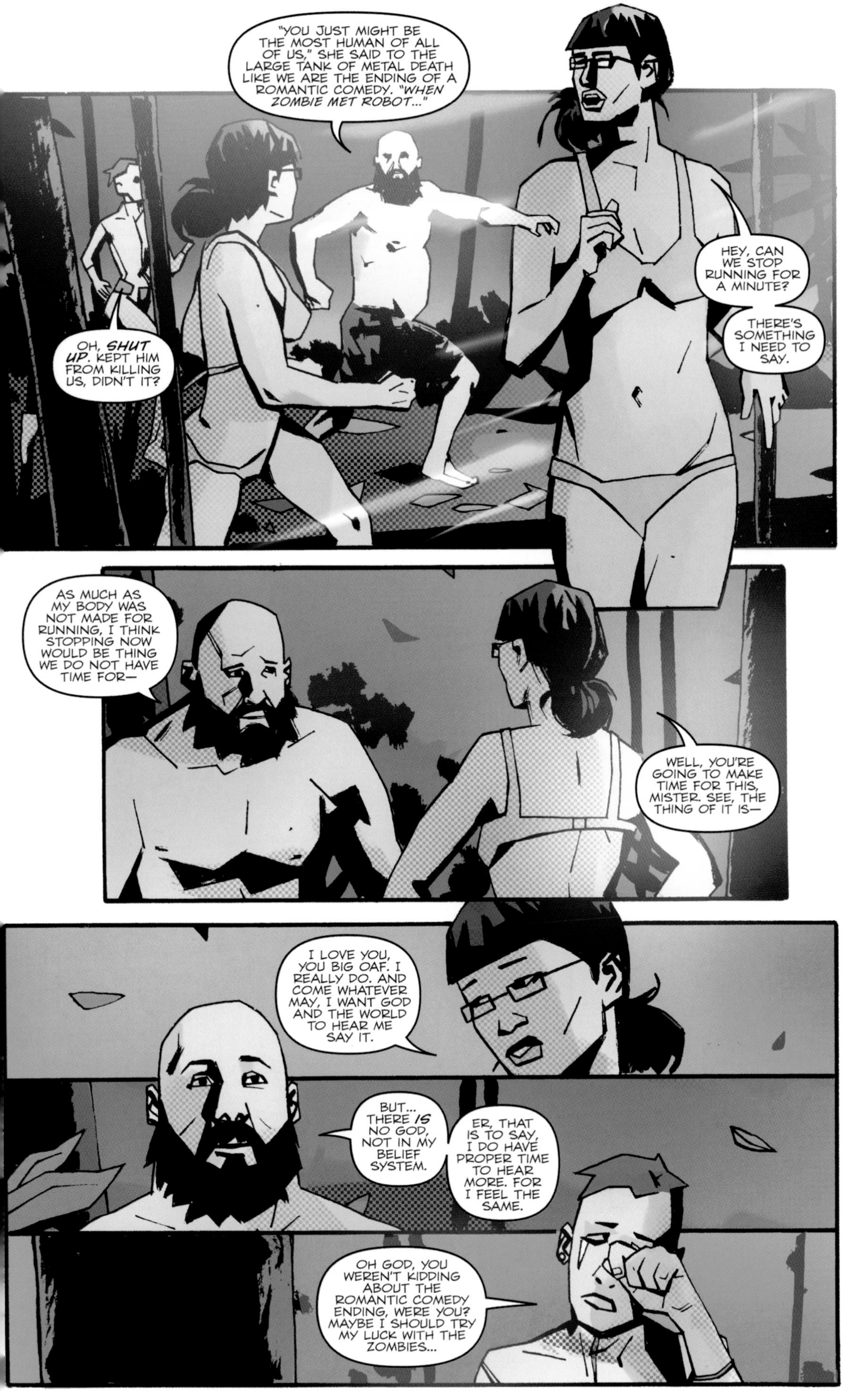
"YOU JUST MIGHT BE THE MOST HUMAN OF ALL OF US," SHE SAID TO THE LARGE TANK OF METAL DEATH LIKE WE ARE THE ENDING OF A ROMANTIC COMEDY. "*WHEN ZOMBIE MET ROBOT...*"
OH, ***SHUT UP***. KEPT HIM FROM KILLING US, DIDN'T IT?
HEY, CAN WE STOP RUNNING FOR A MINUTE?
THERE'S SOMETHING I NEED TO SAY.
AS MUCH AS MY BODY WAS NOT MADE FOR RUNNING, I THINK STOPPING NOW WOULD BE THING WE DO NOT HAVE TIME FOR—
WELL, YOU'RE GOING TO MAKE TIME FOR THIS, MISTER. SEE, THE THING OF IT IS—
I LOVE YOU, YOU BIG OAF. I REALLY DO. AND COME WHATEVER MAY, I WANT GOD AND THE WORLD TO HEAR ME SAY IT.
BUT... THERE *IS* NO GOD, NOT IN MY BELIEF SYSTEM.
ER, THAT IS TO SAY, I DO HAVE PROPER TIME TO HEAR MORE. FOR I FEEL THE SAME.
OH GOD, YOU WEREN'T KIDDING ABOUT THE ROMANTIC COMEDY ENDING, WERE YOU? MAYBE I SHOULD TRY MY LUCK WITH THE ZOMBIES...

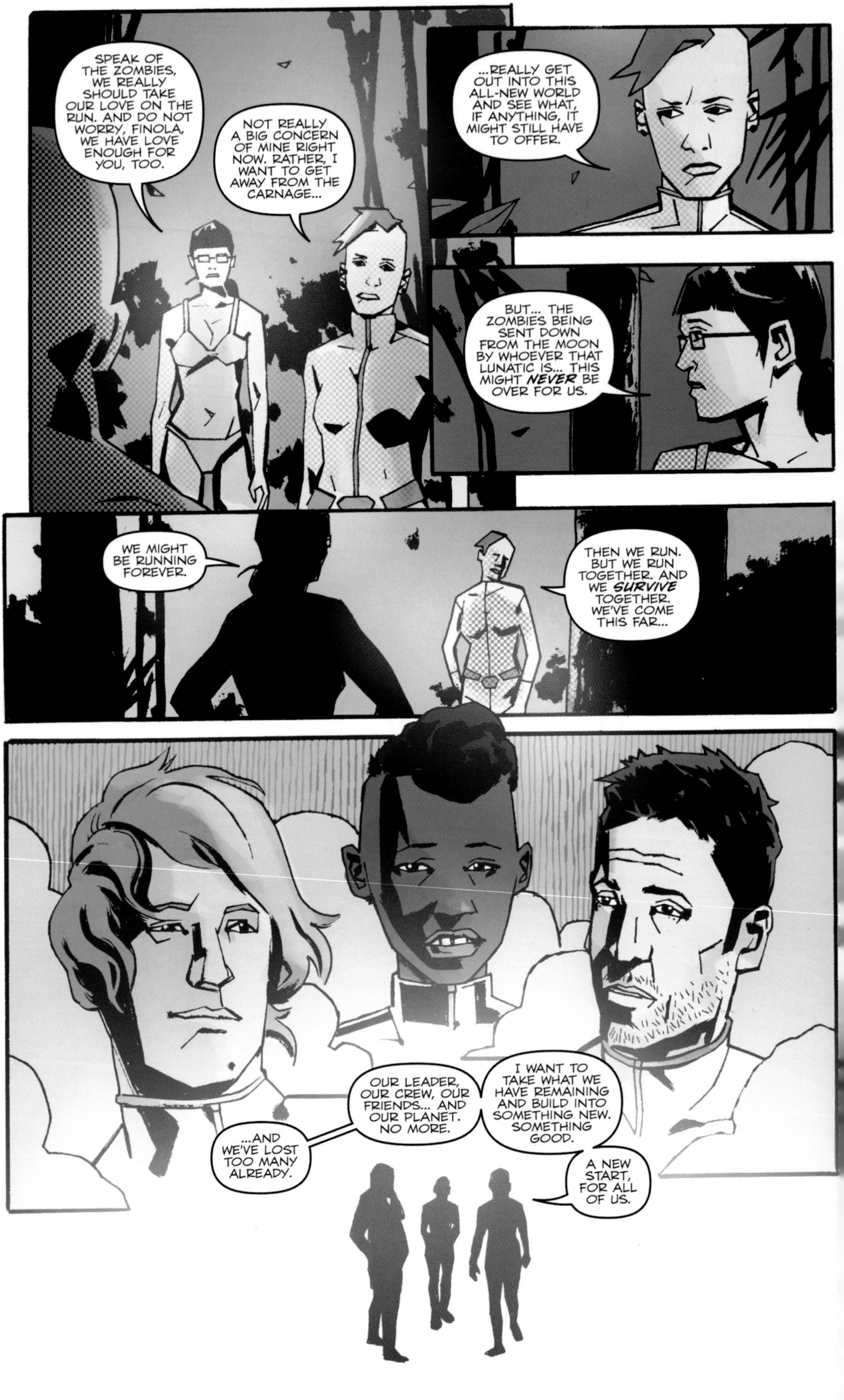
SPEAK OF THE ZOMBIES, WE REALLY SHOULD TAKE OUR LOVE ON THE RUN. AND DO NOT WORRY, FINOLA, WE HAVE LOVE ENOUGH FOR YOU, TOO.
NOT REALLY A BIG CONCERN OF MINE RIGHT NOW. RATHER, I WANT TO GET AWAY FROM THE CARNAGE...
...REALLY GET OUT INTO THIS ALL-NEW WORLD AND SEE WHAT, IF ANYTHING, IT MIGHT STILL HAVE TO OFFER.
BUT... THE ZOMBIES BEING SENT DOWN FROM THE MOON BY WHOEVER THAT LUNATIC IS... THIS MIGHT NEVER BE OVER FOR US.
WE MIGHT BE RUNNING FOREVER.
THEN WE RUN. BUT WE RUN TOGETHER. AND WE SURVIVE TOGETHER. WE'VE COME THIS FAR...
...AND WE'VE LOST TOO MANY ALREADY.
OUR LEADER, OUR CREW, OUR FRIENDS... AND OUR PLANET. NO MORE.
I WANT TO TAKE WHAT WE HAVE REMAINING AND BUILD INTO SOMETHING NEW. SOMETHING GOOD.
A NEW START, FOR ALL OF US.

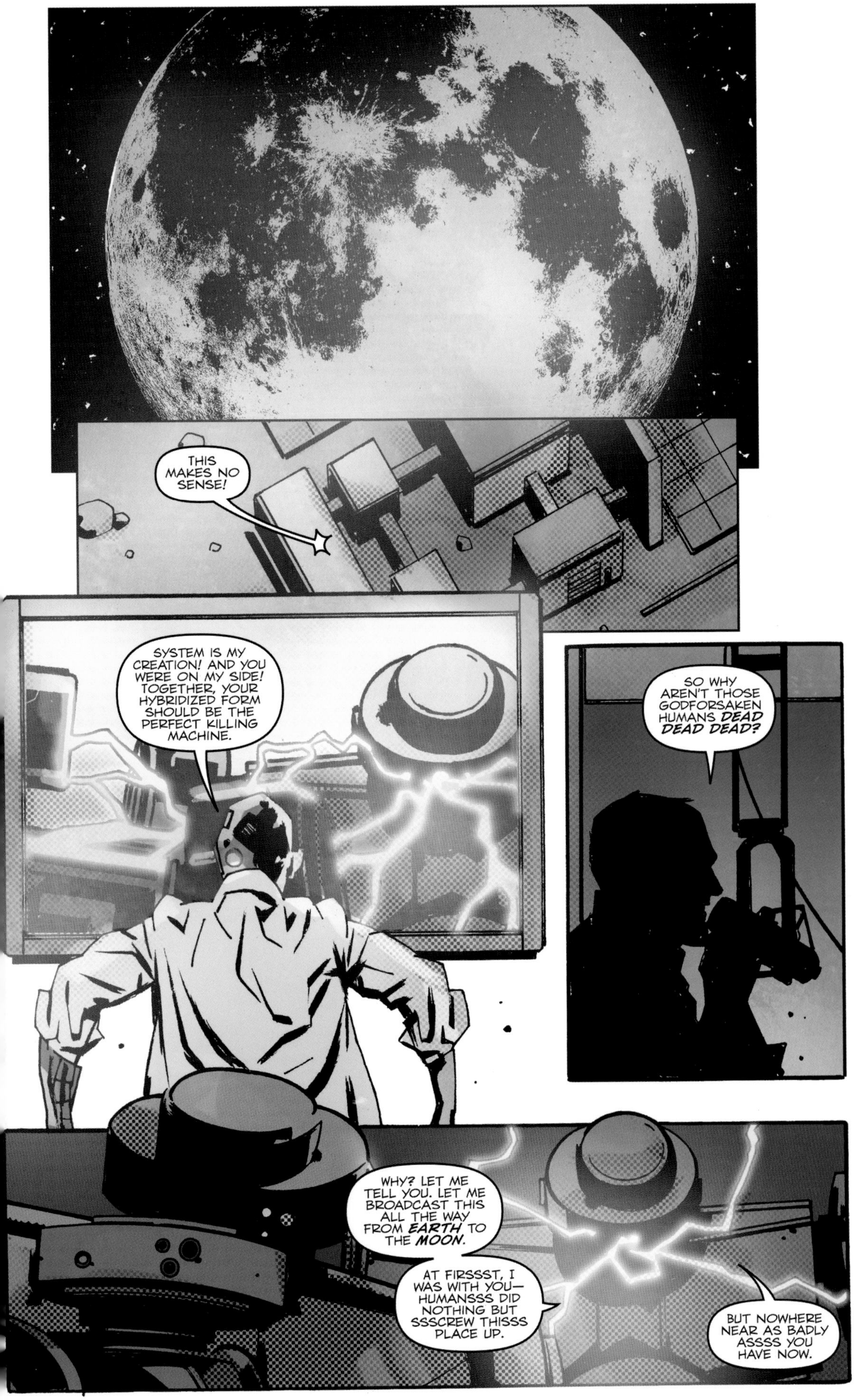

THIS MAKES NO SENSE!
SYSTEM IS MY CREATION! AND YOU WERE ON MY SIDE! TOGETHER, YOUR HYBRIDIZED FORM SHOULD BE THE PERFECT KILLING MACHINE.
SO WHY AREN'T THOSE GODFORSAKEN HUMANS *DEAD DEAD DEAD?*
WHY? LET ME TELL YOU. LET ME BROADCAST THIS ALL THE WAY FROM *EARTH* TO THE *MOON*.
AT FIRSSST, I WAS WITH YOU— HUMANSSS DID NOTHING BUT SSSCREW THISSS PLACE UP.
BUT NOWHERE NEAR AS BADLY ASSSS YOU HAVE NOW.

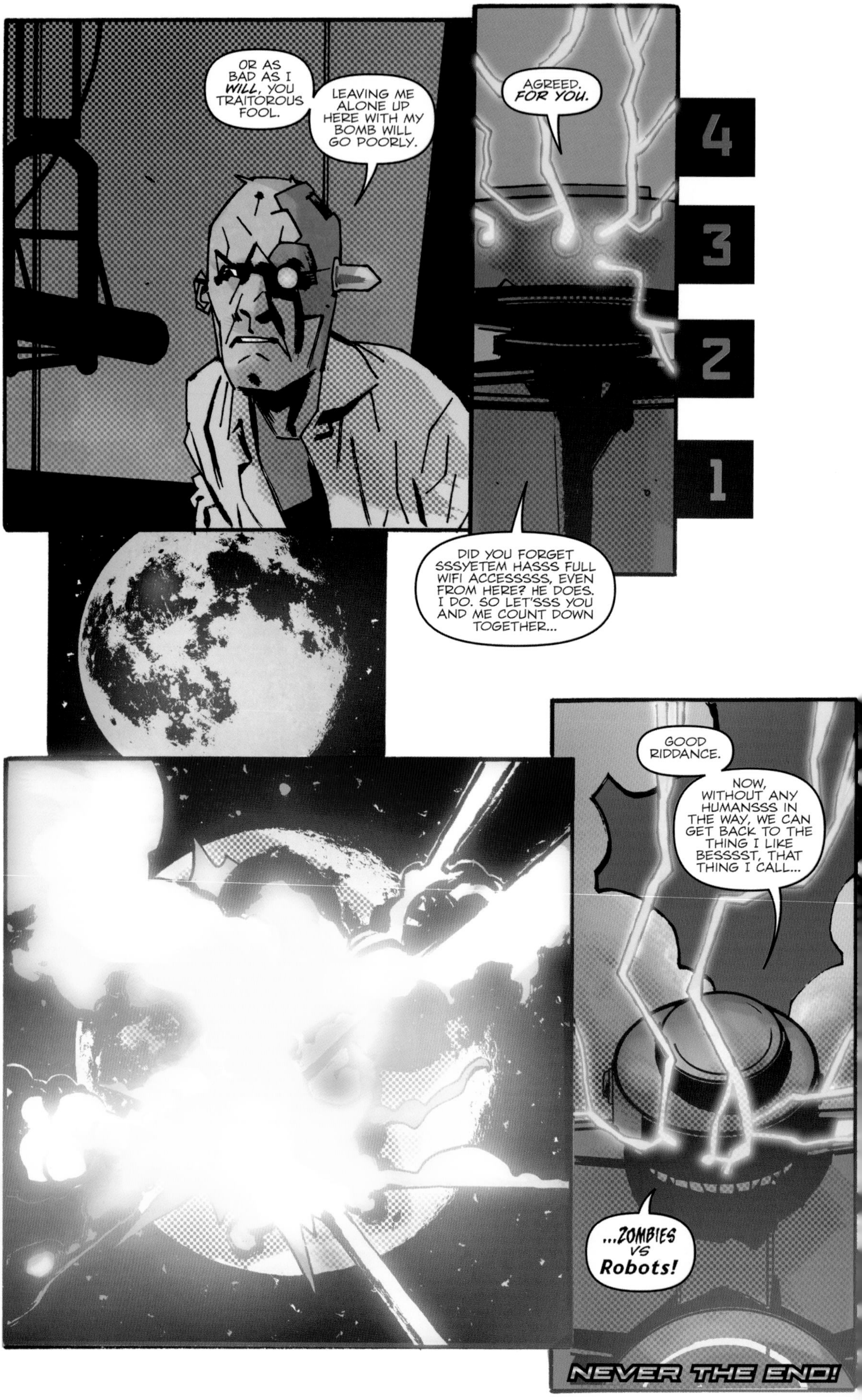

OR AS BAD AS I WILL, YOU TRAITOROUS FOOL.
LEAVING ME ALONE UP HERE WITH MY BOMB WILL GO POORLY.
AGREED. FOR YOU.
4
3
2
1
DID YOU FORGET SSSYETEM HASSS FULL WIFI ACCESSSSS, EVEN FROM HERE? HE DOES. I DO. SO LET'SSS YOU AND ME COUNT DOWN TOGETHER...
GOOD RIDDANCE.
NOW, WITHOUT ANY HUMANSSS IN THE WAY, WE CAN GET BACK TO THE THING I LIKE BESSSST, THAT THING I CALL...
...ZOMBIES VS Robots!
NEVER THE END!

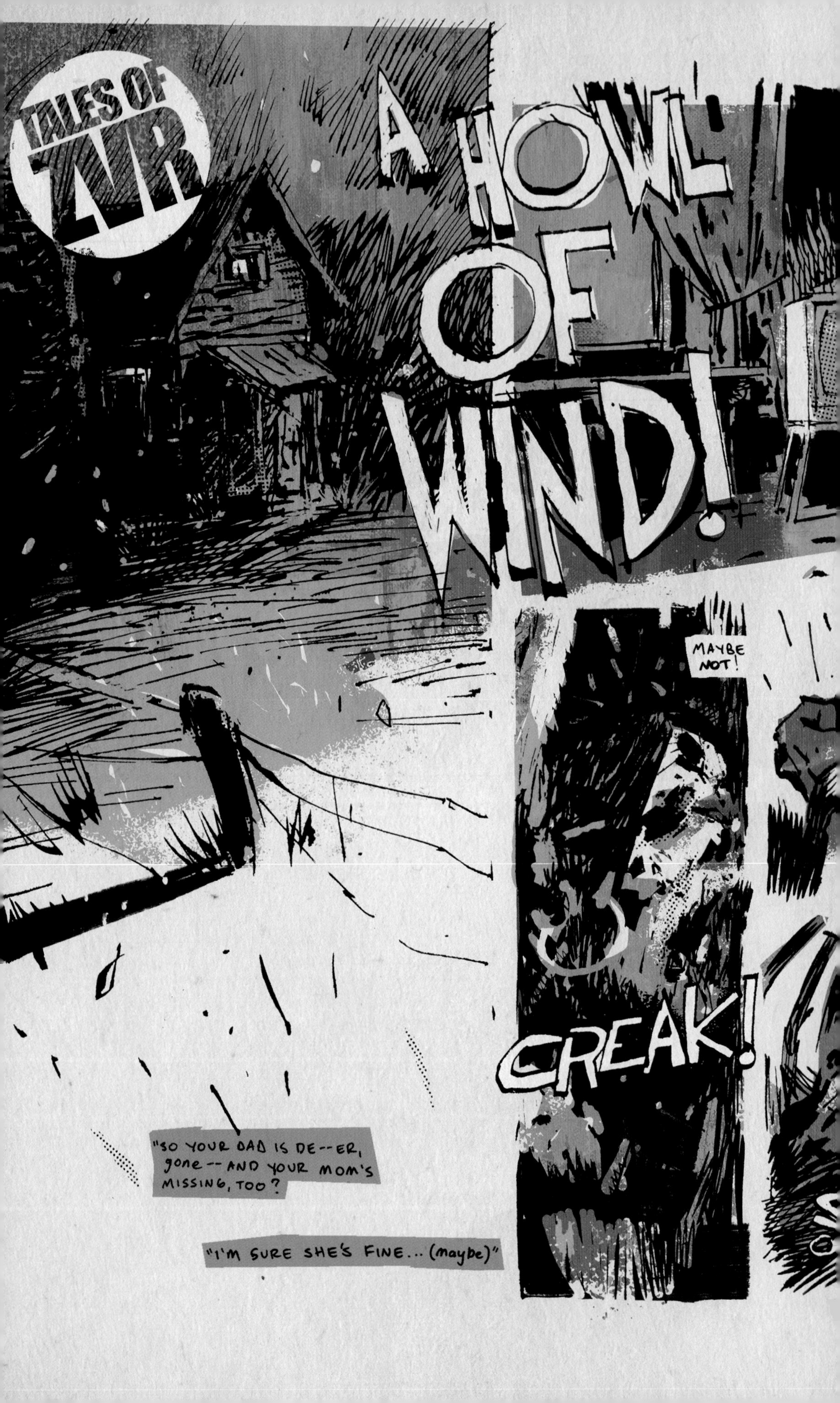
TALES OF ZIR
A HOWL OF WIND!
MAYBE NOT!
CREAK!
"SO YOUR DAD IS DE--ER, gone--AND YOUR MOM'S MISSING, TOO?
"I'M SURE SHE'S FINE... (maybe)"

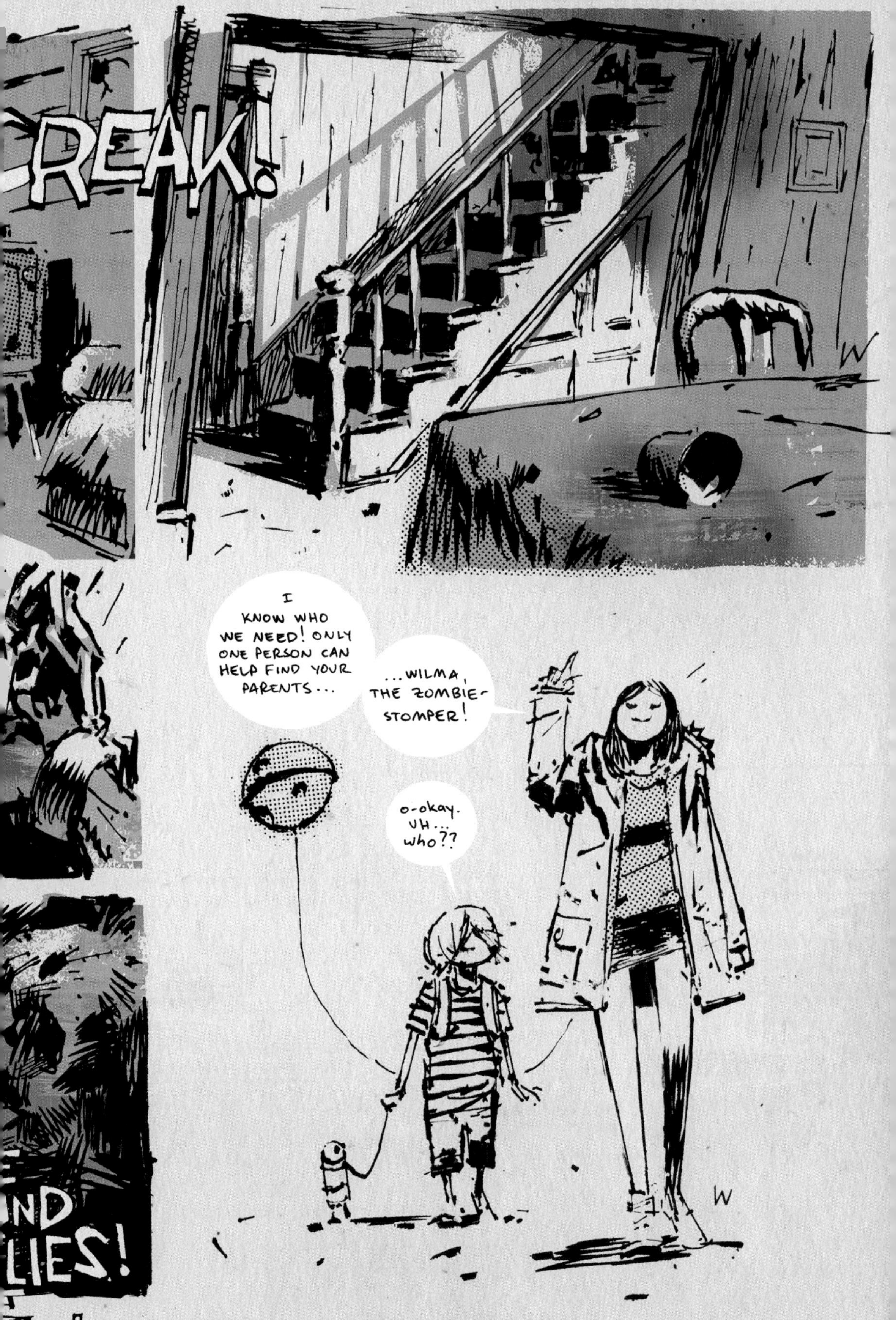

REAK!
I KNOW WHO WE NEED! ONLY ONE PERSON CAN HELP FIND YOUR PARENTS...
...WILMA, THE ZOMBIE-STOMPER!
o-okay. UH... who??
ND
LIES!

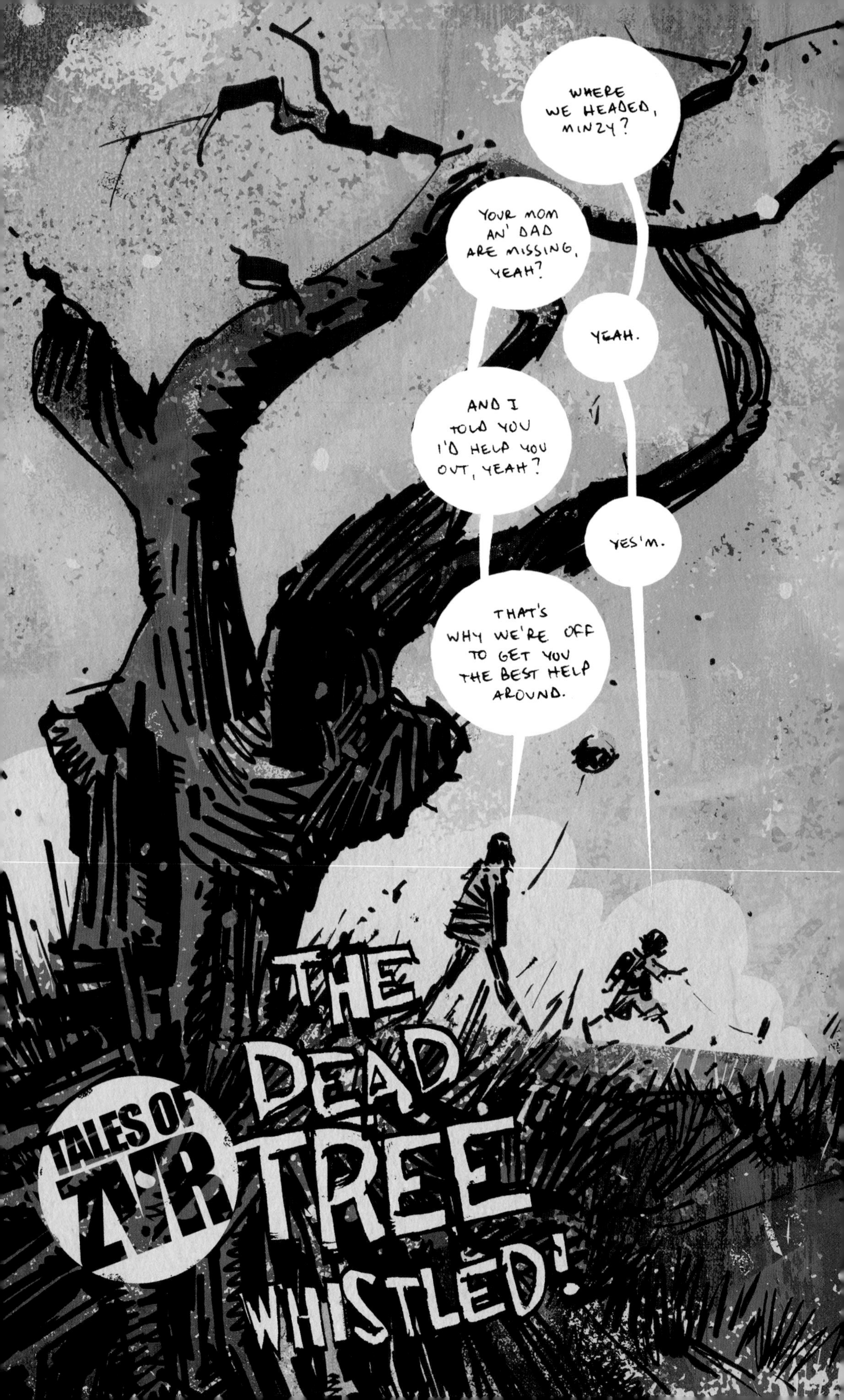
WHERE WE HEADED, MINZY?
YOUR MOM AN' DAD ARE MISSING, YEAH?
YEAH.
AND I TOLD YOU I'D HELP YOU OUT, YEAH?
YES'M.
THAT'S WHY WE'RE OFF TO GET YOU THE BEST HELP AROUND.
TALES OF Z.R.
THE DEAD TREE WHISTLED!

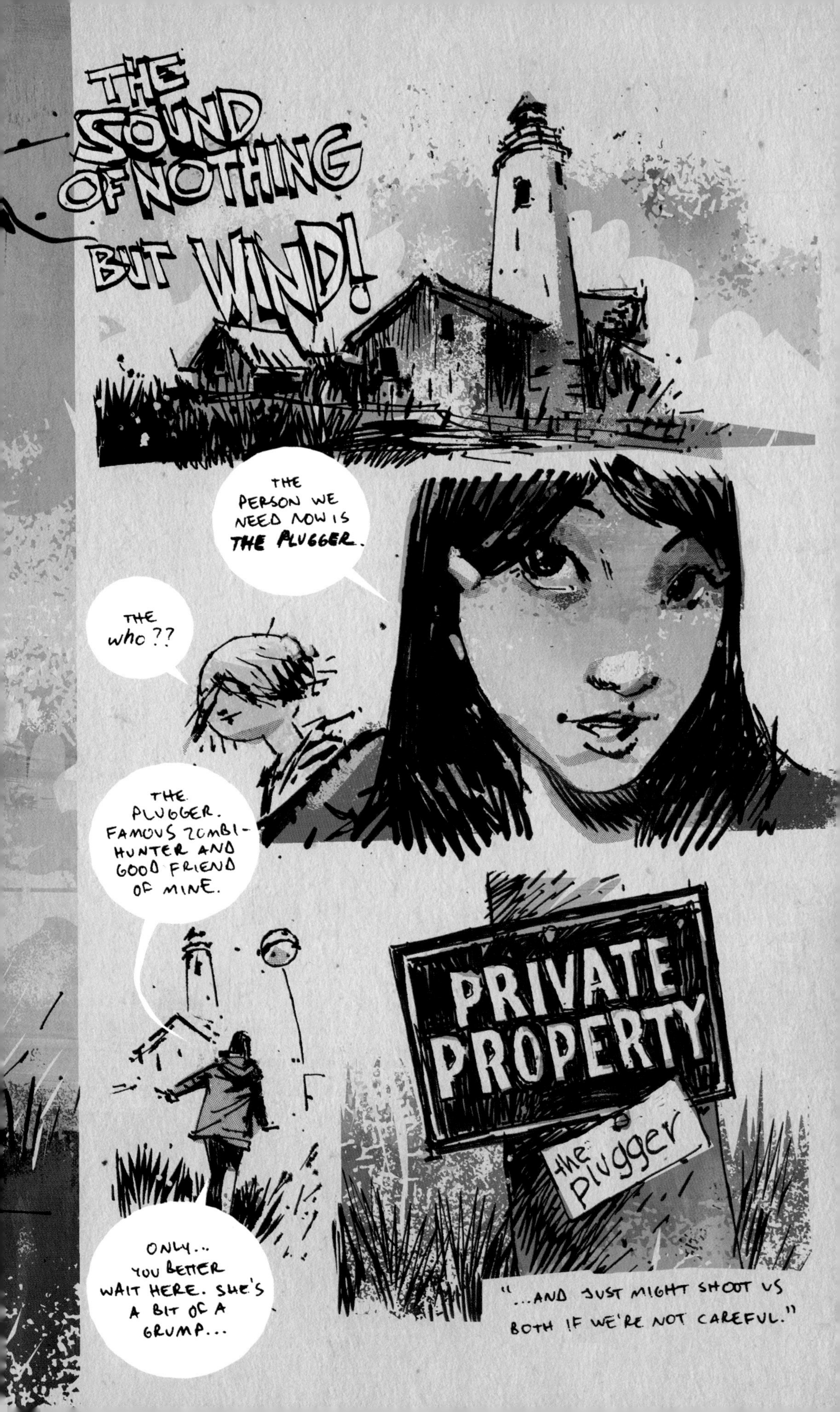
THE SOUND OF NOTHING BUT WIND!
THE PERSON WE NEED NOW IS THE PLUGGER.
THE who??
THE PLUGGER. FAMOUS ZOMBI-HUNTER AND GOOD FRIEND OF MINE.
PRIVATE PROPERTY
the plugger
ONLY... YOU BETTER WAIT HERE. SHE'S A BIT OF A GRUMP...
"...AND JUST MIGHT SHOOT US BOTH IF WE'RE NOT CAREFUL."

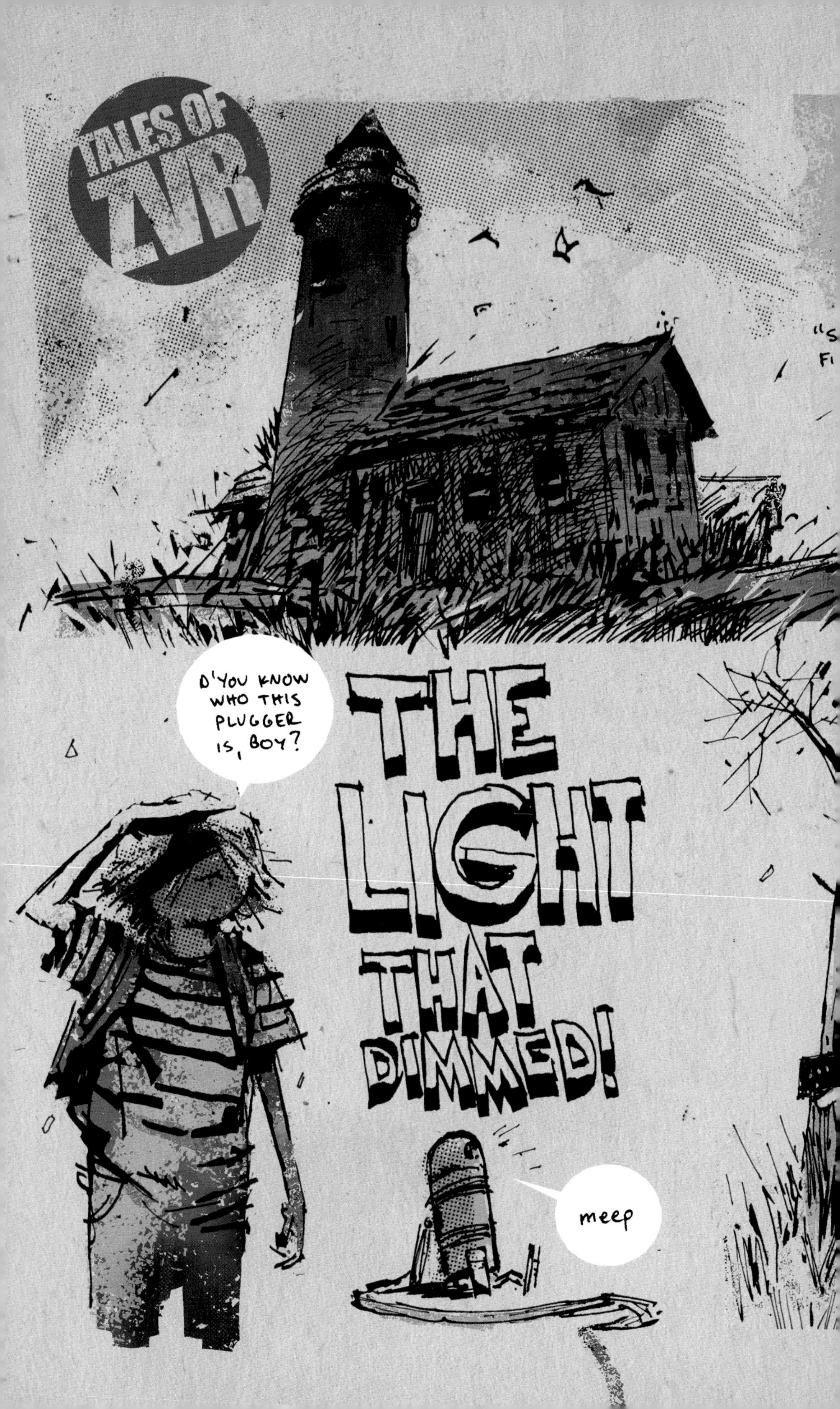
TALES OF ZVR
THE LIGHT THAT DIMMED!
D'YOU KNOW WHO THIS PLUGGER IS, BOY?
meep

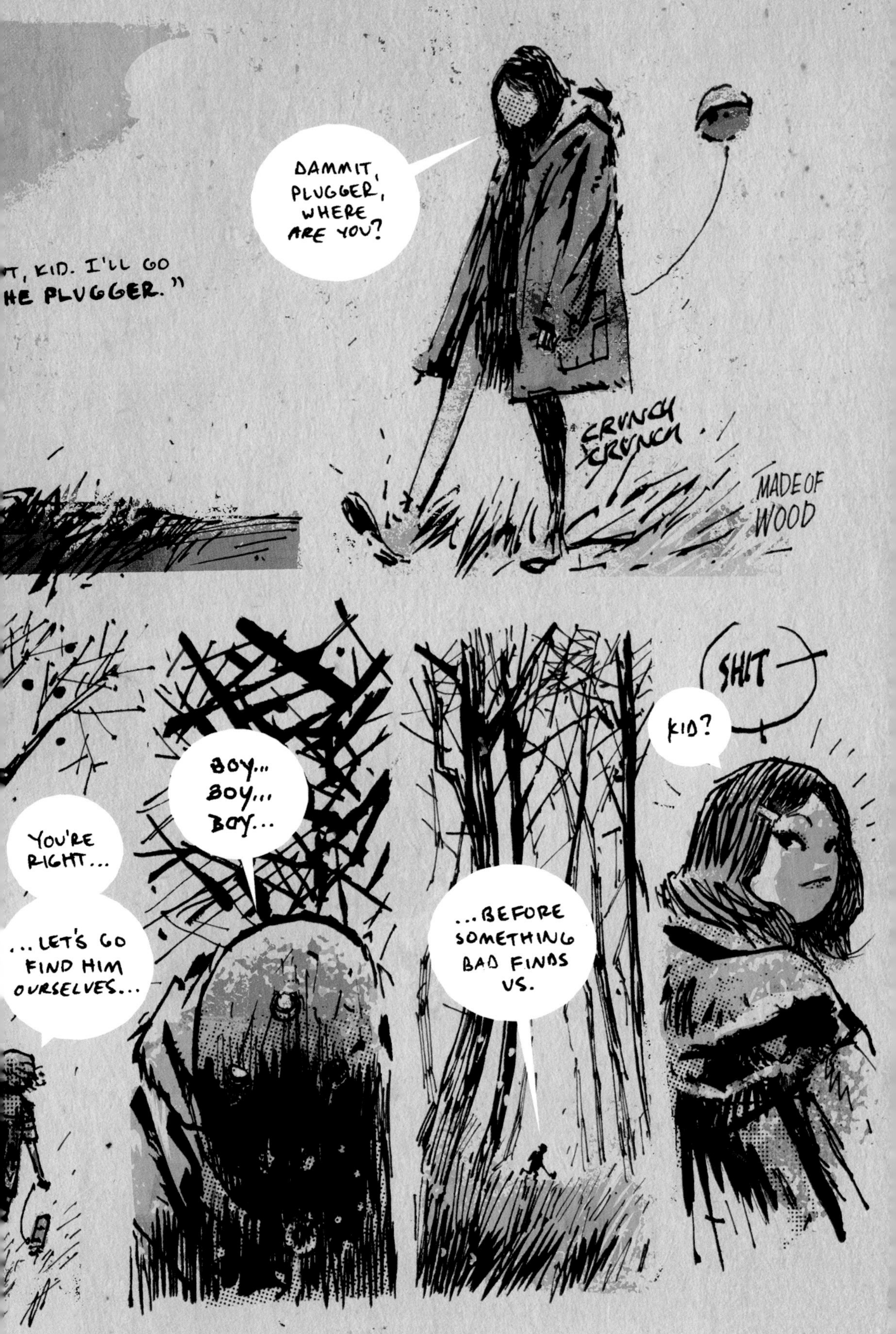
T, KID. I'LL GO
HE PLUGGER."
DAMMIT, PLUGGER, WHERE ARE YOU?
CRUNCH CRUNCH
MADE OF WOOD
YOU'RE RIGHT...
...LET'S GO FIND HIM OURSELVES...
BOY... BOY... BOY...
...BEFORE SOMETHING BAD FINDS US.
KID?
SHIT

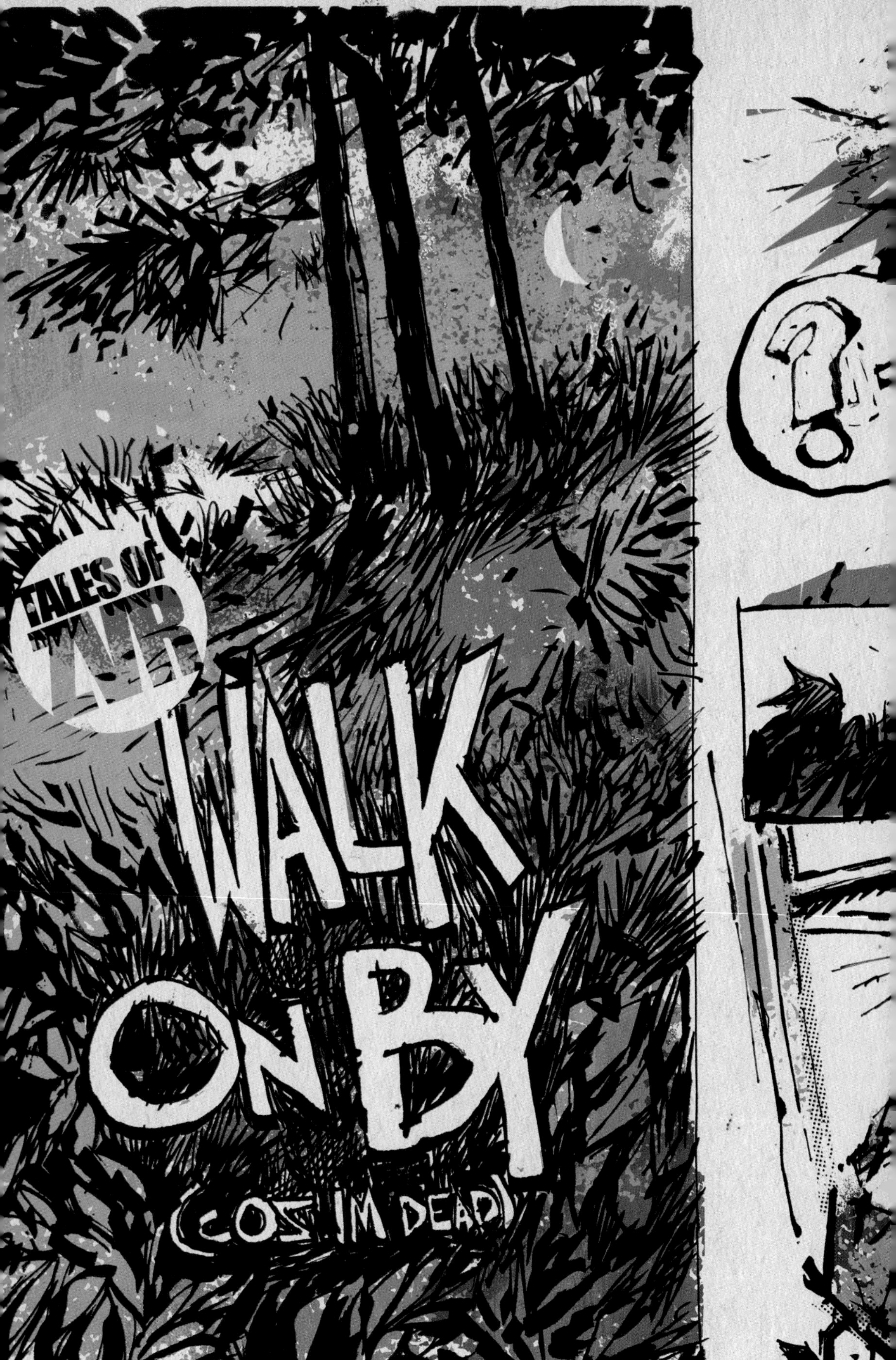
TALES OF ZR
WALK ON BY
(COS IM DEAD)
?

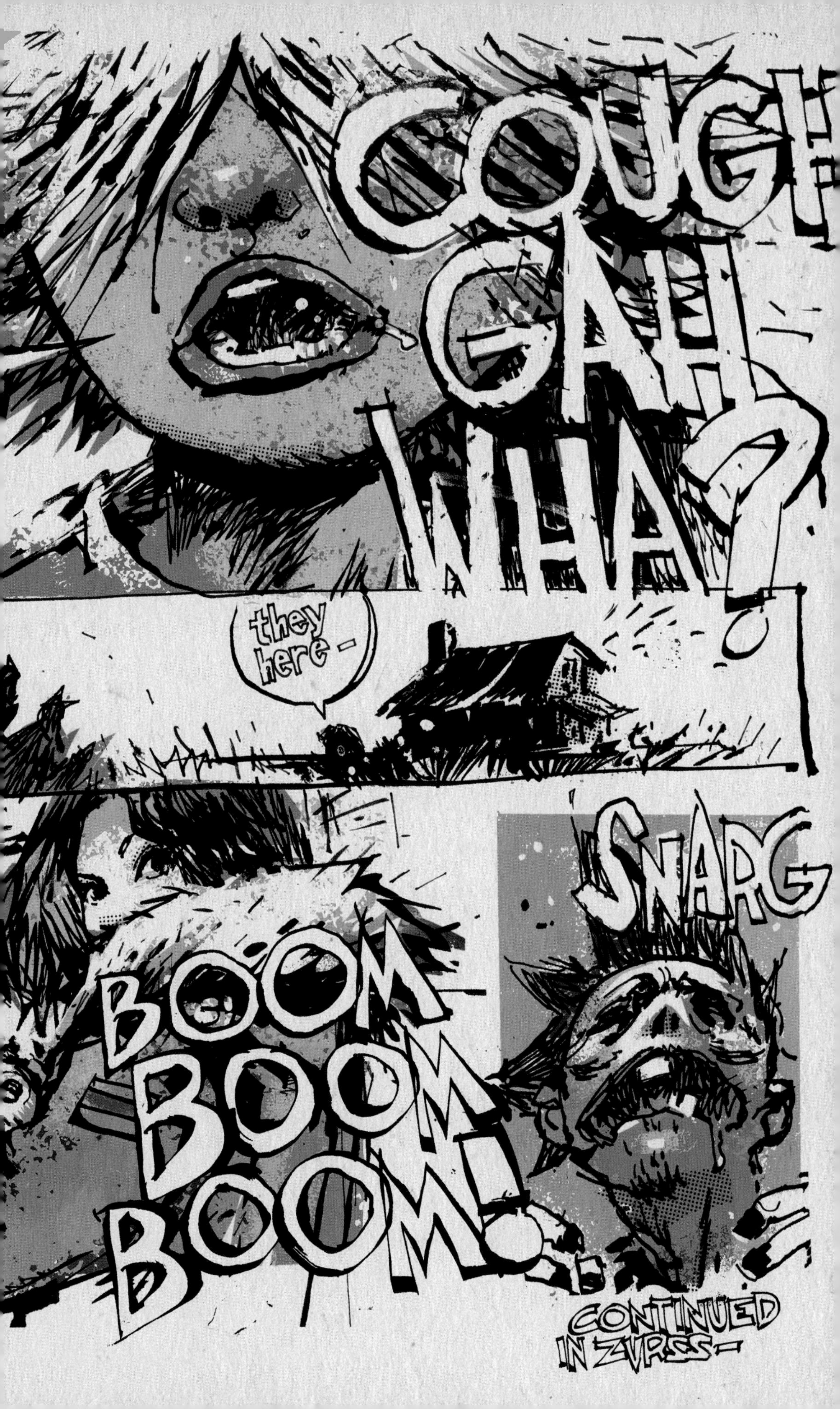

COUGH!
GAH!
WHA?
they here -
SNARG
BOOM
BOOM
BOOM!
CONTINUED IN ZVRSS-

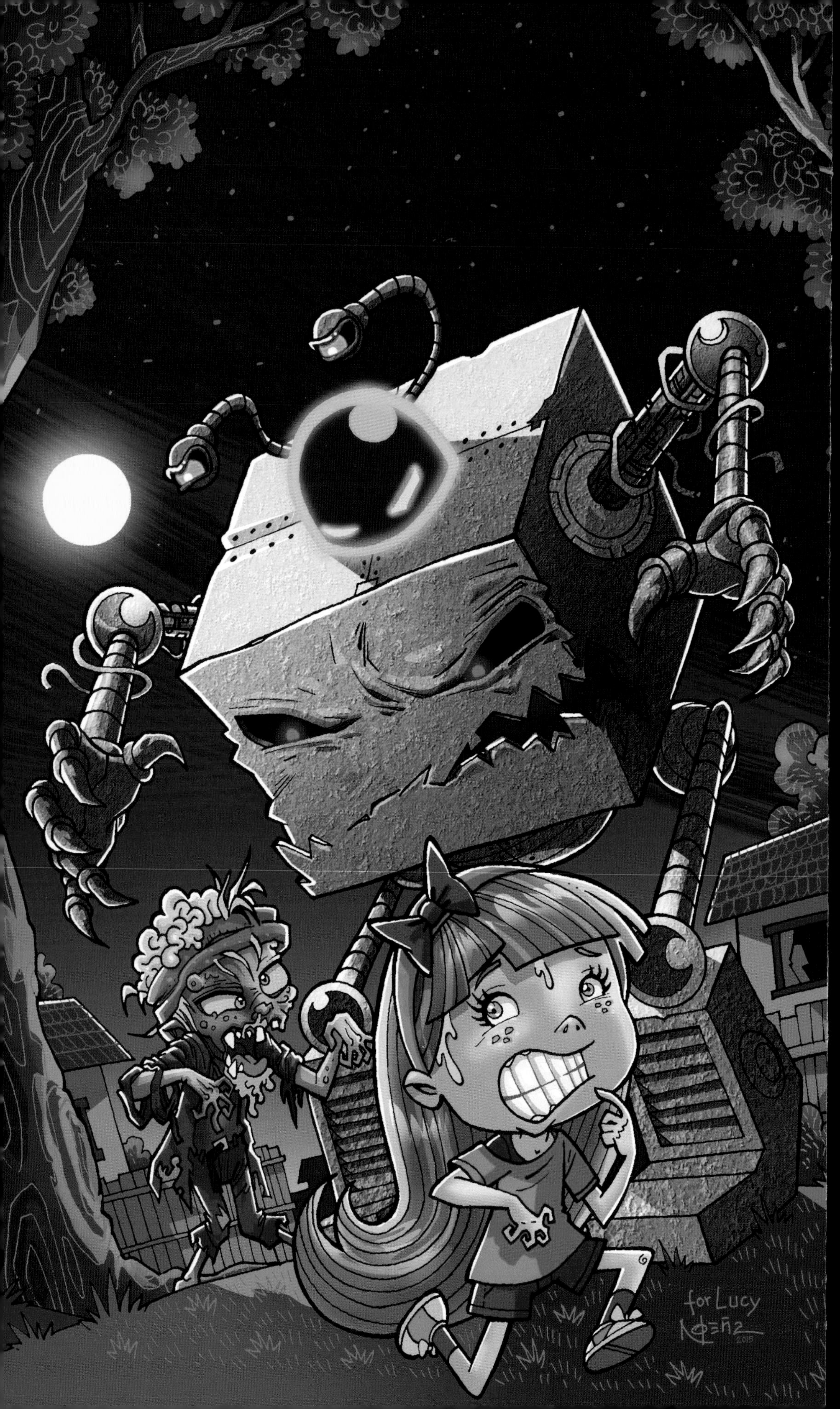
for Lucy

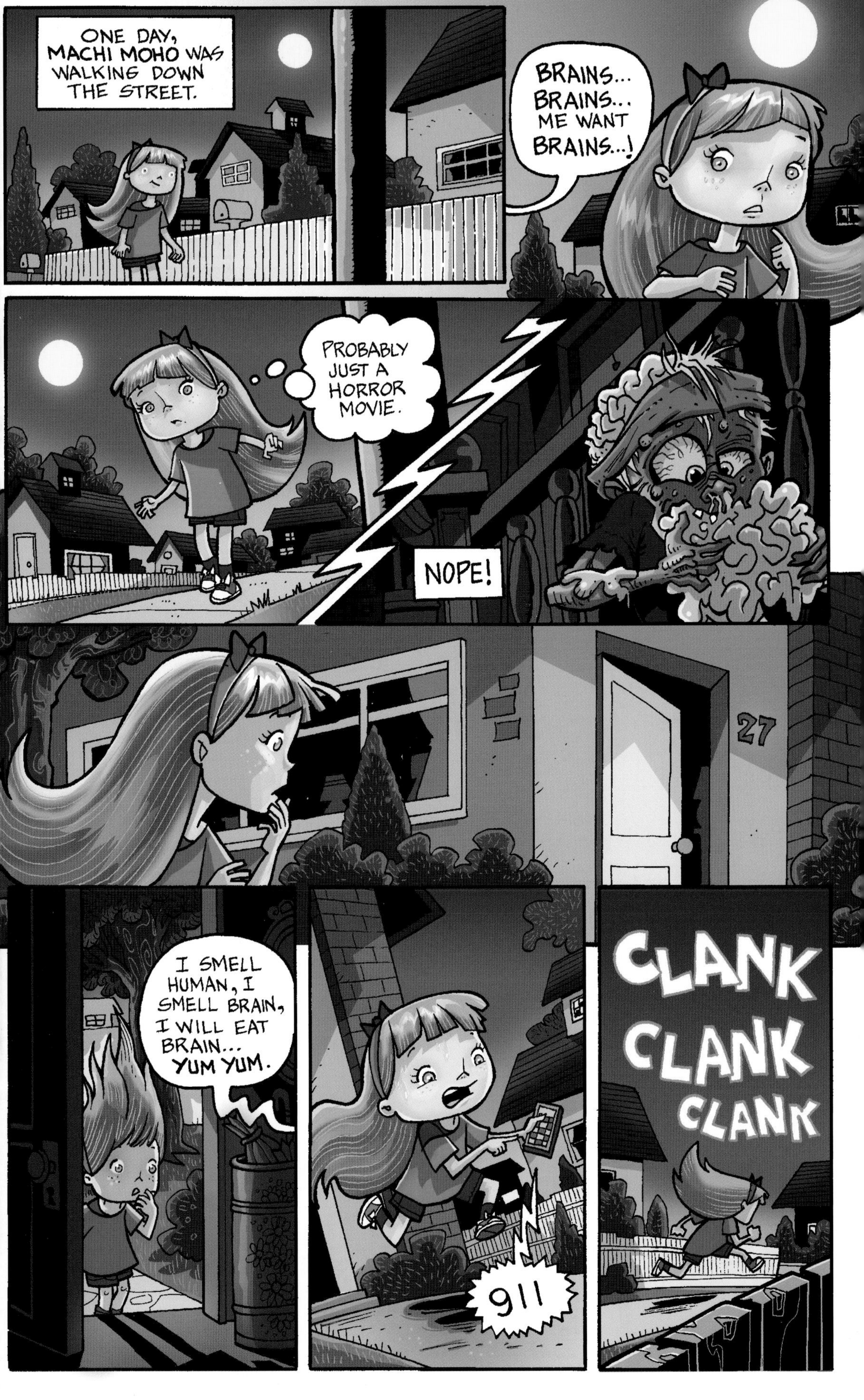
ONE DAY, MACHI MOHO WAS WALKING DOWN THE STREET.
BRAINS... BRAINS... ME WANT BRAINS...!
PROBABLY JUST A HORROR MOVIE.
NOPE!
27
I SMELL HUMAN, I SMELL BRAIN, I WILL EAT BRAIN... YUM YUM.
911
CLANK
CLANK
CLANK

EXCUSE ME, WILL YOU PLEASE LEAD ME TO THE ZOMBIE YOU WERE RUNNING AWAY FROM?

S... S... SURE, FOLLOW ME.

I WON'T BE HUNGRY NO MORE... NO MORE HUNGRINESS... ME WILL EATS BRAINS!

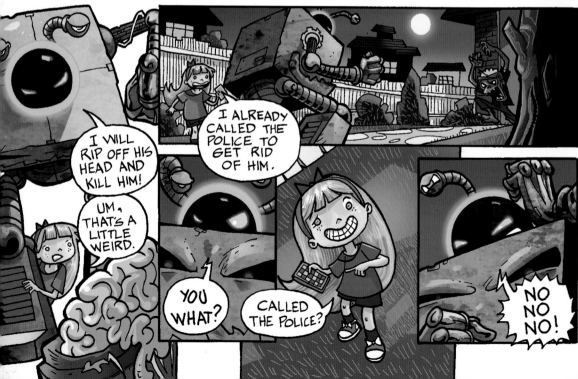

I WILL RIP OFF HIS HEAD AND KILL HIM!

UM, THAT'S A LITTLE WEIRD.

I ALREADY CALLED THE POLICE TO GET RID OF HIM.

YOU WHAT?

CALLED THE POLICE?

NO NO NO!

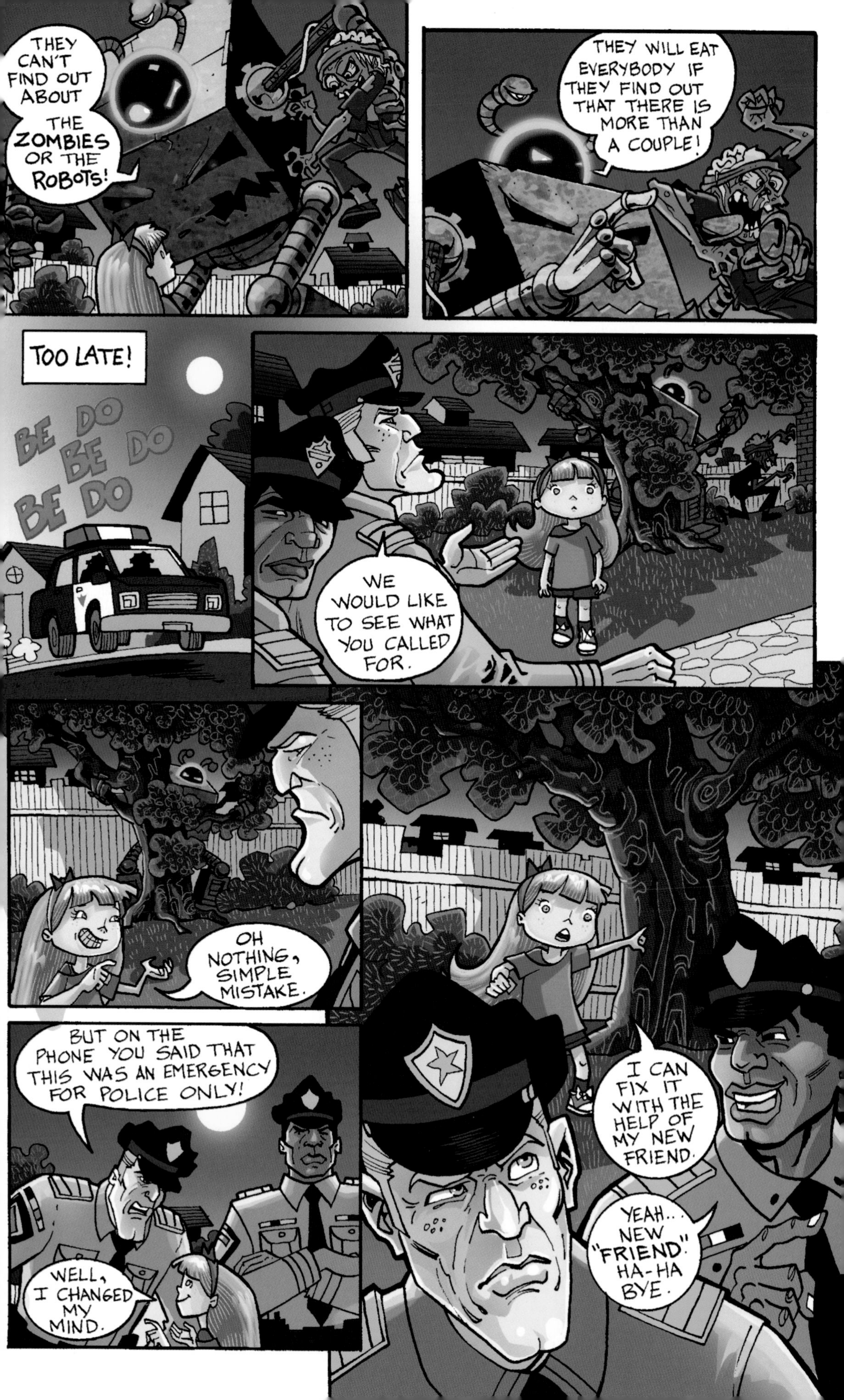
THEY CAN'T FIND OUT ABOUT
THE ZOMBIES OR THE ROBOTS!
THEY WILL EAT EVERYBODY IF THEY FIND OUT THAT THERE IS MORE THAN A COUPLE!
TOO LATE!
BE DO BE DO BE DO
WE WOULD LIKE TO SEE WHAT YOU CALLED FOR.
OH NOTHING, SIMPLE MISTAKE.
BUT ON THE PHONE YOU SAID THAT THIS WAS AN EMERGENCY FOR POLICE ONLY!
WELL, I CHANGED MY MIND.
I CAN FIX IT WITH THE HELP OF MY NEW FRIEND.
YEAH... NEW "FRIEND". HA-HA BYE.

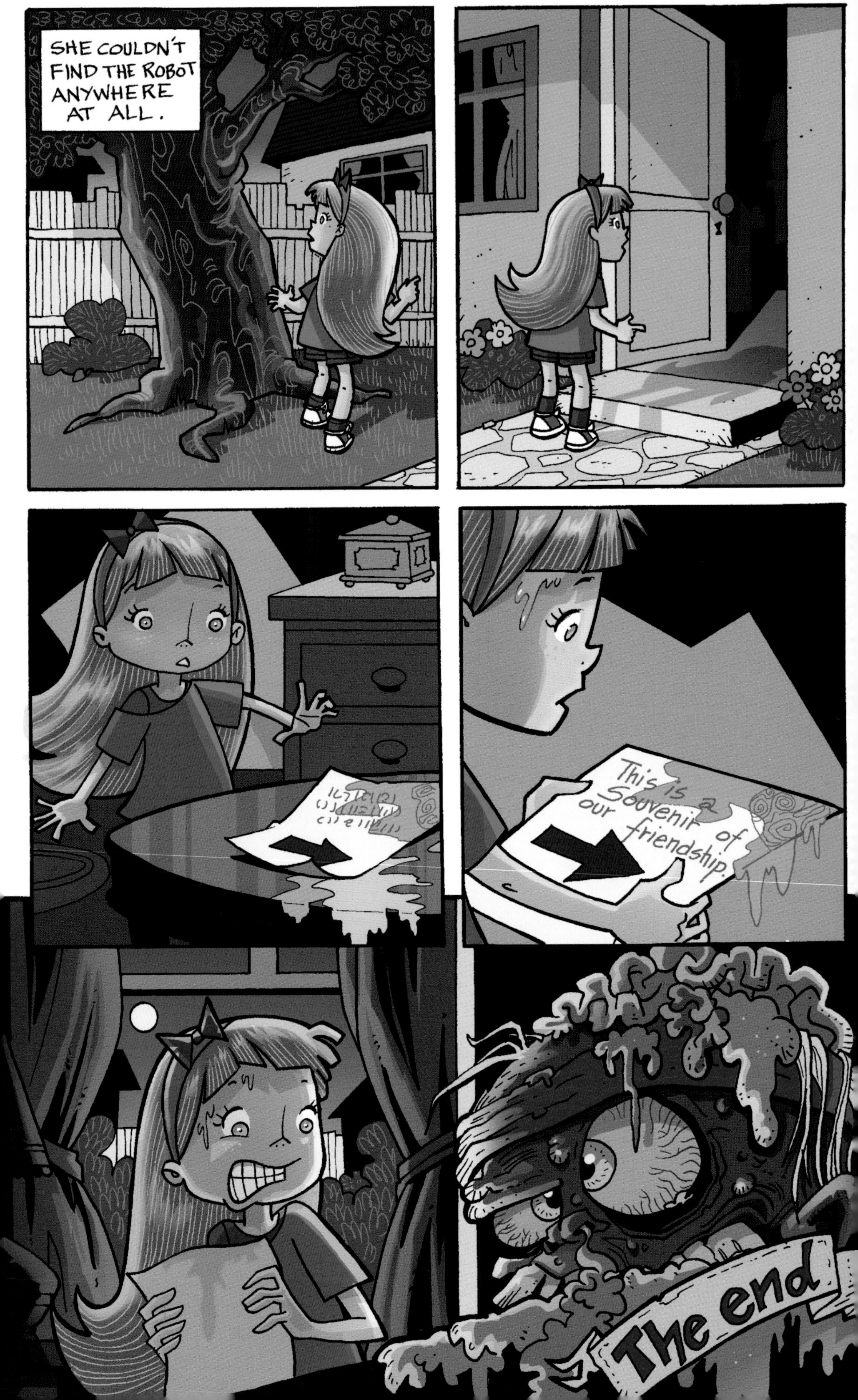
SHE COULDN'T FIND THE ROBOT ANYWHERE AT ALL.
This is a Souvenir of our friendship.
The end

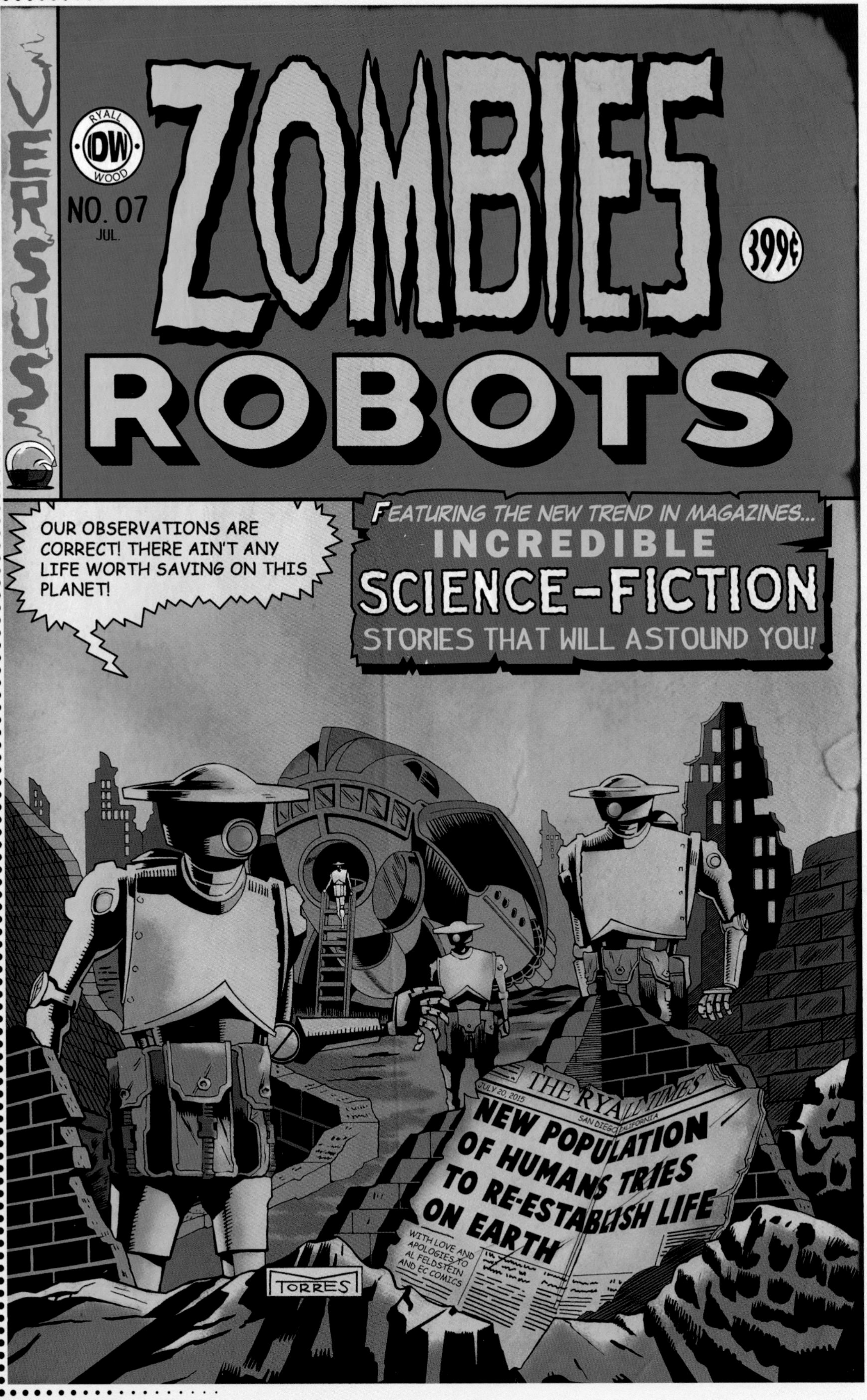
VERSUS
RYALL IDW WOOD
NO. 07
JUL.
ZOMBIES
ROBOTS
399¢
OUR OBSERVATIONS ARE CORRECT! THERE AIN'T ANY LIFE WORTH SAVING ON THIS PLANET!
FEATURING THE NEW TREND IN MAGAZINES...
INCREDIBLE
SCIENCE-FICTION
STORIES THAT WILL ASTOUND YOU!
THE RYALL TIMES
JULY 20, 2015
SAN DIEGO, CALIFORNIA
NEW POPULATION OF HUMANS TRIES TO RE-ESTABLISH LIFE ON EARTH
WITH LOVE AND APOLOGIES TO AL FELDSTEIN AND EC COMICS
TORRES

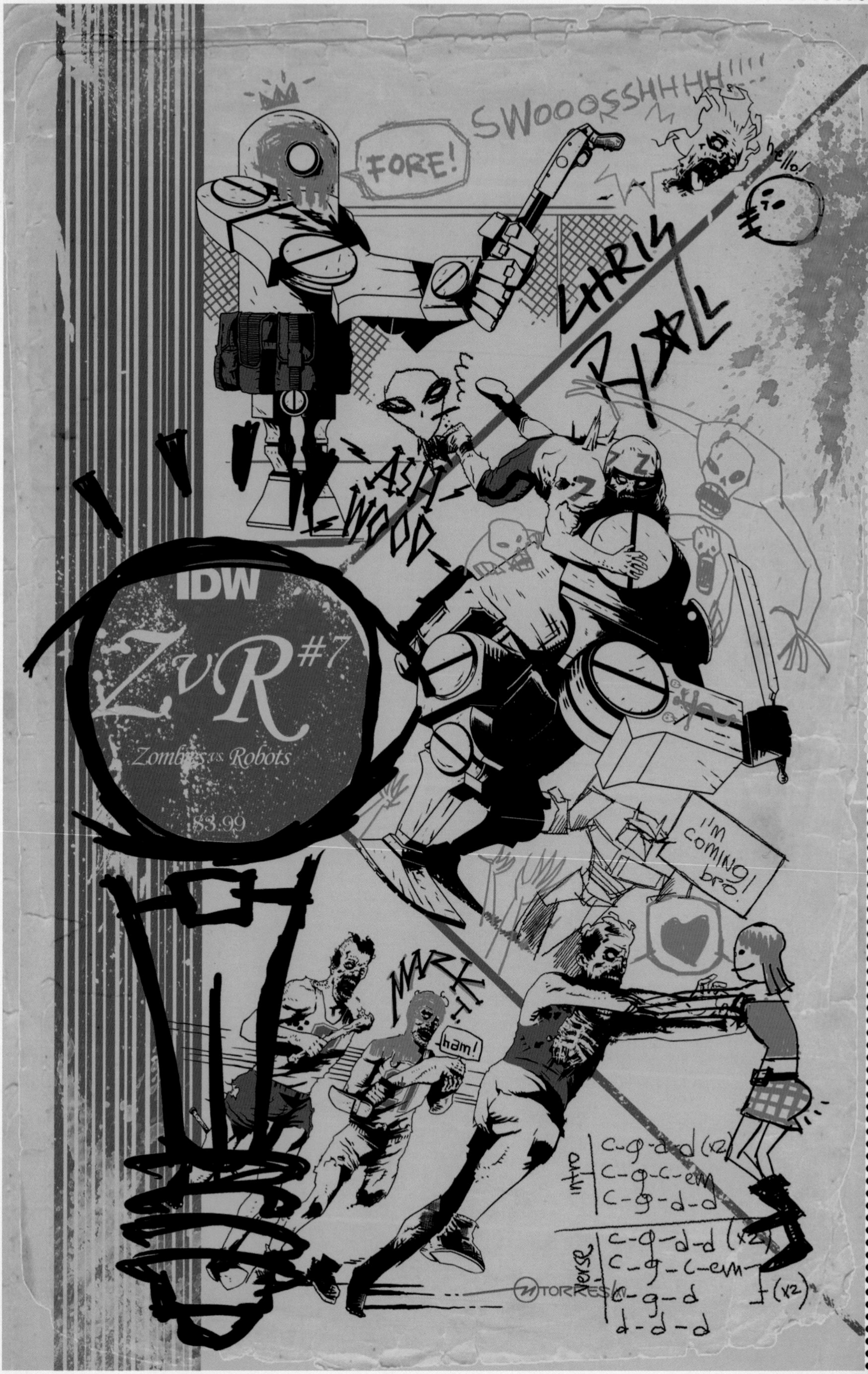
SWOOOSSHHHH!!!!
FORE!
hello!
IDW
ZvR #7
Zombies vs. Robots
$3.99
I'm coming bro!
ham!
intro
c-g-d-d (x2)
c-g-c-em
c-g-d-d
verse
c-g-d-d (x2)
c-g-c-em
c-g-d
d-d-d
(x2)
M TORRES

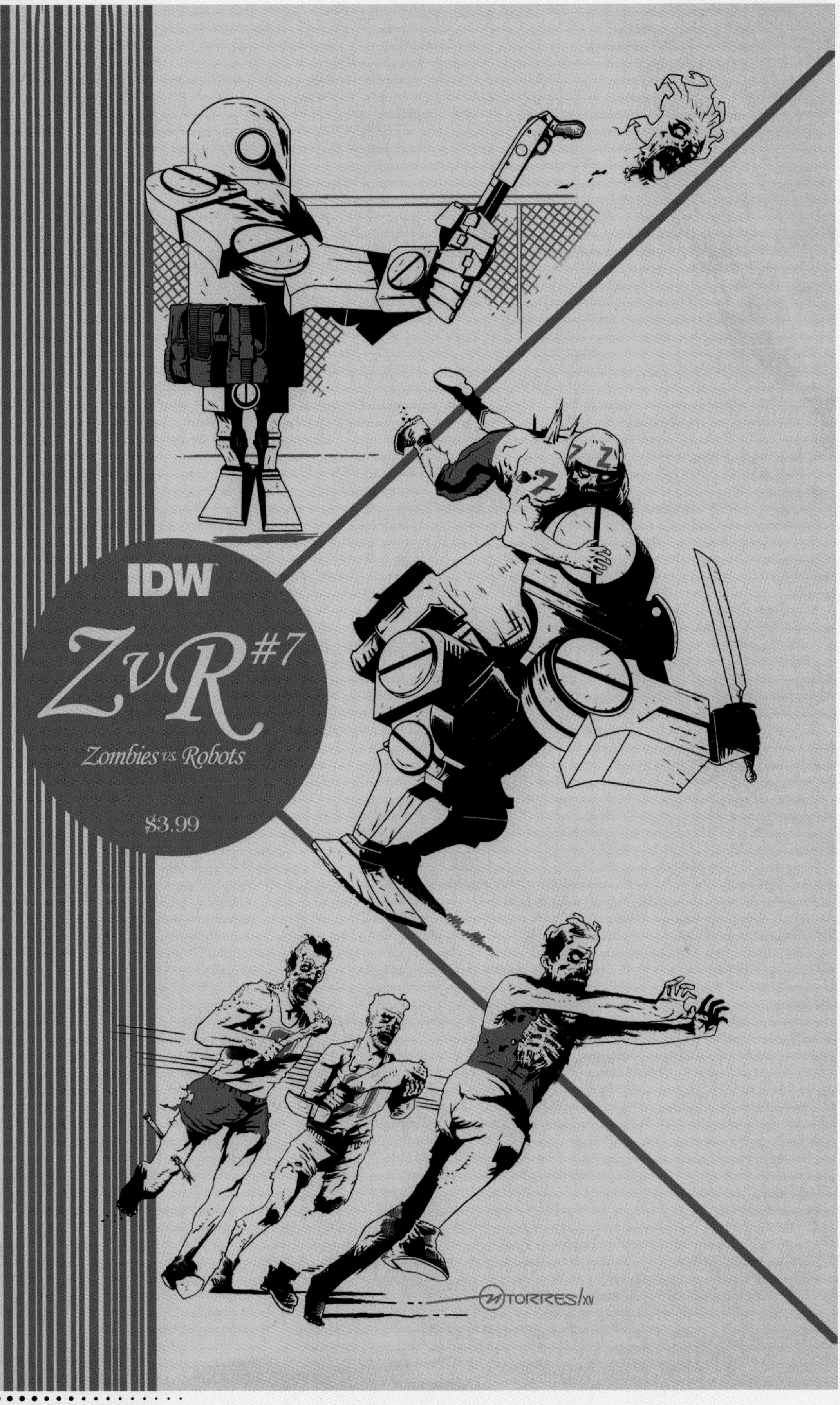
IDW
ZvR #7
Zombies vs. Robots
$3.99
MTORRES/XV

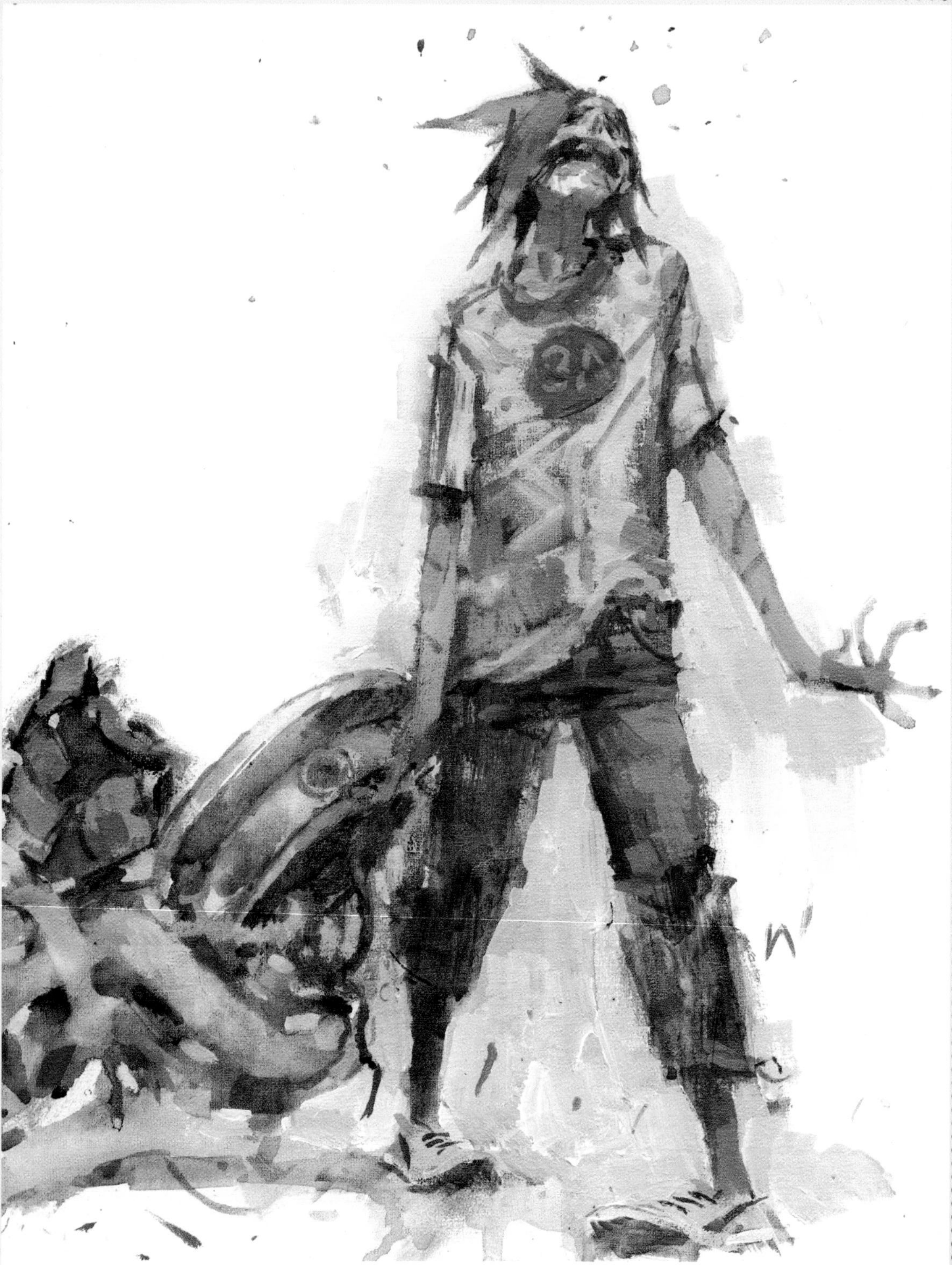
IDW PUBLISHING
RYALL WOOD FUSO SIMEONE
8
ZOMBIES VS ROBOTS

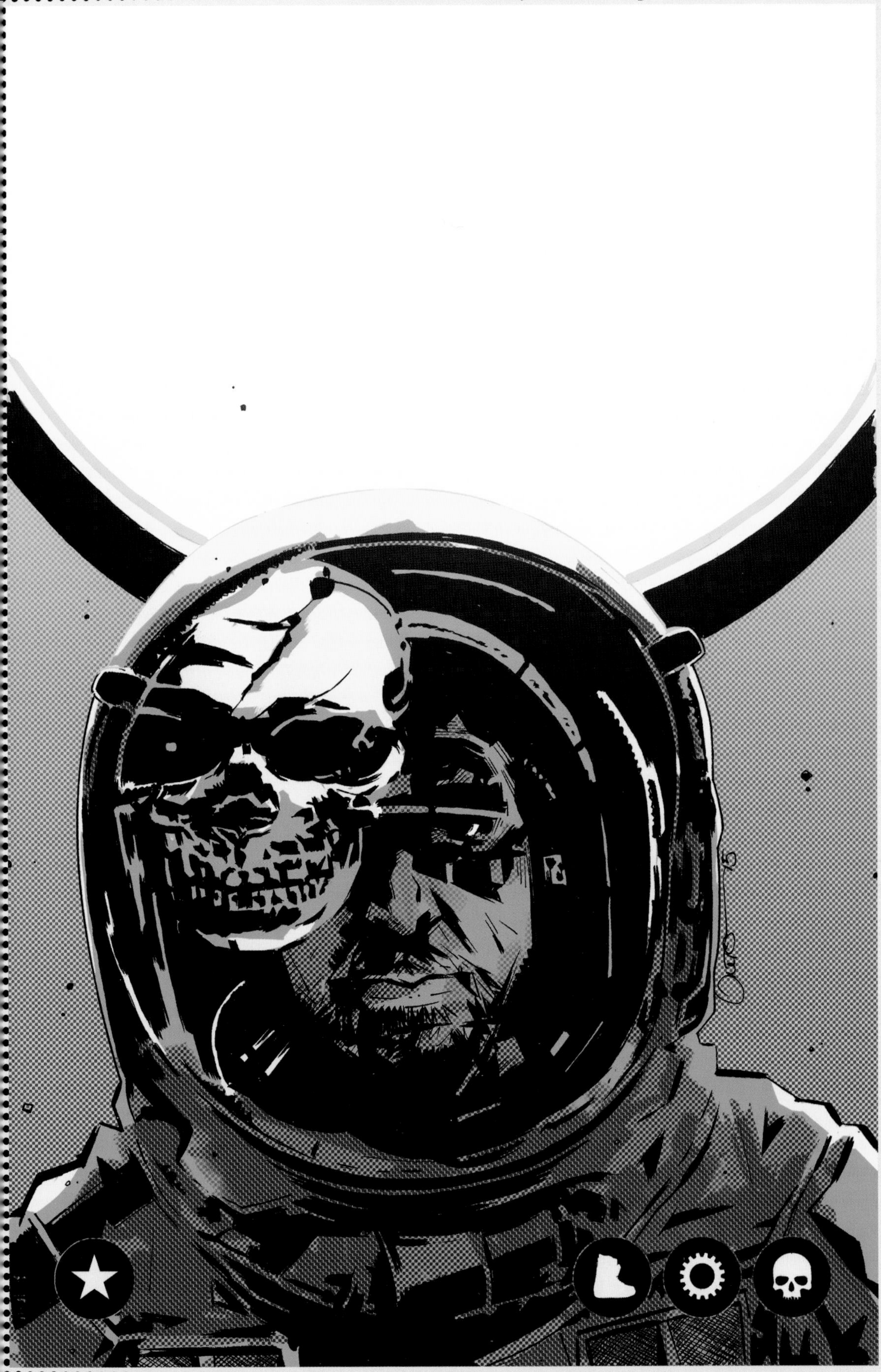

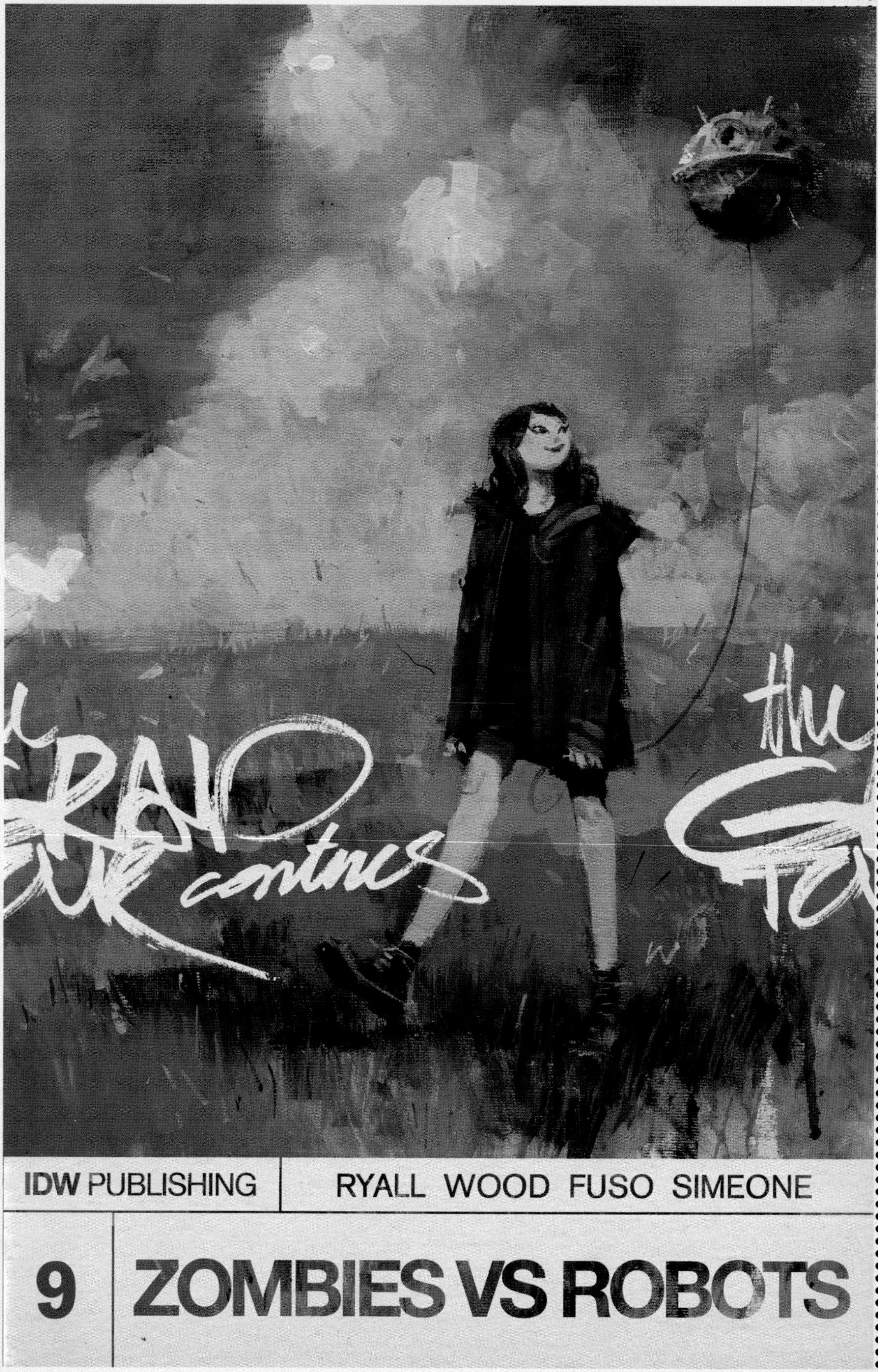
IDW PUBLISHING
RYALL WOOD FUSO SIMEONE
9
ZOMBIES VS ROBOTS

Antonio Fuso, Colors by Stefano Simeone

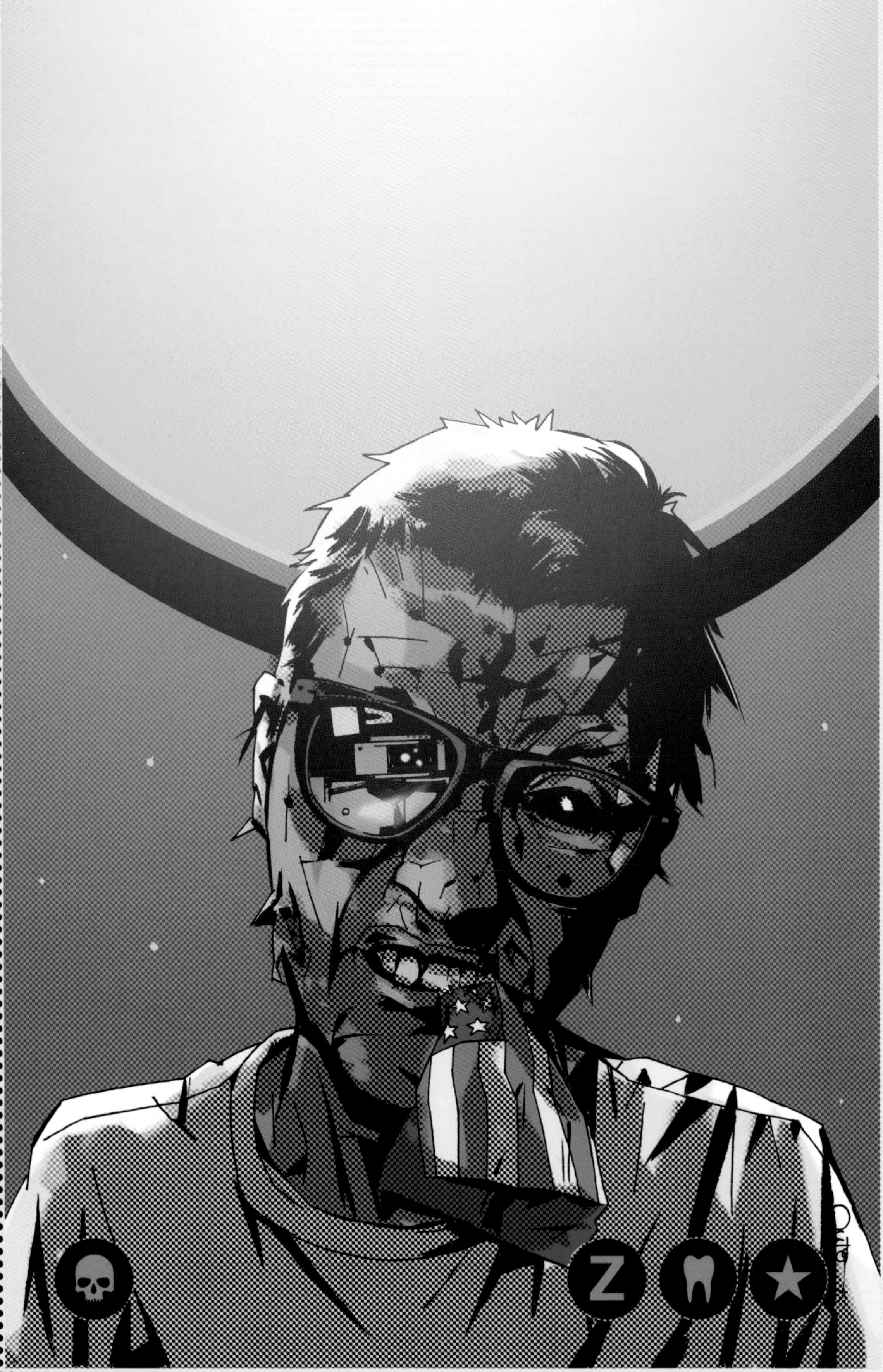

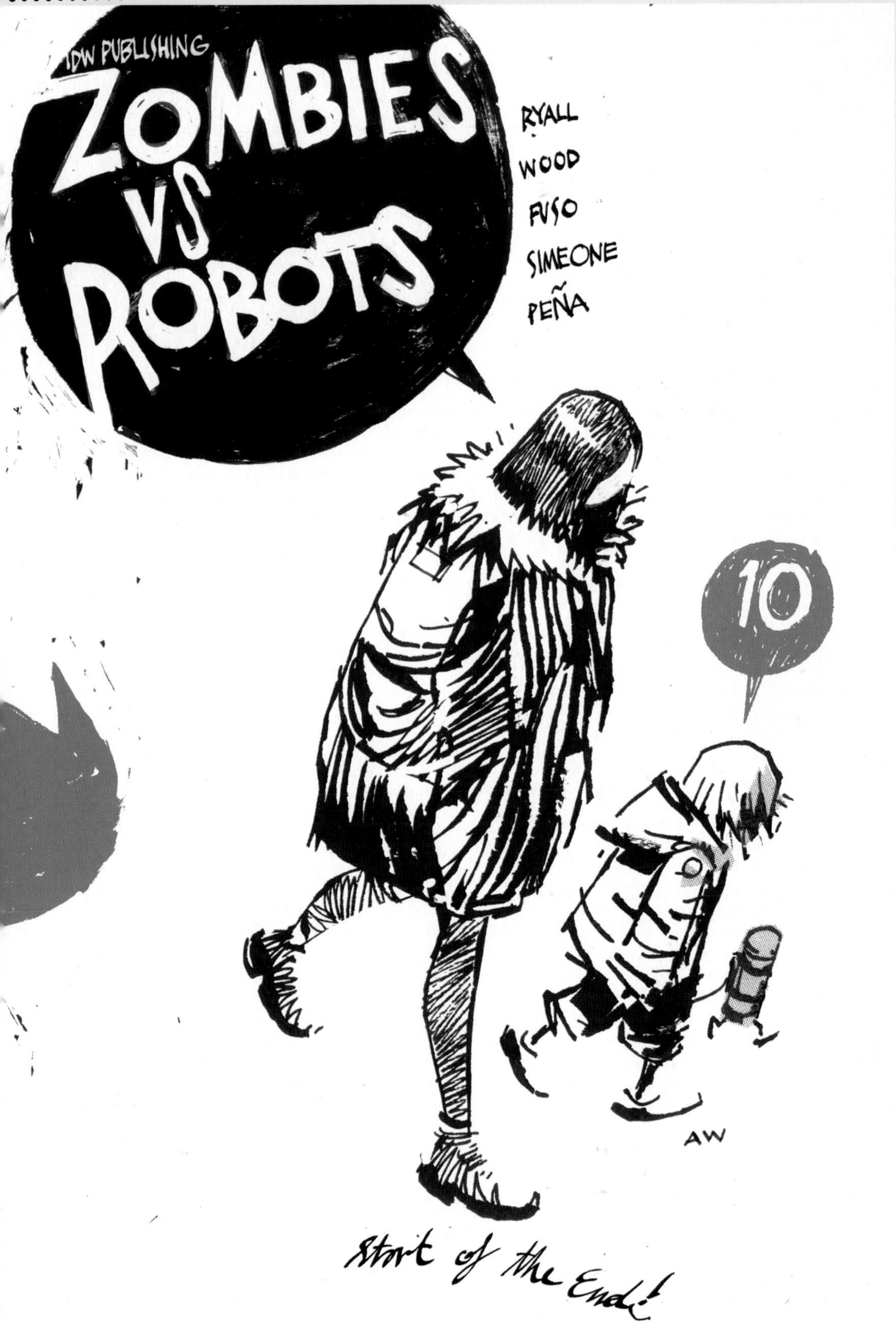
IDW PUBLISHING
ZOMBIES VS ROBOTS
RYALL
WOOD
FUSO
SIMEONE
PEÑA
10
AW
Start of the End!

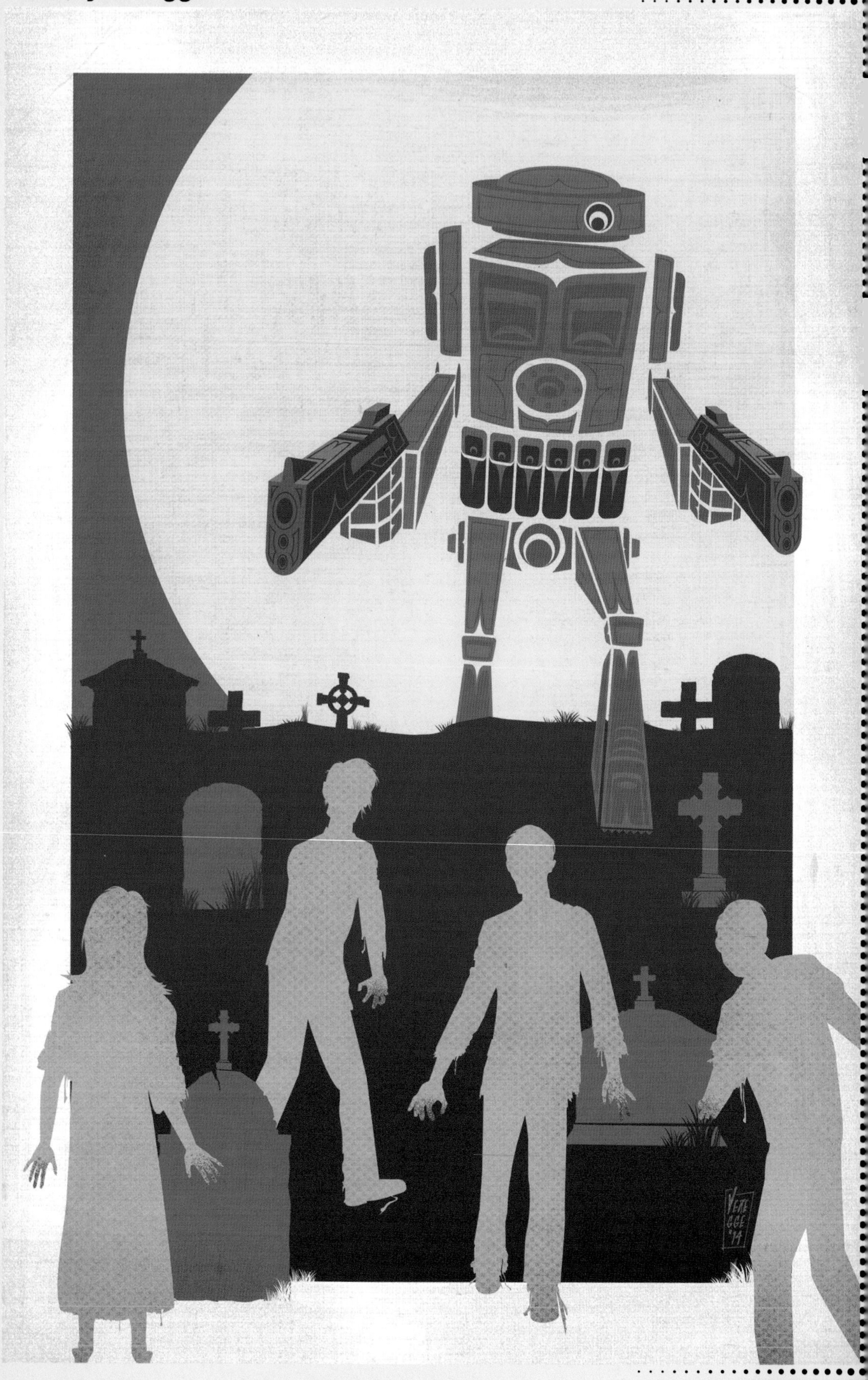
VEREGGE '14

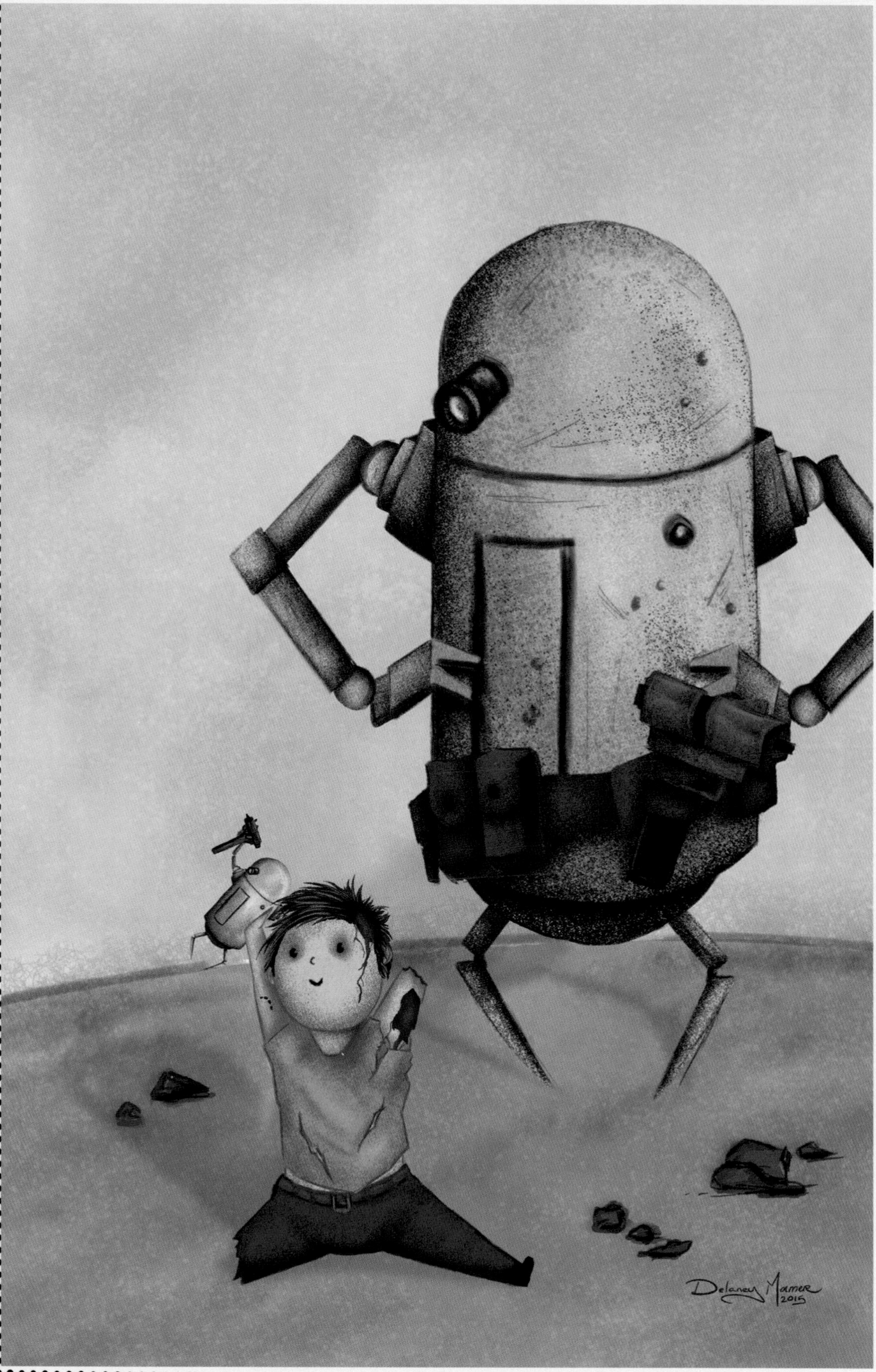
Delaney Mamer
2015

NICO PEÑA PROCESS ART

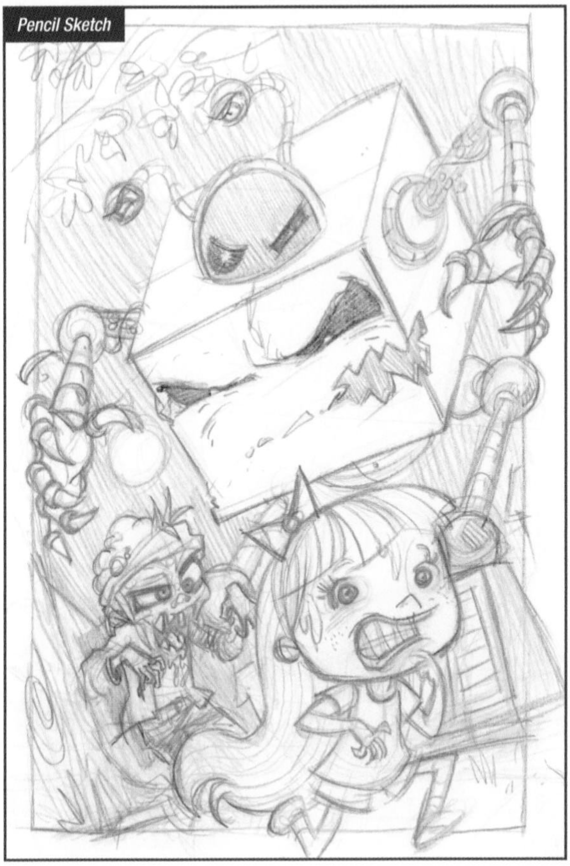

Pencil Sketch

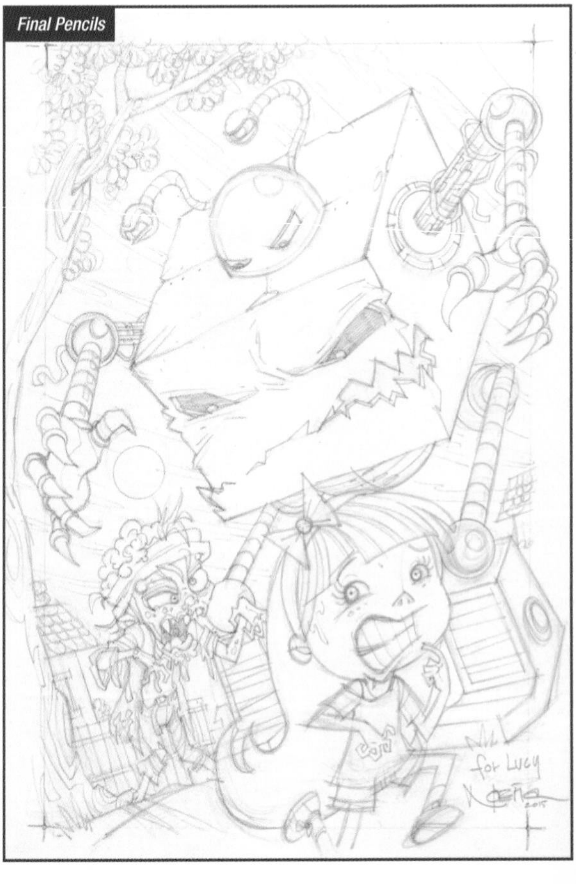
for Lucy

Final Pencils

Final Inks

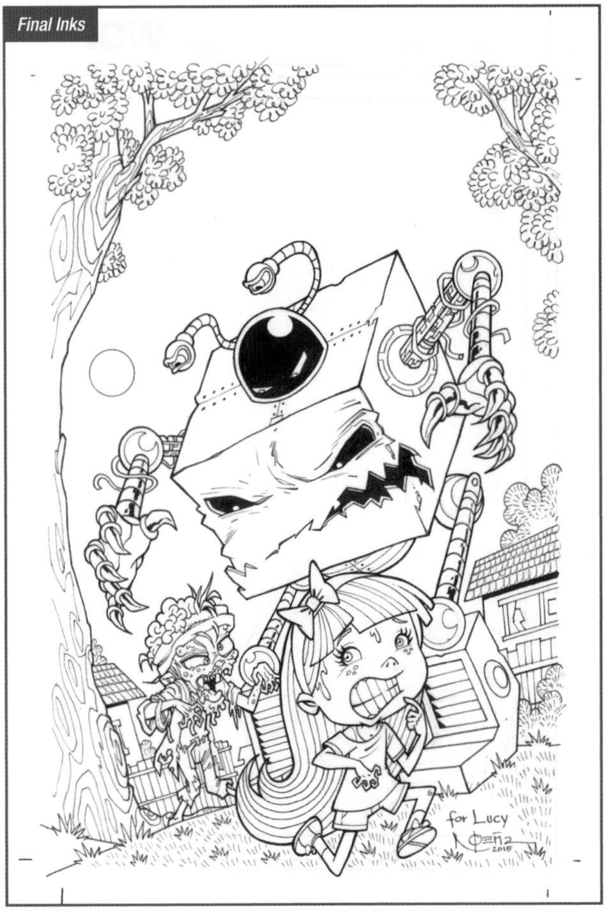
for Lucy

Final Cover Art

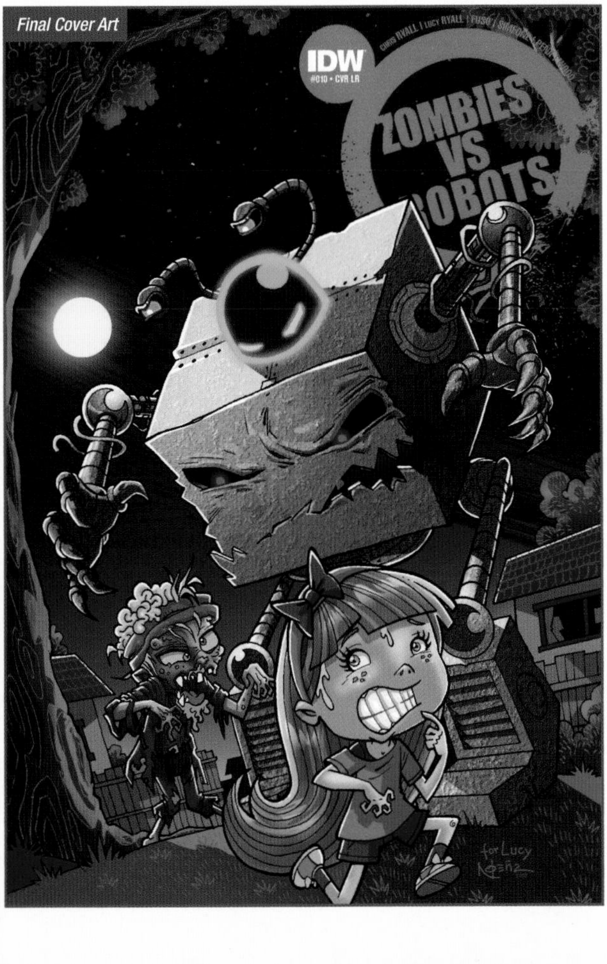
IDW
#010 • CVR LR
CHRIS RYALL | LUCY RYALL
ZOMBIES VS ROBOTS
for Lucy

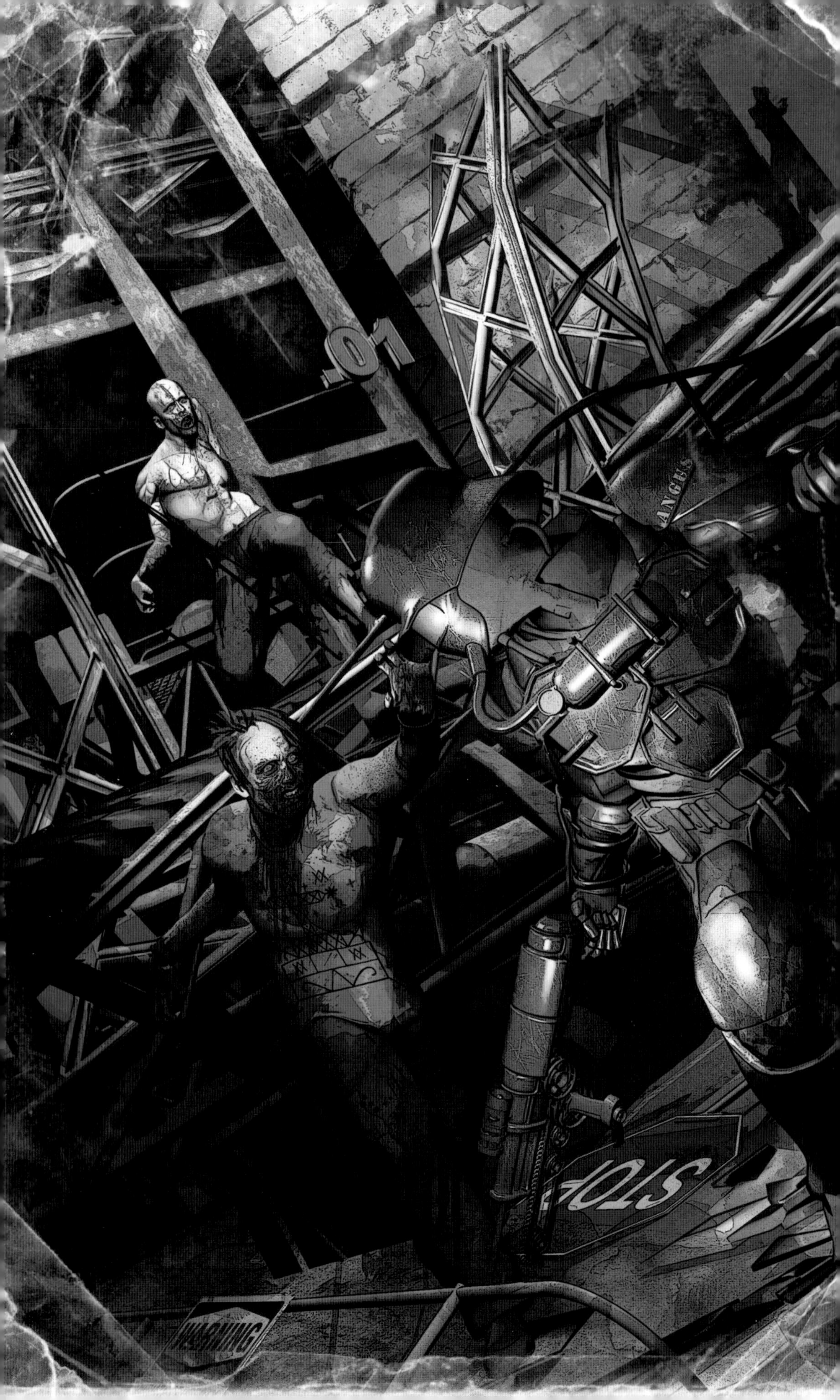
.01
ANGUS
STOP
WARNING

THIS TIME THE Maze was dimly lit. Not completely dark, but with just enough light to make telling the difference between shadow and zombie tricky. Although Angus had prowled the interior of the Maze for as long as he could remember, each time he entered it anew it was slightly different. Sometimes it was brightly lit, or filled with a thick fog. One time it was even flooded with water up to his knees. So it paid to be cautious, the importance

ANGUS: ZOMBIE vs ROBOT FIGHTER

by *Nancy Collins* / illustration by *Fabio Listrani*

of which was drilled into him from the second he woke up to the moment he fell asleep, for as long as he could remember. Even though the Maze was a training exercise, the consequences of his actions inside it were very, very real. Every moment could very well be his last.

He was dressed in a black one-piece garment made of lightweight ballistic fiber with molded, reinforced high-impact protection plates built into the chest, back, shoulders, groin, and legs—all the critical bite-zones zombies instinctively went for. He also wore a pair of knee-high steel-toed boots to protect his shins from crawlers snapping at his ankles, Kevlar gloves to keep his hands and fingers safe from snapping teeth, and a full-face helmet to guard against skeletal fingers stabbing at his eyeballs. The helmet was outfitted with an oxygen recycler, which kept his breath from fogging up the shatterproof face guard.

Suddenly an older, masculine voice spoke in his ear, as if the owner was standing right beside him. "Be on your lookout, Angus. You might not be able to see the zombie, but it can track you down, simply by following the scent of your living brain. It doesn't even need eyes to hunt you."

"Yes, I *know*, Father," he replied, pushing up the visor on the helmet so he could tap the comm-bud nestled in his ear. "I'm not five years old anymore."

"No, you are not," Father conceded. "Tomorrow you will be eighteen."

"*Shhh*," Angus hissed, calling for radio silence. "I think I hear it."

Although the walking dead could no longer speak, they were far from mute. As they shambled about, they gave voice to a constant, toneless moaning. It was an eerie sound, like the wailing of a damned soul trapped in the bowels of some nameless Hell, but at least it served as a rudimentary early warning system. Angus' name for the noise they made was the Zombie Call.

AS HE DOUBLE-CHECKED his weapon—an automatic rifle fitted with a laser sighting system, special explosive hollow-point ammunition, and a detachable chainsaw bayonet for close-quarters combat—a zombie came stumbling out of the shadows to the left of the T-junction.

Although Angus had never met a police officer before, he had seen enough of them on the Feed to recognize their riot gear—or rather, what was left of it. The front of the zombie-cop's bulletproof vest was in shreds, and its face was a mass of dried blood and exposed gum from where the upper lip had been torn away. The zombie walked with its head tilted back, sniffing the air like a hound trying to catch the scent of a rabbit, even though Angus had never seen a dog or rabbit outside the videos in his lesson plans.

The zombie suddenly made a deep, guttural growl, and its head dropped down with an audible *snap* and swung in his direction. A mixture of saliva and blood poured from the former cop's ruined mouth. It had caught the scent of sweet, sweet brain. Angus quickly lowered his face mask to protect himself from the splatter; all it would take would be one zombie bite, or a single drop of zombie blood entering an open wound in his skin, and it would be Game Over. He had to be careful. After all, he was humanity's last hope.

The laser sights swarmed all over the zombie-cop's torso like angry red bees until they coalesced into a single, blinking red triangle located between its filmy, gray eyes. Angus exhaled as he squeezed the trigger, just as he had been taught when he was five years old. The zombie's head disappeared in a spray of skull fragments, coagulated blood, and clotted gray matter.

A buzzer sounded as the body hit the floor, and the roof of the Maze went from opaque to translucent, revealing Father standing in the viewing booth overhead.

"Excellent job, Angus," he said, giving the thumbs-up sign. "When you're decontaminated, come join me in my lab. There is something I must discuss with you."

One of the walls suddenly split in two, and T-1 and T-2 entered the Maze. The modified guardbots stood over six feet tall, with dome-like heads that swiveled completely around on their wide, metal shoulders, so that nothing could sneak up on them. They were equipped with long, segmented arms capped with three-digit graspers, and rolled along on a set of all-terrain wheels that allowed them to move sideways and pivot in place, so they never had to back up in order to turn around. They had been Angus' near-constant companions for as long as he could remember. T-1 sprayed an enzymatic compound that liquefied the zombie's remains, while T-2 vacuumed up the resulting toxic sludge. Once they were finished, the undead waste would be transported to the Disposal Station, where it would be fed into a nuclear digester.

Angus stripped out of his protective zombie-hunting gear in the changing room and fed it to an incinerator unit, then entered the decontamination stall, which sprayed him head-to-toe with anti-microbial disinfectant. While the Z-virus was the most virulent microscopic nasty carried by the undead, it was far from the only one. They *were* walking bags of rotting flesh, after all. Once the scanner-banks deemed him clear, Angus dressed himself in a fresh one-piece jumpsuit and hurried off to join his father in the Hub.

As he stepped onto the moving sidewalk that connected the Training Facility to the central dome that housed their living quarters and Father's laboratory, Angus was suddenly aware of motion above him. He looked up, peering through the foot-thick hyper-acrylic tube-way, as a forty-foot giant squid glided over his head. He yawned. Kraken were an everyday occurrence when you grow up in a secret undersea laboratory base.

His father had built the deep-sea dome, called the Hub, long before the zombie plague became a problem, and in the years since the initial outbreak he had added three smaller annexes, connected via tube-ways. The first was the Training Facility, which also housed the zombie pen; the second was the Garden, which replicated a topside green space; and the third was the Disposal Station, where the liquefied remains of the zombie hunts were incinerated.

Of the three annexes, Angus spent most of his time in the Training Facility. Although Father insisted it was important for him to acquaint himself with the plant life found topside, as this was where he would be transported once he finished his training, Angus found the green, living carpet called grass and the surrounding flowering bushes and leafy trees in the Garden disconcerting. As for the Disposal Station, he had never been allowed inside its doors. Father said it was an environment created by robots for robots, and therefore hostile to human life.

Upon returning to the Hub, Angus reported promptly to the lab. There he found Father staring into a neutron microscope while busily scribbling notes into a computer tablet with a stylus. He was dressed in his usual combination of white lab coat, black turtleneck sweater and faded corduroys, his cowlick as defiant as ever.

"You said you wanted to see me, Father?" Angus prompted.

"Yes, I do," the scientist said, looking up from his work with a weary smile. "By the way, you handled yourself very well today."

"Thank you, sir," Angus replied humbly.

"You know, when I first proposed creating an elite class of human zombie-fighters to combat the plague, everyone said it was a waste of time—it was too easy for infection to be spread through human agents." Father sighed, setting aside his notes. "Why take the risk when we could send battalions of bots to do the job for us?

"I argued that Mankind has a bad habit of relying on technology to get itself out of tight spots—especially those created by technology. Bots are merely tools, Angus. And tools, while useful, have no heart or soul. They simply do what they have been programmed to do, nothing more, nothing less. Ensuring the survival of the human race is just another task for them to complete, no different than loading a cargo ship or recalibrating an engine.

"This is humanity's darkest hour, my son. Now, more than ever, mankind needs a hero, a symbol, to give the people of the world hope. That is why I brought you to this secret laboratory as a baby. That is why I have trained you how to hunt and kill zombies since you were old enough to hold a gun. You know *everything* there is to know about the undead—both their strengths and their weaknesses, and how to defeat them—than any human alive. The human race needs to see one of its own fighting tirelessly for its survival: a hero dedicated to wiping out the zombie menace not because he is *programmed* to do so, but because that is what he was *born* to do. *You* are that hero, Angus. *You* are humanity's last hope."

Angus shifted about in boredom, as this was not the first time he'd heard this rant.

"Tomorrow is a special day for you. It is both your eighteenth birthday and your final day of training. If you complete the Final Test, you will finally be allowed to leave the Hub and start fighting zombies topside."

Angus blinked in surprise. Although he had known this day would eventually come, he had not imagined it would be so soon. "What if I fail the test, Father?" he asked.

"Then you will die and become a zombie, of course."

THE MOMENT THE door to his quarters irised open, the far wall turned translucent and images from the Feed began to stream across its surface. There was no controlling what appeared on the Feed or shutting it off. It played constantly whenever he was in his room. The Feed was comprised of what Father called "programs," but not like the ones that ran the robots. These programs featured humans of all types doing things like solve crime or cure diseases, or have misadventures involving their friends and family, while invisible people laughed in the background. Outside of Father, they were the only examples of the human race he'd ever seen. The zombies didn't count.

Angus had no memory of his mother, since she died shortly after giving birth to him. At least that's what Father said when he asked him about her. Angus sometimes wondered what his mother looked and sounded like, as Father had no photos or videos of her. He wondered if she was a zombie now. He had slain numerous walking dead over the course of his training, some of which had been female. Maybe his mother had been one of them?

He sat on the edge of his bed and stared at the Feed. It showed a young man and woman walking through a forest, surrounded by grass and trees, like the ones in the Garden, except the trees in the Feed weren't growing in plastic buckets and were more than eight feet tall. Angus didn't like how large they were, compared to the humans. Zombies could be hiding behind any one of them, waiting to strike.

Angus continued to watch the young couple as they took out a blanket and spread it on the forest floor. As he watched, his hands clenched themselves in anticipation of a rotting waitress or a decomposing meter-reader lurching out of the shadows. The man and woman began to undress one another, while Angus continued to remain vigilant. Even if there were no zombies in the vicinity, it was still very likely one of the two people could be infected with the Z-virus. At any moment, one of them might find themselves possessed of a ravenous hunger for human brains, and turn on their lover. Within seconds their passionate kisses would easily turn into savage bites, their lustful moans warp into screams.

If his eighteen years of training had taught him anything, it was that inside every human was a zombie waiting to get out.

SOMEONE WAS CALLING his name.

He looked around, trying to identify the source of the voice. He was surrounded on all sides by towering edifices of bark and wood, a thousand times taller than the stunted specimens Father grew under the artificial sunlight in the Garden. The trees were dark and sinister, like the talking ones in the program about the girl with the ruby shoes.

"Angus!"

He turned in the direction of the voice and saw a young woman running through the woods toward a nearby clearing. Her hair was long and loose and the color of gold, and her short skirt and flimsy blouse showed flashes of lithe legs and supple arms. At first he thought she was fleeing zombies, but then he heard her laughter floating on the air. He smiled and gave chase, eager to escape the close confines of the forest.

He found himself on the edge of an open meadow, a hundred times bigger than the carpet of tame grass that lived in the Garden. The young woman was standing at its center, spinning around in a circle, her head thrown back, her arms spread wide as if to embrace the world.

"Isn't it *wonderful,* Angus?" she giggled. "To finally be *free?*"

"Free from what?" he asked, staring at her flawless skin and sparkling eyes. Given that she was the only living woman he had ever seen, she was also the most beautiful. His gaze fell to her low-cut blouse, and her bountiful cleavage. Although he knew he should be scanning his surroundings in case of a zombie attack, he could not look away from her perfectly formed breasts, with their erect nipples straining against the gossamer-thin fabric that covered them. His penis thickened and grew heavy, distracting him even further.

"From *everything*, silly!" she laughed, pirouetting so that she fell into his arms. "From Father, the robots, the zombies, the training—all of it! You're finally free to live your own life!"

"But I'm humanity's last hope," he replied automatically, as he looked down into her perfect face. Her lips were as pink and finely formed as the petals on the rosebush in the Garden. "I'm a zombie-fighter."

"But is that what *you* want to be?" she asked, her voice so hushed Angus was forced to lean in close to hear it. She smelled of grass and flowers, and something else, something familiar, yet he could not pinpoint it. As his erection continued to grow and harden, it blocked more and more of his ability to think rationally.

"Who are you?" he whispered.

"Don't you recognize me?" she replied as she reached up and pulled his mouth down to hers. "I'm your mother."

Although Angus felt confusion, shame, and frustration rise within him, his penis remained rock hard and insistent. He knew he should cast her aside, but he could not bring himself to do so. In the eighteen years of his life, he had yet to know the embrace of another human being. He could not remember Father ever hugging him or picking him up, or even giving him as so much as a pat on the back. All he ever did was smile and give Angus the occasional thumbs-up. The yearning for human contact, if only for a moment's consolation, was so strong he was willing to lower his guard in order to embrace the forbidden.

As his mother's mouth closed on his, the mysterious odor Angus had noticed earlier grew stronger and more distinct. With a horrible start, he finally recognized it. It was the smell of the Z-virus as it turned living flesh into walking meat. He opened his eyes to find the beautiful face with its perfect skin had become gaunt and turned the color of tallow. As he tried to pull away, his mother's eyelids flew open, to reveal the muddied, clouded pupils of the walking dead. He screamed, only to have his mouth instantly fill with blood.

His zombie-mother staggered backward, his lower lip clamped between her teeth, where it hung, pink and bloody, like some pendulous wounded tongue, before being swallowed in a single gulp. Her jaw dropped open and the awful, mindless Zombie Call rose from her deflated lungs.

ANGUS SAT STRAIGHT up in bed, gasping in panic as he clawed desperately at his jaw. He heaved a sigh of relief upon realizing his lower lip was still attached to his face. However, the wailing noise from his nightmare was still ringing in his ears. With a start, he realized it was the breech alarm. That meant zombies had escaped the pens in the Training Facility and invaded the Hub.

He grabbed the emergency zombie-fighting suit from his wardrobe and quickly put it on. He then opened the gun locker at the foot of his bed and took out his weapon. He fired up the bayonet and the electric chainsaw roared to life, sending a reassuring shudder up his arm.

"Father! Please report!" he barked as he tapped the comm-bud in his right ear, but all he heard was the eerie silence of an open line.

As he stepped out into the corridor, his heart was beating so hard the protective chestplate embedded in the suit was throbbing in time with his pulse. Angus' life had been filled with fear from the age of five, when he was first sent into the Maze with a handgun to confront a zombie toddler in a pair of blood-stained pajamas. Every day since then he had faced the walking dead and bested them, whether with firearms, power tools, blunt instruments, or sporting equipment. Although he was confident in his ability to handle the zombie breech, he was also scared as hell. But then, Father said it was good to be afraid, since it was his fear that had kept him alive for so long.

The lights in the hallway flashed red, dyeing everything the color of blood. As he headed in the direction of his father's quarters, he saw a zombie lurch into view. It was what Father called a "husk": more skeleton than corpse, its eyes long withered in its skull. The nose was a shriveled piece of cartilage, but it seemed to have no trouble catching Angus's scent. As the zombie staggered blindly toward him, it began to bite at the air, in anticipation of the meal to come, only to have its lower jaw suddenly snap off and fall onto the metal floor. The exposed tongue writhed about like a slug, looking far more obscene than the desiccated genitals swinging between its mummified thighs.

Angus shouldered his weapon and the zombie's head disappeared in a spray of clotted brains. As the long-dead body dropped to the ground, it revealed another one right behind it. This second zombie must have been an exotic dancer or porn star, judging by its faded, artificial tan and large, equally unreal breasts, which were ghoulishly ample compared to the rest of its desiccated body. The zombie-stripper hissed and lunged forward, swiping at him with long, airbrushed acrylic nails. Since he was too close for the rifle, Angus used the chainsaw instead, parting the zombie-stripper's dyed blonde hair all the way to the brain. He flinched as the blood and gray matter splashed against the faceplate of his helmet, but did not stop until its clouded eyes rolled back in their sockets, showing nothing but yellow.

"T-1! T-2! Are you online? I need a status report!" Angus shouted as he yanked the chainsaw free of the zombie-stripper's skull. He understood why he couldn't raise Father on the comm-bud, but was baffled why the guardbots remained silent. Although he had terminated scores of zombies in the past, it was always with the knowledge that T-1 and T-2 were there to back him up. The idea of combating the undead all by himself made his stomach knot and his heart race even faster. His years of training, however, enabled him to compartmentalize his anxiety and keep it from taking control of his thoughts. While a normal human being in his predicament would piss themselves with fear, Angus's mind was racing to tabulate the number of zombies that might be loose within the Hub.

T-1 and T-2 usually left the undersea base every three months to capture a dozen or so free-range undead for training purposes, and since it was nearing the end of the third quarter, that meant there were probably only four or five zombies left in the pens. The odds weren't impossible—he'd faced as many as ten at once—but that was in the familiar confines of the Maze, under Father's watchful eye. He quickly put those negative thoughts aside; panicking would not get him anywhere but dead.

The portal to Father's quarters was fully dilated. Angus stepped inside, scanning the room for any sign of life. He was not surprised to see the bed had not been slept in, as Father spent the vast majority of his time working in the laboratory, trying to find a means to defeat the Z-virus.

Suddenly he was aware of something wrapping itself around his left leg, followed by a sharp, painful pinch to his calf. He looked down to find a crawler—the reanimated upper torso of a zombie—trying to gnaw its way through his boot and shin guard. Although the creature had been severed at the waist, and was dragging what remained of its guts behind it, it did not seem in the least bit inconvenienced by its bifurcation.

As he pulled his Bowie knife from its sheath and sliced the zombie's head from its shoulders, Angus cursed himself for paying too much attention to eye-level threats. While the hands immediately lost their grip on his leg, the severed head continued to chew on his shin until he plunged the blade into its ear, spearing the decomposing brain like an olive. The crawler's jaws instantly flew open, and the pain in his calf disappeared. He paused just long enough to make sure that the bite hadn't penetrated the outer protective layer of his suit, before heading in the direction of the laboratory. If Father was anywhere, it was there. And if his tabulations were correct, he only had one more zombie to worry about.

As he rounded the corner to the laboratory, Angus spotted his final target. At first, when he saw the thing hobbling toward him, he thought someone had taken a pair of zombies and lashed them together in a grotesque parody of a three-legged race. Then he realized that he was looking at a pair of conjoined twins, fused at the hip and pelvis, so that the left leg of the zombie on the right was the right leg of the one on the left. As it drew closer, he could see that the twin on the right must have been the first to succumb to the Z-virus, since the one on the left was missing most of its face and scalp. The zombie-twins' voices melded into a single, wordless cry of undying hunger as they clumsily made their way toward him, reaching out with their multiple arms as if to pull him into an eternal embrace.

With a mighty shout of anger and disgust, Angus swung the chainsaw's whirring blade down, separating in death that which was never cut asunder in life. The conjoined zombies parted down the middle, toppling to either side. He shot the right-hand twin point-blank, then stomped down on its faceless brother's head as hard as he could, cracking open the exposed skull like an egg and sending spinal fluid and liquefied brains squirting from its ears and nose.

Suddenly the comm-bud came to life, and Father's voice spoke. "Happy Birthday, Angus! You have passed the Final Test! You are now the perfect zombie-fighter!"

He looked up to see the reassuring bulk of T-1 and T-2 at the end of the corridor. They rolled toward him, shoulder to shoulder, just like the zombie-twins he'd just terminated, creating a looming wall of steel. Assuming they were there to clean up the undead, Angus pushed up the visor on his helmet and smiled in welcome. Then a cylindrical tube emerged from T-1's chest and flooded the corridor with knock-out gas.

He woke up staring at the ceiling, feeling drugged and strangely numb, as if his body was a million miles away. His vision kept going in and out of focus and his ears seemed awash in white noise.

"Where am I?" he asked, looking around at his unfamiliar surroundings.

"You are in the Disposal Station," Father's voice said, sounding strangely distant.

Angus frowned in confusion. "I thought you said only robots could survive the conditions inside the Disposal Station?"

"That is true."

As he struggled to sit up, Angus saw he was lying on a long metal table. Next to him was an identical slab, but this one held a young, Caucasian male missing the top of his skull. With a dull start of horror, he realized he was staring at his own body.

He looked down at himself, in hopes that what he had seen wasn't real, only to recoil at the sight of a metal torso and a pair of robot hands. Although it felt as if his limbs were deadened to all sensation, he managed to get to his feet.

As he glanced down at the shiny metal surface of the table, he saw the reflection of a shatterproof hyper-acrylic skull, inside of which could be seen a human brain floating in a bath of synthetic cerebrospinal fluid and covered in numerous electrodes and wires. In place of eyes, the see-through skull's sockets contained a pair of unblinking, hi-def cameras.

When he was finally able to look away from the horrifying visage, he realized Father was standing opposite him, dressed in a white lab-smock, the front of which was smeared with blood. "There is no need to be alarmed, Angus," Father smiled, speaking in the same calm, reassuring tone of voice he had used for as long as the boy could remember. "The vertigo and sensory deprivation are temporary until your brain becomes accustomed to your new inputs. You will find your new body works just as well—even better—than the one you were born with. Not only will you be faster, stronger, and able to see spectrums and hear frequencies impossible to the human eye and ear, you are now impervious to hunger, cold, heat, and fatigue. You will be a tireless warrior in the battle against the undead plague."

"How could you do this to me—?" Angus intended the words to be a shocked, heart-broken wail of betrayal. Instead, they were spoken in the dry, inflectionless voice of a robot. "I'm your son! Your own flesh and blood!" he tried to scream as he punched Father in the face. To his dismay, the blithely smiling scientist didn't even flinch, although the blow should have fractured his jaw. The only visible damage was a sizable gouge underneath Father's right cheekbone, revealing a steely skeleton underneath his synthetic skin. "You're a robot?" Angus gasped in surprise. Despite the horror of his own predicament, he was still shocked by this revelation.

"Yes, I am a robot," Father replied, pointing a remote control unit at the newly minted cyborg. "A sci-bot, to be exact. I was created in the image of, and programmed by, the human scientist who originally created the Hub, in order to assist him in his work. And to avoid any further damage to either of us, I am shutting down the connections to your motor system."

What little sensation Angus was receiving from his new body abruptly disappeared altogether. He tried to raise his arm and move his legs, only to find them inert as lead ingots. "What happened to my real father and mother? What did you do to them?"

"You have no parents, as humans understand the words," Father replied flatly, no longer bothering to hide his robotic voice. "You are a clone; one of the A-Series. You are the fourteenth, in fact, to undergo training in this facility. To save on downtime, the clones are born as five-year-olds. The first was called Aaron, the second was Absalom, the third Ace, and so on."

"What happened to the others?"

"They are dead; killed during training. Most of them perished the first time they were sent into the Maze, save for the once called Ajax—he managed to survive until the age of six. Every time one of the A-Series is slain or becomes infected, a new one is decanted. You are the first and only A-Series to survive to adulthood and complete the training program."

"You're telling me my entire life has been an insane lie—why go through the pointless charade of pretending to be my father?"

"I am unable to make a decision or have an opinion as to the logic behind my creator's thought processes. However, a search of available data banks shows considerable discussion among my creator's peer group as to his mental health in regard to this matter. However, as he possessed a sizable private fortune, he proceeded with his plans, regardless of government or societal approval.

"My creator was convinced that the parent-child bond was the most effective way to make sure the clones were indoctrinated with the drive to keep the human race alive. He personally oversaw the training of clones Aaron through Aeneas. However, he eventually succumbed to the Z-virus and was added to the zombie pens, fifteen years ago. His zombie was the first one you encountered during the Final Test. It was kept 'alive' during this time by feeding it the occasional clone—starting with the B-Series. It was his last order to be destroyed by his own zombie-fighter as part of the Final Test.

"My creator made adaptations to my AI in order for me to continue his project, allowing me a certain amount of what humans once called 'free will.' It was my creator's intention that his ultimate zombie-fighter be humanity's savior, despite the fact the human body is weak and uniquely susceptible to the Z-virus. This was illogical, as robots are clearly physically superior when it comes to combating zombies. I therefore came to the logical conclusion that to send you out into a world full of cannibal zombies clothed in nothing but flesh and blood was counterintuitive to my creator's goal. By placing your brain inside a robot body, I am able to complete my programming. The nuclear battery housed in your robot body should keep your brain alive for at least two thousand years, which, according to the master computer system, should be long enough for you to find and kill every zombie topside."

"*Two thousand years?*" Angus wanted to scream, but the best he could do was turn up the volume on his voice until it distorted. "How many zombies *are* there?"

"The last census estimated the world's human population at 10.5 billion. Following the outbreak of the Z-virus, the human population was believed to be 7.6 billion. According to the master computer system shared by the bot nation, I would estimate the current number of zombies to be seven billion, five hundred million, nine-hundred ninety-nine thousand, nine hundred ninety-eight."

"You mean there are only *two* humans left alive on the face of the Earth?"

"That figure includes you, of course," Father pointed out. "The other is an infant female being kept in an underground bunker, surrounded by a phalanx of bot protectors and caregivers. Now that you have finished your training, and assumed your new form, you will be transported topside by T-1 and T-2. Good luck, Angus. Upon your human wits and strength rests the future of Mankind!"

"Fuck you, Father! Fuck you, you cocksucking soulless machine! I'm going to kill you, you motherfucking robot! You hear me? I'm going to come back and tear your grinning metal head off and shove it up your—"

"It will be better for your transition if you go offline during transport," Father smiled, pushing yet another button on the remote. The stream of profanity spilling from Angus's speakers abruptly cut off.

Having fulfilled its programming, Father turned away as the twin workbots trundled the cyborg off to the jet-sled. The zombie-fighter was fully trained and on its way to save humanity. The sci-bot sent a wireless message via one of the servicebots to the Hub's mainframe and ordered it to prepare the next clone in the A-Series—Aoen—for decanting.

WHEN ANGUS CAME back online it was to find himself standing alone in the middle of a city. Everywhere he looked there were towering blocks of steel and glass rising into the sky. After a lifetime spent in a dome at the bottom of the ocean, his first sight of the bright blue emptiness overhead was enough to paralyze him with amazement and anxiety. His sense of wonder ended, however, upon seeing the dead bodies—some of them stacked up in piles two stories high. Despite the horribleness of his situation, he was relieved his sense of smell had yet to return.

The windows of the storefronts and shops that lined the boulevard were shattered, their contents strewn in the gutters, mixed in with paper money and other trash. Here and there were burned-out military vehicles scattered among their civilian kin, like so many abandoned toys. As a boy he had studied the different topside cities shown on the Feed and dreamed about the day he would finally be free to explore them on his own. But now, not only did Angus not know which city he was in, he did not care. New York, London, Paris, and Beijing were all alike now, weren't they? Dead is dead.

Just then the auditory receptors that replaced his ears picked up a noise. It was very faint, but quickly grew in volume. At first he thought it was what his lesson plans had called wind, whistling through the concrete and steel canyons of the city. Then he recognized it. It was the Zombie Call. Only he had never heard it this *loud* before.

Seconds later, pale, rotting faces appeared at the empty windows, and shuffling figures filled the open doorways. Some still had eyes, while others made do with empty sockets, yet all of them sniffed the air like the ones he used to hunt in the Maze. Ever since the last living human in the city had been torn, screaming, limb from limb, they had lain dormant, hidden within the abandoned skyscrapers, desecrated churches, and burned-out shopping malls. But now they were being drawn from their hidey-holes, like maggots wriggling from a long-dead corpse, lured forth by the smell of human brains—the only living brains for thousands of miles. They came pouring forth, in all their funereal glory, driven by a hunger greater than the grave, crawling over one another until they were an amorphous tidal wave of rotten flesh, all teeth and clawing, groping hands. There was no need to wonder where they might be hiding—all he had to do was stand there, and they would come to him.

Years of training took over, and Angus began instinctively killing the zombies out of fear for a life that was no longer mortal. The first zombie might have been a woman at one time. It was hard to tell. He grabbed its head with one metal hand and squeezed, only to have it pop like a ripe zit.

By the end of the first day, Angus had to admit Father had been right. A robot body made it very easy to kill zombies. By his calculations, he was killing one zombie every two seconds, each minute of the day, since neither he nor they slept. That meant there were 43,200 down, and only seven billion, five hundred million, nine-hundred ninety-eight thousand, five hundred fifty-eight to go.

That's when he started to scream.

He was still screaming a month later.

And had taken two steps.

Name: *Ashley Wood*
Location: *AUS / HK*
Specialty: *Auteur*
Published Works: *Too many to list, google it!*
Statement: *Why not!*
Future projects to watch for: *Ashley Wood*

Name: *Chris Ryall*
Location: *San Diego, CA*
Specialty: *Writer/co-creator of ZvR, Groom Lake, The Colonized, The Hollows, Onyx*
Published Works: *The above titles, plus many other comics; recent works include String Divers and Dirk Gently's Holistic Detective Agency.*
Statement: *"I'm looking forward to handing over the keys to the ZvR franchise to my new ZvR writer/10-year-old daughter, Lucy."*
Future projects to watch for: *Rom the Space Knight*

Name: *Lucy Ryall*
Location: *San Diego, CA*
Specialty: *Writer*
Published Works: *"One Day," Zombies vs Robots #10*
Statement: *"Robots will always beat zombies because zombies are just really dumb."*
Future projects to watch for: *Fifth grade; would love to someday write Archie comics.*

Name: *Paul Davidson*
Location: *Whitley Bay. UK*
Specialty: *Artist*
Published Works: *X-Men: Legacy, Magneto, Judge Dredd*
Future projects to watch for: *To be Announced creator-owned title.*

Name: *Antonio Fuso*
Location: *Rome, Italy*
Specialty: *Artist*
Published Works: *G.I. JOE: Cobra and Drive (IDW),*
Millennium Trilogy Graphic Novel adaption (Vertigo)
Statement: *Long life to comics!*
Future projects to watch for: *Driven, Kriminal, dEUS*

Name: *Jay Fotos*
Location: *Tempe, AZ*
Specialty: *Colorist*
Published Works: *Locke & Key, TMNT, Land of The Dead,*
The Great and Secret Show, Godzilla, Transformers,
Zombies Vs Robots, Mars Attacks Judge Dredd, '68,
Frazetta Comics, Spawn.
Statement: *Jay Fotos has been working professionally in*
the comic industry in every aspect from writing, inking,
penciling, coloring, lettering, design and pre-press
production for more than 15 years.
Future projects to watch for: *www.jayfotos.com*

Name: *Stefano Simeone*
Location: *Rome, Italy*
Specialty: *In ZvR, I'm the colorist. Usually I write,*
draw and ink.
Published Works: *Butterfly for Archaia, Eternal for*
Boom!Studios, three graphic novels for Bao Publishing,
Statement: *"Such a pretty zombie, such a pretty robot."*
Future projects to watch for: *I'm working on my fourth*
graphic novel and on a sci-fi project.

Name: *Nicanor "Nico" Peña*
Location: *Queretaro, Qro. Mexico*
Specialty: *Artist (Pencils, inks and color)*
Published Works: *Squids, Cut The Rope, Littlest Pet Shop,*
and Zombies vs. Robots
Statement: *Working on more stuff for IDW!*
Future projects to watch for: *Strawberry Shortcake*

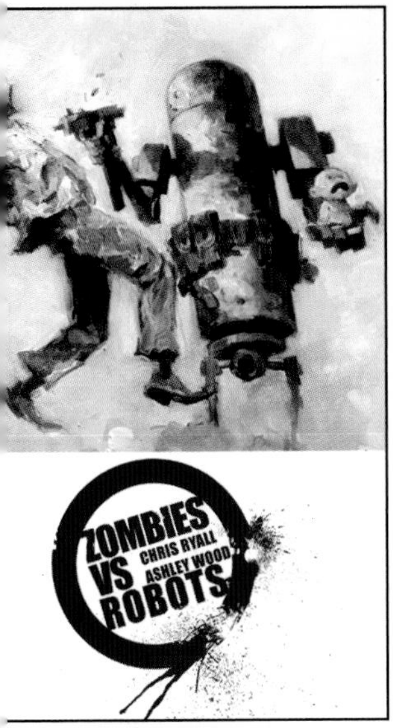
ZOMBIES
VS
ROBOTS
CHRIS RYALL
ASHLEY WOOD

ZOMBIES VS ROBOTS
OVERSIZE HC
FC • $19.99 • ISBN: 978-1-60010-052-9

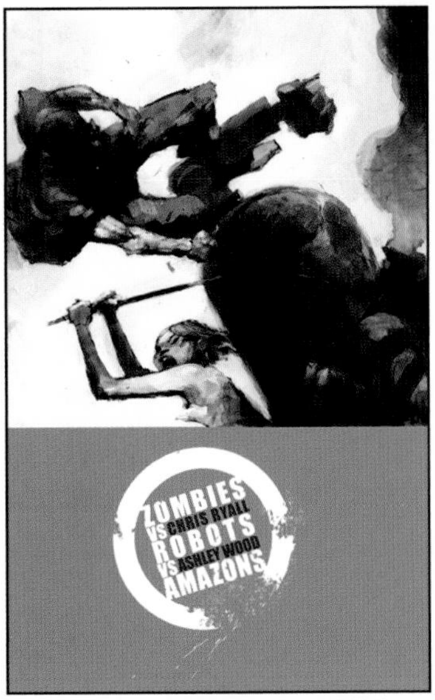
ZOMBIES
VS
ROBOTS
VS
AMAZONS
CHRIS RYALL
ASHLEY WOOD

ZOMBIES VS ROBOTS VS AMAZONS
OVERSIZE HC
FC • $19.99 • ISBN: 978-1-60010-163-2

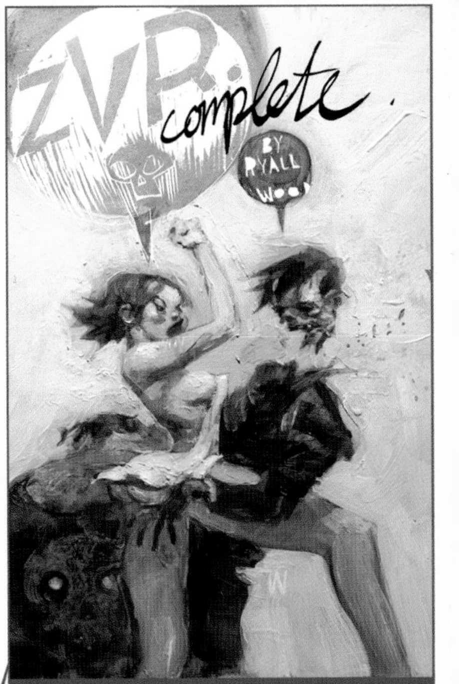
ZVR.
complete
BY
RYALL
WOOD

THE COMPLETE ZOMBIES VS ROBOTS
HC • FC • $29.99 • ISBN: 978-1-60010-809-9
SC • FC • $19.99 • ISBN: 978-1-60010-328-5

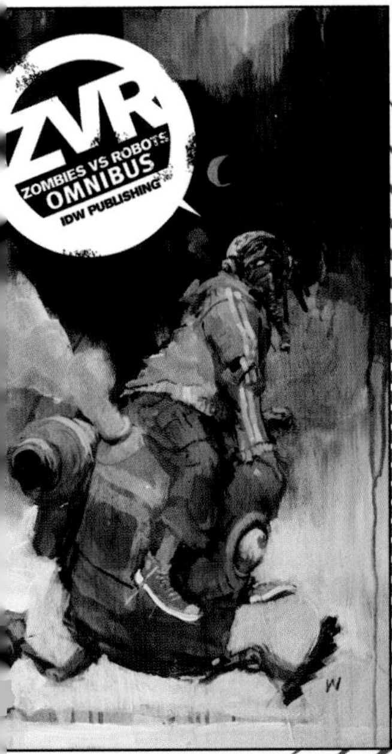
ZVR
ZOMBIES VS ROBOTS
OMNIBUS
IDW PUBLISHING

ZOMBIES VS ROBOTS
WARBOOK OMNIBUS
SC • FC • $29.99 • 440 PAGES
6" X 9" • ISBN: 978-1-63140-213-5

ZOMBIES VS ROBOTS AVENTURE

HC • FC • $24.99 • ISBN: 978-1-60010-717-7
SC • FC • $17.99 • ISBN: 978-1-60010-869-3

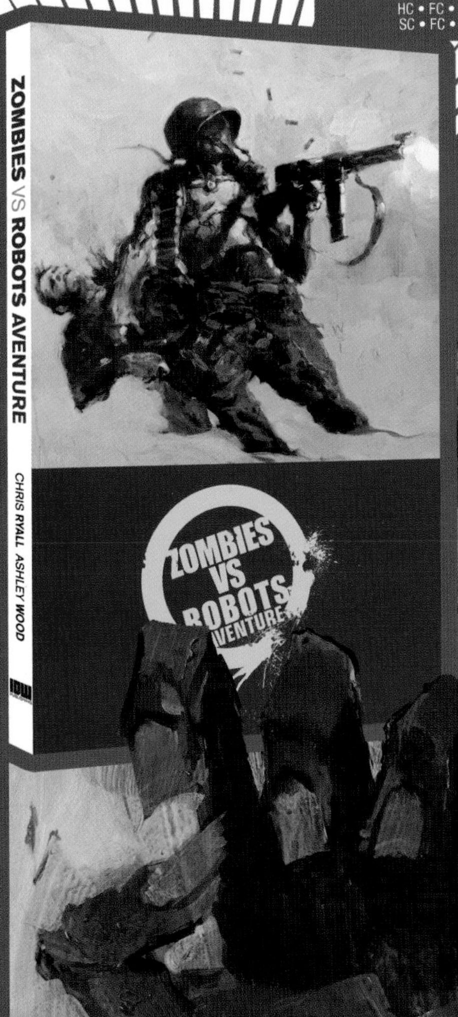
ZOMBIES VS ROBOTS AVENTURE
CHRIS RYALL ASHLEY WOOD
IDW
ZOMBIES
VS
ROBOTS
AVENTURE

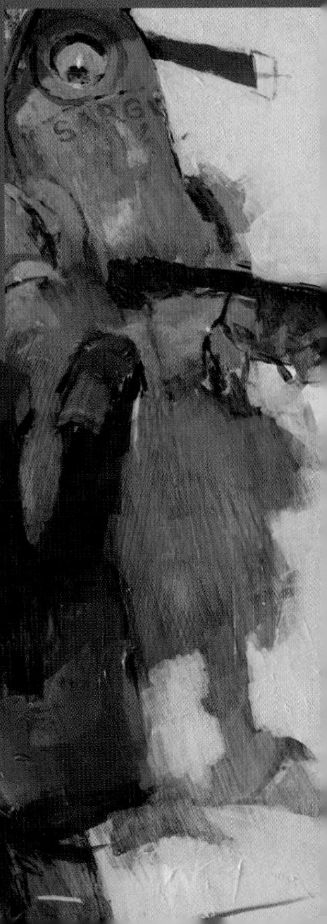

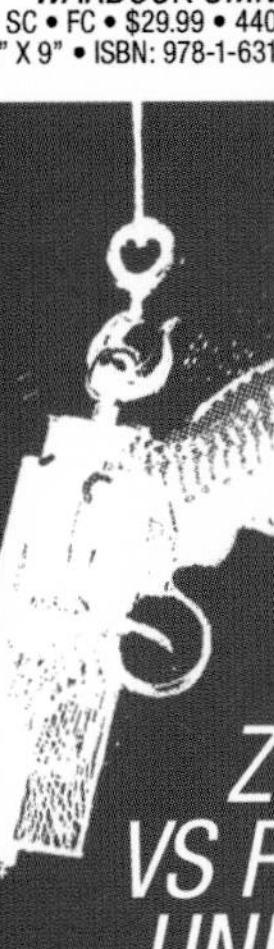

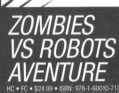

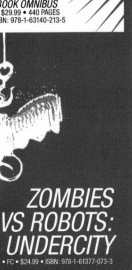

ZOMBIES VS ROBOTS: UNDERCITY

HC • FC • $24.99 • ISBN: 978-1-61377-073-3